Sheriffmuir, 1715

Sheriffmuir, 1715

The Jacobite War in Scotland

Stuart Reid

Frontline Books, London

Sheriffmuir, 1715: The Jacobite War in Scotland

This edition published in 2014 by Frontline Books,
an imprint of Pen & Sword Books Ltd,
47 Church Street, Barnsley, S. Yorkshire, S70 2AS
www.frontline-books.com

ISBN: 978–1–84832–732–0

CIP data records for this title are available from the British Library

For more information on our books, please visit
www.frontline-books.com, email info@frontline-books.com
or write to us at the above address.

Printed and bound by CPI Group (UK) Ltd, Croydon, CR0 4YY
Designed and typeset in 11/14 point Bembo by Wordsense Ltd, Edinburgh

Contents

Illustrations

Maps

Introduction

THE JACOBITE RISING OF 1715 has always tended to occupy an undeservedly obscure position in Scottish history. Both the risings that preceded it and followed it (apart from the even more obscure affair of Glenshiel) featured dashing leaders and dramatic battles. Bonnie Dundee and the Battle of Killiecrankie form one bookend, and Bonnie Prince Charlie and Culloden the other. Between them stands an uncharismatic leader in the form of John Erskine, Earl of Mar, and a correspondingly indecisive battle on the Sheriffmuir, famous only for the fact that both sides ran away.

In large part, the absence of daring deeds and the sound and fury of battle may be attributed to the fact that Sherrifmuir was never conceived of as a military campaign but as a political revolution. To be sure, the Jacobites would raise armies, and arguably a good one in Scotland, but in effect these were intended to aid the civil power rather than overthrow it. Consequently, although some good work has been carried out in recent years discussing the political and social background to the Jacobite rising of 1715, comparatively little attention has been paid to the ultimate argument of kings. This book is therefore intended not as a discussion of Jacobitism and the failure of the Jacobite movement in 1715, but as a military history of the rising. More particularly it is aimed at explaining how the Battle of Sheriffmuir occurred where and when it did, who fought there and above all what really happened on that high moorland on a cold November day. Towards the end of the American Civil War, an officer named August Kaust observed that: 'In battle men are very apt to lose their heads and do absurd things.' That was certainly true of both sides at Sheriffmuir.

As always the author is indebted to a goodly number of people for their advice and encouragement in writing this book, not least the ever patient staff of the library of the Literary and Philosophical Society of Newcastle upon Tyne. Particular mention must however be made of Dr Tony Pollard, of Glasgow University's Archaeology Department, who very kindly confirmed that his own site investigations on the battlefield suggested that I have located it in the right place.

Note:

Once upon a time it was customary for historians to link the regiments involved in the campaign with the more familiar numbers and territorial titles which they would bear in later years. However, the brisk process of disbandment and repeated amalgamation since the Second World War has rendered such an exercise quite pointless. In the narrative which follows regiments are therefore normally referred to by the name of their then commanding officer. An exception is Colonel George Preston's Regiment, which was more famously known as the Cameronians. As Preston's Regiment fought at the Battle of Preston (indeed it was the only regular infantry unit to do so), it is referred to there as the Cameronians in order to avoid confusion.

As to individuals, with so many Scots bearing the same surname residing in close proximity, it was necessary to distinguish between them by reference to their land. Thus John Gordon of Glenbuchat was normally referred to simply as Glenbuchat, and this convention is followed here. Confusingly, however, when more than one individual resided at a particular place the convention was reversed. Thomas Drummond of Logiealmond was not therefore referred to as Logiealmond, but as Logie Drummond. Conversely Alexander Gordon of Auchintoul appears to have invariably been referred to as General Gordon rather than as the laird of Auchintoul.

Chapter 1
A Parcel of Rogues

As with all insurrections, the background and the chain of events that led to the Jacobite rising of 1715 were complex and the rebellion itself by no means inevitable. Nor were those ultimately engaged in it united in their ideals or in their motives. It would probably be true to say, however, that straightforward loyalty to the Stuarts as the rightful lawful kings of Britain did not figure highly, if indeed it figured at all as a significant factor in bringing men out.

For some it was a matter of genuine political or religious conviction, but often enough that conviction had more to do with party or family loyalty, or with deep-rooted personal antipathies rather than properly reasoned consideration. Moreover political opposition or a simple unhappiness with the *status quo* was one thing; actually taking up arms against the state with all the awful penalties for rebellion which would follow failure was quite another. The question of exactly why men chose or were at the very least compelled by one means or another to 'come out' is therefore a worthy subject of study in itself, beyond the scope of a military history of the rising. Nevertheless the course and nature of that campaign was in some measure dictated by those factors.[1]

The Stuart Kings of Britain

The early background at least is straightforward enough. In the year of our Lord 1603, James VI of his name, King of Scots by the grace of God and the will of his people, found himself served heir to the aged Virgin Queen, Elizabeth, and her twin kingdoms of England and Ireland. He was thus the first king – or more accurately emperor – of all the islands of Britain, for in practice and law there was then no such kingdom. He was at one and the same time King of Scots and, as James I, also King of England and Ireland, but they were still two entirely independent realms – as his son Charles I discovered to his cost.

Religion, or rather its practical application, was at the root of the troubles. Belief in God was absolute and governed the lives of great and small, but the devil as always lay in the detail. Early in the sixteenth century Henry VIII of England had embraced the Protestant reformation primarily in order to abrogate to himself supreme authority over the English church, and ultimately its lands and its revenues. With religious and secular life so closely intertwined at every level it was regarded as essential that the church should be the mouthpiece of the state rather than of the papacy in Rome. No monarch could afford to be preached against or have defiance urged from the pulpit. Church and state needed to be as one, and there was a perceived danger that Catholics might not only attempt to overthrow the state in order to restore the authority of the papacy, but would also make common cause with their co-religionists abroad in order to accomplish it.

In Scotland there was a similar but subtly different dimension to this potential for conflict, in that the Protestant reformation, modelled in this case on the teachings of John Calvin, in Geneva, was not sponsored by the Crown but carried through in defiance of it. Unlike Calvin's Geneva there was no question of establishing a theocratic republic, but nevertheless the Scots Kirk would soon prove to be an extremely powerful force in secular as well as religious life. Therefore, when Charles I decided to remodel the Scots Kirk on Episcopalian or High Anglican lines, reimpose a hierarchical structure of bishops and repossess the former landholdings of the old Catholic Church in order to finance these reforms, he not only alienated the Kirk but also managed to upset a substantial proportion of the laity as well.

In 1638 a National Covenant was widely signed throughout the country, pledging a substantial part of the population, both great and small, to opposing the king's religious reforms. In two short wars in 1639 and 1640 the king's attempts to reassert his power in Scotland were not only decisively rebuffed, but his authority in his other kingdoms was also thereby fatally weakened. A calamitous civil war or rather series of civil wars then followed in all three kingdoms, and by the time they all ended twenty years later Charles I was dead – executed by his own subjects – and men had died on battlefields as far apart as the Orkneys and the Scillies, and from Flanders to Virginia.

In England the bloodless restoration of Charles II in 1660 was brought about through a pragmatic reconciliation of the religious and secular issues, which had led to the civil wars. While many differences remained, English politicians on all sides were heartily united in a near-paranoid desire to re-establish stability at all costs and avoid a similar rupture in the future.

In Scotland unfortunately the position was rather different, in that there had been no reasoned resolution of the political divide. Peace between the various factions had in effect been imposed by Oliver Cromwell's army, and while the return of the king saw the restoration of independence to a conquered Scotland it also meant a resumption of unfinished business.

The Episcopal hierarchy desired by the king's father (Charles I) was duly reimposed on the Kirk, whereupon the stauncher Presbyterians, or Covenanters, responded by establishing conventicles. These were alternative services conducted, often in the open air, by those ministers ejected from the official Kirk for refusing to acknowledge the authority of the bishops. When the authorities inevitably attempted to suppress the conventicles, they were met with armed resistance, which soon developed into a counter-insurgency campaign chiefly in the Ayrshire and Galloway hills. The so-called 'Killing Times' was a vicious and protracted struggle, which at one point saw a Highland Host unleashed on the Covenanters to plunder and intimidate the refractory in a conscious imitation of Louis XIV's dragonnades. More seriously civil disobedience and occasional acts of terrorism on the part of the Covenanters was also punctuated by two major uprisings in 1666 and 1679, crushed in full-scale battles at Rullion Green and Bothwell Brig, respectively. A third rebellion in 1685, led by the 9th Earl of Argyle in concert with the Duke of Monmouth's ill-fated bid for the English throne, was also summarily dealt with, but by now Charles II had been succeeded by his brother James VII and II, and that meant trouble.

It was not simply that James VII and II was openly Catholic, although that certainly provided the public justification for his eventual downfall. Rather he was altogether far too able an administrator. Being anxious 'not to go on his travels again', Charles II had managed the two realms well enough by adopting what might be described as a policy of masterful indolence, while affairs of state were actually delegated to a succession of all too expendable favourites. James VII and II was different; not only did he incline to despotism, but he also possessed the organisational talents and energy to exercise it efficiently with the aid of an army, which he expanded at an alarming rate. It was this combination that so terrified the increasingly marginalised political establishment on both sides of the border.

Characteristically, when the crisis came with with the landing of James's Dutch son-in-law, Prince William of Orange, in Torbay late in 1688, James offered his

Scottish subjects no concessions. Instead a promise of pardon to all returning to their duty by 31 March was accompanied by threats of 'infamy and disgrace . . . in this world and the Condemnation due to the Rebellious in the nixt'.[2] Unfortunately James himself, instead of fighting, had already fled to France. Not surprisingly on 4 April 1689 the Scottish Estates, or Parliament, responded to his ill-timed bluster by unambiguously declaring that James had 'forfaultit the Croun'. A week later they underlined the fact by the formal adoption of the Claim of Right, a declaration which asserted that, by transforming what was a limited legal monarchy into an arbitrary and despotic power, James had violated the Scots' constitution. What his royal grandfather, James VI and I, would have made of that might easily be imagined, for it was his formulation of the doctrine of the divine right of kings which had indirectly led to that earlier civil war. The Claim of Right firmly repudiated that particular notion, for it harked back to the foundation of the modern Scottish state and the Declaration of Arbroath, in 1320, which asserted that the king ruled only by the will of his people and that, if he abused the power thus entrusted to him or otherwise failed them, he could be set aside and the Crown offered to another.

In this case of course that alternative was James VII and II's undoubtedly Protestant daughter Mary, and her husband Prince William of Orange – or, as he was more familiarly known, Dutch William. The fact that William had not and never was to set foot in Scotland was probably no bad thing, for the Scots had long been used to going their own way. When Charles I made his own disastrous experiment in benevolent despotism, the result was the emergence of a Scots republic in all but name. Now once again the real power rested or appeared to rest with the Scots Parliament, backed up by a militant Kirk, shorn once more of its bishops.

Revolution and Rebellion

The transfer of power from James VII and II to William II and III, although in the end surprisingly smooth, was not by any means a foregone conclusion. In the early months of 1689 the streets of Edinburgh were thronged in traditional Scottish fashion with the armed supporters of the rival factions, each seeking to intimidate the other. In a dramatic replay of the old Whiggamore Raid, in 1648, thousands of Covenanters from the southwest were joined by the clansmen of the Earl of Argyle, all urging recognition of Dutch William as their lawful sovereign. James's few remaining supporters on the other hand were notably fewer in number, disorganised and demoralised, especially after the arrival of that hectoring letter on 16 March. The Duke of Gordon still held Edinburgh Castle in James's name, but that seemingly was their sole advantage.

With the capital becoming increasingly unsafe, talk turned to establishing a rival 'convention' of James's supporters at Stirling. On the evening of 18 March 1689, one of his last remaining loyal officers, John Graham of Claverhouse, Viscount Dundee, led a little troop of fifty men out of the West Port and headed for Stirling only to find the gates barred against him. At that point Claverhouse returned home, but when news arrived of a declaration of forfeiture against him, and rumours of a warrant for his arrest, he decided to fight and defiantly raised the royal standard outside Dundee.

Raising an army to follow that standard soon turned out to be a vastly discouraging business. The truth of the matter is that the Scots were never at that time sentimental about the Stuarts, and even in the northeast of Scotland he found few volunteers. Although the area had been the Royalist heartland during the civil war in the 1640s and was again to be a hotbed of Jacobitism in the later risings of 1715 and 1745, its people were sharply divided. The fact that the Duke of Gordon was supposedly still a committed supporter of King James might have counted for something if he had not been rather too conveniently shut up in Edinburgh Castle. Even if the Gordons were for the king, all too many of the other local families were for the Protestant succession, if only to spite the Gordons.

Nevertheless Claverhouse eventually found sufficient of the Highland clans willing to follow him and in the summer of that year won a stunning victory just above the Pass of Killiecrankie. With the Scots government's only field army lost there, victory might have beckoned, but Claverhouse himself was among the dead, and without him the cause was lost. Indeed it is questionable whether it could have succeeded even if he had lived, because, notwithstanding his bright new title as Viscount Dundee, he was still at bottom just John Graham of Claverhouse, a minor laird and colonel of horse of no consequence beyond his loyalty to his king. There was simply put no appetite for an uprising in the name of King James either among the traditional leaders of the country, or among the common people.

The Union

That there should apparently be such a dramatic alteration in attitude by 1715 was down to a number of interdependent factors, largely centring on the Act of Union in 1707.

The scheme of uniting the two kingdoms originated with Dutch William. He had no children, and following the death of his wife, Mary, an Act of Settlement was passed in June 1701. This laid down a Protestant line of succession to the English throne, first through James's surviving daughter, Anne, and then failing any heirs of her body, through her aunt, Sophia of Hanover, and her heirs.[3]

This Act of Settlement obviously had no legal or practical effect in Scotland for so long as it remained a separate kingdom. Notwithstanding, Anne Stuart was indeed duly proclaimed Queen of Scots on William's death in the following year, but there was no guarantee that her northern subjects would be equally complaisant when she in turn shuffled off her mortal coil. A full union between the two countries was therefore seen as necessary to ensure both the Protestant succession and the continued political stability of the two kingdoms.

A step of this magnitude naturally took some time to achieve, but by 1706 Queen Anne was able to appoint thirty-one commissioners on either side, who after nine weeks of discussion arrived at a workable if far from satisfactory settlement. Subject to ratification, which in Scotland at least took place against a somewhat tumultuous background, the two kingdoms were to be united under the style of Great Britain on 1 May 1707, with a common flag, coinage and legislature, and the Protestant succession was assured in accordance with the English 1701 Act of Settlement.

Although Scotland was to retain its own laws and legal system and the established (Presbyterian) church, turning the country into North Britain was a deeply unpopular move. Ironically those Scots politicians who had most eagerly supported the Union found their influence and consequent prestige dramatically diminished in the much bigger British parliamentary theatre. The hoped-for benefits at first proved largely illusory, and conversely English interference in Scottish affairs was greater than had been anticipated. The Scottish Toleration Act of 1712 for example dismayed the Presbyterians by legally sanctioning Episcopalian worship, and in the following year an alteration in the malt tax applied the same rate across both kingdoms. In principle this ought to have been beneficial. Indeed, the proposers' intention was that in England it should be brought down to the then lower Scottish rate. Instead somehow the reverse occurred, and Scots farmers found themselves paying the higher English rate – which would prove a significant grievance factor in 1715. On the other hand the benefits offsetting these and other examples of a casual disregard for Scottish interests were hard to find, save for the ultimate justification of ensuring the Protestant succession.

Yet even that was by no means inevitable, for in some quarters both north and south of the border hopes remained that Anne, who disliked her aunt Sophia, might yet be persuaded to allow the throne to revert to her Catholic half-brother – the would-be King James VIII – at her death.

Whigs and Tories

The nuances need not detain us here. Suffice to say that broadly speaking there were two political parties with the capacity to form a government. In England, the Whigs, while including a significant number of aristocrats, were largely made up of lesser landed gentry and businessmen, who were strongly Protestant in faith and outlook, and sometimes consciously saw themselves to be the successors of the Parliamentarians of the Civil War. Conversely the Tories saw themselves both as monarchists and supporters of an established Church of England, perceived to be under threat from Presbyterians and other schismatic dissenters. Fear God, honour the king, might not unfairly be taken as their watchword. Nevertheless, although they were accused not always unfairly of leaning towards Jacobitism, fundamentally they were not so very far apart from their Whig opponents, colleagues and neighbours. Their differences were more a matter of party than principle and, had the incoming George I seen fit to favour them, the overwhelming majority were prepared to accommodate rather than oppose him.

Scotland, not surprisingly, was a different matter. Once again party accounted for much, but the religious divide was sharper and unreconciled bitterness remained. For the most part the Whigs were at one with their English colleagues. However, while they largely accepted the Union, their Tory counterparts perceived that its dissolution would require King James to be sitting on the throne. Thus almost by default Scottish Tories, more than their English counterparts, inclined to Jacobitism. Nevertheless this was by no means an inevitable position because it was not a question of a sentimental desire to see the Auld Stuarts back again, but a complex series of economic, political and religious issues for which James represented a possible solution.

Further complicating the issue, and at the same time offering a means of facilitating that particular solution, was the continuing war with France. Although periodically punctuated by short-lived peace treaties, this had been waged for decades against a background of Louis XIV's largely successful aim of turning France into the foremost power in Europe. Indeed Dutch William's principal aim in securing for himself the twin thrones was to bolster Holland's position by bringing Scotland and England into the Grand Alliance against King Louis. In this, despite the distraction of a prolonged campaign in Ireland, he was spectacularly successful both in the short term and in ensuring that the alliance survived his death. It did more, for it also paved the way for the Duke of Marlborough's great victories over the French at Blenheim, Ramillies, Oudenarde and Malplaquet, between 1704 and 1709.

Against that background, Louis XIV was prepared to offer first the exiled King James VII and II and then his son more than just sympathy, for a Stuart restoration would at the very least take Britain out of the alliance. The best opportunity to do so came in the immediate aftermath of the Union, when popular opposition to it was at its height. An expedition was accordingly fitted out in 1708 to carry the would-be King James VIII to his ancestral kingdom. Whether this would indeed have succeeded in bringing him to his throne or simply plunged the two kingdoms into another destructive civil war is a moot point, but it would certainly have crippled if not removed Britain as a major player in the European war. In the event and seemingly because the French admiral had misconstrued his orders, it was never put to the test. Having arrived off the Fife coast and failing to be greeted by the expected recognition signals, he declined to put James ashore and instead allowed himself to be chased out to sea by the Royal Navy. Another possible landing at Aberdeen was similarly aborted, so back they all went to France, having given the government of Great Britain an almighty fright but accomplished nothing else.

Two years later the political situation took another interesting turn with the coming to power of a Tory government at Westminster and a radical shift in British foreign policy. Notwithstanding the glamour of Marlborough's victories the country was by then weary of war and the concomitant drain in blood and treasure to sustain it. Peace rather than victory was sought and eventually accomplished by the Treaty of Utrecht in April 1713. From a Jacobite point of view this development was at once a setback, since one of the clauses required James's expulsion from France; thus the prospect of a second French expeditionary force effectively evaporated. On the other hand the treaty removed a serious political obstacle to his return at a time when Queen Anne's days were clearly numbered, her Tory government was not implacably opposed to a second restoration, and the German alternative monarch was coming to be seen in some quarters as unnecessary and unwelcome.

This is not to say of course that James would have been warmly greeted had he slipped across the Channel immediately following Anne's death on 1

August 1714, but he was unlikely to have been actively opposed. As it was, he sat tight in Bar-le-Duc waiting for a call that never came. Meanwhile at home, in a complicated sequence of political manoeuvring, the Tories let power slip through their fingers. In came a Whig administration and so too did George I.

Enter Bobbing John

To his credit the new king was initially prepared to accommodate those Tories supportive of the new regime, but for the most part he was rebuffed, not through Jacobite leanings but a deep-seated political antipathy towards the Whigs. Consequently a clean sweep was made, so comprehensive that not only were the Tories excluded completely from government, but there was also little prospect of their coming back into power at any point in the foreseeable future.

In England this reversal was far from accepted gracefully insofar as the grandees of the party grumbled and plotted, and further down the social scale there was widespread rioting directed against the Whig administration. Nevertheless such expressions of frustration, although public and sometimes spectacular, remained largely superficial. Letting off steam was one thing, encompassing the overthrow of the state was quite another, as those who sought to capitalise on the unrest discovered to their cost.

The situation in Scotland was quite different, because a much more serious opposition had emerged, centring around the Earl of Mar. While lately a Tory, his Jacobite credentials were far from deep rooted. A career politician, he had first entered the Scottish Parliament in 1696 as an acknowledged supporter of King William and thereafter steadily rose in prominence, becoming a privy councillor two years later, a joint secretary of state in 1705 and in the following year a Knight of the Thistle and one of the Scottish commissioners in the pre-Union negotiations. Afterwards Mar served as a secretary of state in the Earl of Oxford's Tory administration under Queen Anne. Turned out with the rest of the Tories in August 1714, and with his former ministerial salary well in arrears, he faced financial ruin. It has plausibly been suggested that his sudden decision at this point to adopt an anti-Union stance and rally opinion behind a movement to have it dissolved was not motivated by nationalism, but the hope that he would make sufficient of a nuisance of himself to be bought off with a position under the new regime. Mar had been a Whig before and, although he had since established Jacobite contacts, he could no doubt bring himself be a Whig once again.[4]

If so it was a forlorn hope, and in any case Mar became heavily involved in active Jacobite plotting in the summer of 1715. In July he penned a blunt memorandum to King James, endorsed by other prominent Jacobites, stating that while 'the generality of the people are extremely averse from the Court and the Ministry (whom they hate and despise) and well inclined to a restoration' there was little prospect of a general uprising in his favour unless he landed with a force of regular troops at his back. Conversely, should he bring such an army, a landing in Northumberland or in the northeast of Scotland would afford him the opportunity to rally considerable numbers of volunteers to his standard, including large numbers of Highland clansmen who would not require a great deal of training to be of use.[5]

Therein lay the rub, for while the French government was prepared quietly to provide arms and the ships to carry them, the ailing Louis XIV was not likely to commit troops or officers, and that included James's uncle, the very able Duke of Berwick. Any support would have to be clandestine and deniable, and even that vanished with Louis's death in August. The Jacobites were going to be on their own.

In the meantime, in Scotland at least, King James's putative supporters continued with their preparations. Arms and ammunition were landed, although far from sufficient as it would turn out, and horses and men were prepared for a rising scheduled to begin on 30 July. At this stage they were still relying on that French landing, and as the projected date came and went without any sign of either James or the lily banners of France, the rebels sensibly lay low. But then the Earl of Mar arrived.

Afterwards his enemies suggested that Mar had been prepared to accommodate himself to George I right up until the moment the king publicly snubbed him at a royal levee on 1 August. On the contrary, both his immediate actions and the degree of organisation involved show that his appearance at the levee was no more than a diversion. That same evening he and a professional soldier, Major-General (later Lieutenant-General) George Hamilton, slipped aboard a boat at Gravesend, which carried them north to the Tyne and a rendezvous with another boat, which eventually landed them at Elie in Fife.[6] Once ashore Mar made his way north on about 10 August, avoiding Perth and travelling through Atholl and over the Spittal of Glenshee to reach Deeside, where he establshed himself in his own country at Invercauld Castle outside Braemar.

There, as the frustrated authorities in Edinburgh acknowledged, he was safe for the time being. Immediately he busied himself, as he had on the journey north, with sending letters to known or anticipated Jacobite supporters, inviting them to a tinchal, or great hunt, at Braemar. There are various estimates as to the numbers who responded, but they certainly included the marquises of Huntly and of Tullibardine, the Earl Marischal and the earls of Erroll, Seaforth and Linlithgow as well as an impressive number of viscounts, lords and other gentlemen great and small. Even though it seems unlikely that the earls of Carnwath and Nithsdale, and other southern notables such the Viscount Kenmure, did not actually make it, there was no doubt that the tinchal was an impressive gathering, quite unlike John Graham of Claverhouse's little band.

No one of course was in any doubt as to the real reason behind the summons, but strangely enough the assembled great and the good did go out and enjoy a day's hunting on 26 August. Whether their minds were concentrated on their sport is of course a different matter, for that evening the entertainment was rounded off by sinking a considerable quantity of whisky punch and toasting the success of the intended rising.[7]

Just over a week later, on 6 September, the standard was formally raised at Braemar.

Chapter 2
The Crown Gathers its Forces

NATURALLY ENOUGH THE GOVERNMENT, which was pretty well informed as to what was going on, immediately started mustering and moving its forces to contain and deal with the Jacobite threat. Neither side, however, notwithstanding their mutual bluster, was at first in any position to initiate hostilities against the other. This is therefore a convenient point at which to pause and to look at how the respective armies were to be raised and brought together, how strong they were and how they were organised, equipped and trained for battle. In so doing we obviously need to take the British Army as our starting point, first and foremost in its own right, but also as the pattern against which to compare and contrast a rebel army that endeavoured to emulate it, yet was in its own way a very different organisation.

The British Army
Strictly speaking the British Army, or at least the regular army, was an institution of no great antiquity since it had only been formed as recently as 1708 by amalgamating the previously separate Scottish and English armies. Even then the majority of its regiments dated back to only Dutch William's time in the 1690s. It was nevertheless a very good army, but it is also important to appreciate it was in a sense no longer the army that the great Duke of Marlborough had led to victory at Blenheim, Ramillies and Oudenarde.

Inevitably that army had been quite savagely reduced in size at the end of Queen Anne's War. From a high of seventy-three battalions of infantry exclusive of the foot guards during the war, there were just thirty-one battalions remaining by the beginning of 1715, together with four troops of horse guards, two of horse grenadier guards, eight regiments of horse and six of dragoons.

Constitutionally the army's existence was in any case always precarious, and since 1689 it had rested on the annual passage of what was termed the Mutiny Act. The preamble to this Act unambiguously declared: 'The raising and keeping a standing army within the United Kingdom in time of peace, unless it be with the consent of Parliament, is against law.' The Act then went on to set out the rules and legal framework by which the army was to operate and conduct itself (hence the Mutiny Act), and most important of all it set out exactly how many officers and men Parliament was prepared to pay for in the coming financial year. Thus, despite having just reduced the size of the army by more than half, Parliament was persuaded, in view of the growing signs of unrest, to vote in early 1715 to support an increased British establishment for the coming year of 15,851 officers and men. In addition, since 1699 a further 12,000 officers and men were authorised to be carried on a quite separately administered Irish establishment funded out of the revenues of that kingdom, for a combined total of just under 28,000 men.

Outwardly the separation between the British and the Irish establishments was merely an administrative one, insofar as there were not actually two separate armies and regiments were transferred freely between the two.[1] On the other hand, while the figure of 12,000 men on the Irish establishment was fixed by law, paid for out of the Irish exchequer and not subject to the whim of an ever parsimonious Westminster Parliament, those men were intended as a permanent garrison for that country. Thus the disposable strength of the army was supposedly limited to those regiments carried on the parent British establishment.

Out of that establishment, standing garrisons had to be found for Gibraltar and Minorca in the Mediterranean, for New York, Newfoundland and Nova Scotia, and for Jamaica and the other Caribbean colonies. In Britain itself guards and garrisons had also to be provided for London (the foot guards and horse guards) and the royal dockyards and such-like places. All in all therefore the actual number of marching regiments that were available at the beginning of 1715 to deal with a possible Jacobite emergency was quite inadequate. Increasing the size of the British establishment to just under 16,000 men was a good start, but, in order to raise the additional men quickly enough to be of any use, it was necessary to reactivate no fewer than fourteen regiments of dragoons and at least nine regiments of foot.[2]

When units became surplus to requirements at the end of a conflict it was rare for them to be completely disbanded. Instead they were officially reduced to a cadre – or, as those concerned more pithily termed it, broken. This process entailed discharging all of the rank and file, or occasionally drafting them into other units, but retaining the officers, who were placed on half pay. This normally served as a form of pension, but the officers drawing it could be recalled to active duty at any time if their services were required.

Returning the officers to full pay was one thing, but recruiting their regiments afresh was quite another. Most were returned onto the establishment as of 22 July 1715, just weeks before the Jacobite rising began, but it is unlikely that all of them were fully recruited at that date, let alone properly trained. Cavalry regiments of course also required to have their horses trained, and no doubt more than a few of their troopers needed to be taught to ride them. Nevertheless the new regiments made an absolutely vital contribution in the coming campaign: five out of General Wills's six cavalry regiments at the Battle of Preston were reactivated units, while at Sheriffmuir Lord Mark Kerr's Dragoons was reactivated as of 31 January 1715.[3]

Infantry

As to the units themselves, the infantry, often referred to as the Foot, was by far the larger and most important element. Regiments at this time were identified neither by numbers nor by territorial titles, but by the name of the commanding officer, who effectively owned it.[4] At this period he was still expected to lead the regiment, unless also exercising a higher appointment. For example at Sheriffmuir Colonel Archibald Douglas, Earl of Forfar, was present with his regiment, but in charge of a brigade. Similarly William Evans led a cavalry brigade, while his lieutenant-colonel, Henry Hawley, commanded his regiment.

British infantry regiments normally comprised a single battalion of ten companies, each of which was led by a captain, who might also double up as one of the regiment's three field officers; the colonel, lieutenant-colonel and major, who collectively commanded the regiment. The captain was assisted by a couple of subalterns and three sergeants, but as the army was on a reduced peacetime establishment he at best had no more than thirty-five men under his immediate control. The battalion therefore should have had a total strength of 350 men exclusive of officers and senior non-commissioned officers (NCOs). Such at least was the theory, but few units were fully recruited up to even this relatively modest figure at the outbreak of the rising. A return of troops in the camp at Stirling on 29 October 1715, two weeks before the battle of Sheriffmuir, revealed an average of just 302 men in each regiment.[5]

All of the men were clothed in red woollen coats, worn over long waistcoats, knee breeches and stockings, and topped off with a largish hat. The hat was supposed to be fashionably cocked up in the form of a tricorne, but was more usually slouched on active service. The uniform may not have been particularly elegant and often lacked many of the decorative embellishments worn in later years, but it was very practical and well adapted to a winter campaign in Scotland.

Fighting equipment included a buff leather belt around the waist, supporting a sword, which was of little practical use but still regarded as the indispensable badge of the soldier. Another belt slung over one shoulder supported a black leather cartridge box, containing 8–12 rounds sitting on the right hip, while a duffel bag like knapsack and tin canteen were slung over the other. The primary weapon carried by all but officers was the firelock musket and bayonet. This was a .75-calibre weapon and its soft lead ball was a potent man-stopper.

One of the ten companies was designated as grenadiers and distinguished from the ordinary or battalion companies by the wearing of mitre-shaped cloth caps rather than cocked hats. Originally their function had been to spearhead assaults on fortified places, for which purpose they were issued with grenades to toss over walls and palisades, hatchets to help tear openings and caps, which could be jammed down on their heads, allowing each grenadier to sling his firelock and so free both hands. Latterly that specialist role had all but disappeared, along with the hatchets and the grenades, but the men retained their caps and were still regarded as the elite of the battalion. Accordingly they were always kept recruited to their full establishment at the expense of the other companies, not by drawing off the tallest men, but the steadier and more experienced ones.

Officers were expected to carry half-pikes, or espontoons, while sergeants bore halberds. These were as much a badge of rank as a weapon. Grenadier officers might carry firelocks, but otherwise firearms were not used by officers. An officer's job was to control his men, not to be distracted by the loading and firing of his personal weapon. Two junior officers were, however, allotted the task of carrying the battalion's flags or colours. The king's colour was a large union flag, while the regimental one matched what were termed the facings displayed on the soldiers' cuffs and linings, and they often at this period bore the colonel's own personal coat of arms. These colours were extremely important. They had a practical function in marking the centre of the battalion and of course in identifying the regiment in the smoke and chaos of the battlefield. However, there was also a more important spiritual purpose, in that they represented the honour of the regiment. To lose a colour was unthinkable, and therefore the corollary was that a regiment that did lose its colours had self-evidently been destroyed or at least so badly beaten as to be unable to protect them. Hence the importance placed on captured colours by contemporaries as a tangible measure of victory.

Infantry Tactics

Although the company was the basic building block of an infantry battalion, its function was largely administrative, and the tactical organisation of the battalion was quite different. The grenadier company was split into two halves and deployed to guard both flanks of this line, which provided the justification for keeping that company fully up to strength and allowing it an additional subaltern. The rest of the battalion was then ideally counted off into twelve equal-sized platoons of between twenty and thirty men apiece, without regard to their companies. These platoons were in turn grouped into four grand divisions, each of three platoons, for manoeuvring purposes.[6]

At the same time these temporary platoons were also numbered, usually in series of threes. This was to facilitate the fire control system known as platooning. There were a number of variations of this which could be employed. At its simplest, on the word of command to open fire being given, only those platoons allocated to the first firing would deliver a volley, followed in turn by those of the second firing and then by the third. By that time it was expected that the platoons of the first firing should have reloaded and would be ready to continue the cycle. This served two very basic purposes. In the first place it is fallacious to regard firelock muskets as clumsy, inaccurate and slow to reload. The process of loading was straightforward and easily learned. With a modicum of practice it was easy to fire twice in the space of a minute, and in the excitement of battle that rate could just as easily be doubled. The problem then lay not with the rate of fire but with the corresponding tendency when hurrying to shoot high and to expend ammunition too quickly. Officers were constantly enjoined therefore to control and steady the firing, and above all to ensure that their men levelled their firelocks properly. Breaking down the firing line into manageable platoons not only facilitated this control, but also ensured that with volleys constantly rippling up and down the line there was no point at which a complete battalion was left frantically reloading its empty weapons.

It was an article of faith among most British officers that platooning was superior to the French system of firing by whole ranks. This was seemingly justified by wartime experience under the great Duke of Marlborough, but it could be a complicated procedure and required endless practice. In peacetime the ordinary dispersal of units in quarters and on policing duties, especially in Ireland, made this problematic at a battalion level. All too often, in the event of a prolonged firefight, platooning degenerated into what the French called *feu à billebaude* – each man simply loading and firing in his own time. The assumed superiority of the British system of firing was based on the premise of course that the soldiers would be fighting against similarly trained and equipped ones, and that both parties would close to within no more than 20–30 metres of each other before halting and engaging in a static firefight. How they would fare against an opponent who did not obligingly halt, but attempted to close with cold steel, remained to be seen.

Cavalry

So much for the infantry. Cavalry units were variously designated either as horse or as dragoons. By the middle of the eighteenth century the distinction would become fairly meaningless, but at this period they were still two quite different branches of cavalry. The former were heavy battle cavalry, often armoured at least with a breastplate, and always well mounted. Dragoons for their part were originally no more than mounted infantry and so carried muskets strapped to their saddles, instead of carbines.[7] They also tended to be rather less well mounted, and slightly later in the eighteenth century it was reckoned that a mount for a trooper of horse cost between £15 and £20, while a trooper of dragoons made do with a nag costing between £12 and £15.[8]

Nevertheless there was a growing feeling that dragoons were much more useful, and as it happens, with the exception of the Bays at Preston, only dragoon regiments were actively employed during the campaign of 1715. Those serving under Argyle in Scotland largely performed in the mounted role, relying upon broadsword and pistol, but at the Battle of Preston the five dragoon regiments, which made up the bulk of General Wills's forces, fought dismounted as infantry.

With some exceptions both types of cavalry regiment normally mustered six troops, each with a peacetime establishment of four officers, four NCOs and about thirty-five men or troopers. Once again this was difficult to achieve, and although augmentations were authorised the 29 October return from Stirling revealed an average of just 168 troopers in each regiment, rather than 210.

While individual troops of horse or dragoons might occasionally be detached to act independently, this organisation was again primarily an administrative one. In action the regiment would normally be divided in two squadrons, each comprising three troops.

Once dismounted, dragoons were expected to be proficient in platoon firing and consequently devoted a sizeable amount of time each year to practising infantry drill while their horses were put to grass. Mounted tactical doctrine, as practised by both horse and dragoons, was very straightforward. Under the Duke of Marlborough the importance of shock action had been stressed. This required the squadrons to close up tightly, the troopers riding knee to knee and moving at no more than a trot in order to maintain a solid compact mass with as straight a front as possible. Such a formation was reckoned sufficient to break up a less compact formation, either in the initial charge, or if necessary by literally pushing through it. Pistols, of which each officer and trooper had a pair, were not to be drawn in the charge since that would encourage both parties to stand off and simply blaze away at each other rather than closing. By way of emphasis Marlborough had allowed his troopers only three rounds apiece. There was also a tendency to use pistols against any formed bodies of infantry who had obligingly failed to run away since it was very difficult to force horses onto resolute lines of bayonets.

Artillery

Strictly speaking, in Britain the train of artillery was not at this period a part of the army proper but was a quite separate organisation answerable to the Board of Ordnance. The basic unit was the company, but once again this was primarily an administrative unit and actually included three different grades, as well as specialist tradesmen.

The lowest grade were what were termed matrosses. Their task was simply to do the heavy labouring work associated with guns, to lend a hand moving them and to fetch and carry ammunition and stores. In time, if they had the attitude and the application, they might progress upwards first to become fireworkers and then gunners, but the unskilled nature of their work often saw ordinary infantrymen being drafted in to help. Having learned the basics as matrosses, fireworkers were trained in some of the more arcane mysteries associated with gunpowder and pyrotechnics including the use of mortars and explosive charges. The third grade, including the officers, were gunners, accounted fit to handle whatever type of cannon was made available to them.

Although all would have agreed with the then Lieutenant-General Henry Hawley in 1746 that to march anywhere without an artillery train would be silly, guns actually played very little part in the 1715 campaign and those that did contrive to be fired were generally very small. This was very largely a reflection of the near total absence of proper roads north of the Forth, which meant that transporting guns other than by sea was generally problematic.

Deployments

That aside, all in all, the British soldier was well equipped, had tried-and-tested fighting methods, which optimised his weapons, and was led by men who knew their business. The problems were that sometimes training was sketchy, that there were far too few soldiers, and none of them was in the right place when the Jacobite rebellion began.

Ironically, despite the government's foreknowledge of trouble, most of the existing regiments were not deployed in Scotland but in England when the rising actually began, for it was there where unrest appeared to be greatest in the early months of 1715. There were a whole series of pro-Jacobite (or at least anti-government) riots in Oxford, the southwest and in the Midlands. Worse, the pro-Jacobite Duke of Ormonde was actively engaged in planning an uprising in the West Country, when he abruptly lost his nerve and fled to France in July. In the end none of this excitement turned into anything serious, but with no civilian police force available to contain the widespread disorder it fell to the army to deal with it. Scotland by contrast was relatively quiet and so virtually ignored. Indeed there were afterwards bitter complaints that the rising would never have got off the ground if there had been a substantial number of troops in Scotland at the outset.

Notwithstanding all the efforts to increase the size of the British establishment by raising new regiments, it was literally too little and too late. When the crisis came just weeks later it was necessary to mortgage the Irish garrison. Even then the first Irish contingent – a regiment of dragoons and two regiments of foot – did not arrive in Edinburgh until sometime around 24 August, fully three weeks after Mar went north and began raising his followers. However, their arrival in turn allowed Lieutenant-General Thomas Whetham to send Major-General Joseph Wightman forward to Stirling, with two regiments of dragoons and three regiments of foot. All in all the whole lot probably mustered not much more than 1,000 men, but they were at least sufficient for the moment to secure the vitally important bridge over the Forth until further reinforcements could arrive. Orders were immediately sent ordering up those reinforcements in the form of two more cavalry regiments from northern England, but once again it was the Irish garrison which had to be called on to find a third one, together with a second infantry brigade.

Given the popular stereotype, which invariably pictures tartan-clad Scottish Highlanders pitted against English Redcoats, it is worth digressing for a moment to look closely at Wightman's little army. Of his two dragoon regiments, one – Portmore's – is better known to history as the Royal Scots Greys, while Major-General John Hill's was newly raised, quite unfit for service and soon withdrawn. Of Wightman's three regiments of foot, two were unambiguously Scottish: namely the Earl of Orrery's Royal Scots Fusiliers; and Shannon's Edinburgh Regiment, later to become the King's Own Scottish Borderers. The third regiment was the Buffs. Supposedly a quintessentially English regiment, it had been commanded since 1707 first by the Duke of Argyle and then by the Earl of Forfar, and under their patronage it had gradually absorbed a considerable number of Scottish officers and men.

The Scottish character of the British Army was shortly to be firmly underlined by the appointment of a new commander. Lieutenant-General Whetham's post as Commander-in-Chief Scotland, which he had occupied since 1712, was primarily an administrative one. To actually lead the army in the field and at the same time engage effectively with the local authorities, the government turned to John Campbell, 2nd Duke of Argyle. His qualifications for the job were obvious. Born in 1678 he was not only one of the most powerful noblemen in Scotland in his own right, but he was also an unquestioned supporter of the Protestant succession, and above all a thoroughly competent professional soldier who had made a name for himself under the Duke of Marlborough and afterwards served in Spain. Known to his own people as Red John of the Battles, Argyle was still, at the age of thirty-seven, very much in his prime and well able to pursue his new task with vigour as well as ability, local knowledge and a strong measure of common sense.

After an interview with the king on 8 September Argyle got on the road at once. By 12 September he was at Boroughbridge in Yorkshire, complaining of the tardy progress of the two dragoon regiments ordered north, before arriving in Edinburgh two nights later. Next morning he formally inspected the castle and its garrison, congratulated them on having just fought off a Jacobite attempt to seize the place. He then settled down to find some more men.

Local Forces

In addition to the army's existing and sometimes hastily recruited regular forces, there were two other sources of men available to Argyle. As the crisis approached, informal and often enthusiastic offers were made by the Whig gentry to raise local volunteer units, or associations as they were termed, but by and large these were very properly declined. The situation was then delicate enough without what would have amounted to armed vigilante groups roaming around the countryside. Nevertheless once the rising actually began it was a different matter, and the lord lieutenants were expected to mobilise the militia in each county.

Except in Edinburgh, there was no longer an established Scottish militia organisation by this time, but there was still a residual obligation for fencibles, that is, those capable of bearing 'arms defencible' to turn out at the behest of the civil authorities. Similarly in England the authorities were expected to be able to call out what was rather more grandly termed the posse comitatus. This was all very well, but it naturally turned out to be a fairly *ad hoc* affair since there was no established procedure for organising, leading, arming, equipping or even feeding those levies. In practice, other than the fact that the volunteers were more likely to have taken the trouble to arm themselves properly, there was probably very little difference between fencibles and volunteers, since it boiled down to how effective the lord lieutenants and other local authorities actually were in raising men and persuading them to do their duty.

How much effort was expended in doing so obviously depended to a very large extent on the support of the regular army. With Argyle and his regulars sitting in Stirling, the Earl of Buchan had no difficulty in raising, organising and maintaining a battalion locally, which was to do good service in guarding Stirling bridge during the Battle of Sheriffmuir. Likewise, when Mackintosh of Borlum slipped across the Forth in October 1715, Edinburgh was defended against him not only by its town guard (an armed police force recruited from old soldiers) but also by a part-time militia regiment[9] and a 400-strong volunteer regiment, whose soldiers were paid sixpence a day by the Common Council. They and other Lothian fencible units were consequently willing enough to come in from the countryside to help blockade the Jacobites in Leith and afterwards at Seaton House.

Otherwise their employment could be a little more problematic, and typically they tended to be very reluctant to move far from home or to serve for any length of time. Over in the west, Argyle's younger brother, the Earl of Islay, had little difficulty in calling out substantial numbers of Campbell clansmen to defend Inverary against the Jacobites under General Gordon. However, as soon as that particular local threat evaporated, they all went home again. In part this reflected a widespread dislike of Islay himself, but it underlines the importance of personal leadership in persuading men to move out of their local area. By contrast, 120 volunteers from Paisley and another 400 from Ayrshire were persuaded to mount a successful 'expedition' up Loch Lomond way.

By far the best of these fencible units was in fact the three-battalion-strong Glasgow Regiment of Volunteers. This regiment was exceptional in being willing to serve outside its home area for a prolonged period, and it benefited immensely from being commanded by the redoubtable Colonel John Blackadder. One of the original officers of the Cameronians, he not only trained the Glasgow Volunteers properly but also provided quite exceptional inspirational leadership. Although never put to the test, it is likely that they would have proved the equal of regular units. Afterwards Blackadder was rewarded by being appointed deputy governor of Stirling Castle.

For the most part these and other fencibles were so far as possible organised and equipped in the same manner as regular troops. For example, shortly before the town was taken over by the rebels, the Aberdeen town council recommended the provost 'to buy two hundred stand of Armes, viz., guns and bayenotts for the use of the towne, with all convenient diligence'.[10]

How these various units were distinguished from the rebels is not entirely clear, for they must all have looked very similar. Regular troops primarily relied on their red coats for identification since their black cockades were not visible at any distance. Instead both blue or occasionally green cockades were variously worn by volunteers in 1745 and it seems likely that their forebears did likewise in 1715.

Their opponents of course famously wore white ones . . .

Chapter 3
The Jacobites

Aftr their dramatic victory at Prestonpans in 1745, the Jacobites would very consciously promote the impression of their being a Highland army, but this was far from the case thirty years earlier. Although it may at first seem strange that the rebels in 1715 should assume themselves to be capable of raising a conventional army, it is important to recall that few of the British Army's regiments were older than the century. Indeed a significant number of regular units were still in the process of being raised even as the rebellion began. Consequently, while most of the rebels can have been under no illusions about the task in front of them, the various earls, lords and other magnates great and small took it for granted that they could raise their tenants and followers and transform them into an army.

It would take time of course to turn them into proper soldiers, but the Highland clans at least were assumed to be already well armed and of a naturally war-like disposition. This, as we shall see, was a touch optimistic, and ultimately the chief reliance would have to be placed on conventionally equipped and trained soldiers recruited in the lowlands or on the highland estates of the magnates.

Ordinarily, for example, the Marquis of Huntly's men, raised in the hills around Glenlivet, Strathavan and Strathbogie, would be accounted Highlanders, and indeed his early preparations seemingly included the provision of tartan coats and trews for his men. Nevertheless contemporaries did draw a very clear distinction between those Highlanders who were tenants, vassals and followers of magnates such as Huntly, and the wilder men from the west, who were clansmen, following their own chiefs. So far as soldiering was concerned, the simple difference was that, given the will and the instructors, the former were capable of being disciplined and trained, while the latter were not.

The trick of course was raising those tenants and vassals in the first place. While they were not clansmen subject to the whim of their chief, as late as 1745 and arguably beyond there was a tacit assumption that they were obliged to follow and serve their lord in all his undertakings. However, although some dutifully turned out, others proved recalcitrant and even openly defiant, as a well-known letter from Mar illustrates. Disappointed in the numbers actually appearing from his Aberdeenshire estates, he wrote to his baillie, John (Black Jock) Forbes of Inverernan, on 9 September, instructing him to:

> let my own Tenants in Kildrummy know, that if they come not forth with their best Arms, that I will send a Party immediately to burn what they shall miss taking from them. And they may believe this not only a Threat, but, by all that's sacred, I'll put it in execution, let my Loss be what it will, that it may be an example to others. You are to tell the Gentlemen that I'll expect them in their best Accoutrements, on Horseback and no Excuse to be accepted of.[1]

As it happens there is a sequel to this letter, for some of these very tenants from Kildrummy would later obtain testimony that they:

> were forced and Compelled to go out in the unhappy Rebellion much against their inclination, And that they did to be free of the same, Flee from their houses for severall dayes, And that by My Lord Marrs order, Parties were sent, who did sett fire to their houses and corn yards, And after they had absconded for severall dayes, They were taken prisoners by the saids parties, And were sent prisoners to Braemar, where my Lord Marr then was.[2]

It was very much a continuous process, and on 10 January 1716, hoping to make good the losses at Sheriffmuir, the Chevalier issued a proclamation 'requyreing all noblemen, barrons, heritors, wodsetters,[3] and others able to bear armes, to repair to the camp at Perth with ther best horses arms, and accutriments'. Thus for example the Jacobite town council in Aberdeen resolved to:

> raise a troup of thirty horses, well provided with armes and all accutriments; as also produced a scheme thereof, and of the expensis of the same extending to four thousand pund Scots money, which should be proportioned and stented upon the inhabitants . . . and the said troupe be added to and made a part of the Earle Marischalls squadron of horss.[4]

Unfortunately there is then a break of three months in the records before they resumed under a loyalist administration in April, so it is difficult to tell how well these plans were realised. The likelihood is that the troop was never raised or at least never completed. Indeed, coming so late in the day, the proclamation might appear more optimistic than otherwise, but it is significant in showing that once James arrived an attempt was made to activate the fencible system rather than relying on volunteers and their followers.

Organisation

Nevertheless, having once assembled their men, voluntarily or otherwise, Mar, Huntly, Panmure and the others then needed to form them into proper regiments. These by and large were organised in very similar fashion to their regular counterparts.

This was not always to the liking of those concerned. When the Earl of Southesk turned up at Perth with thirty horse and 150 foot, he was allowed to keep his cavalry troop, but after some grumbling his infantry were taken from him and added to the Earl of Strathmore's Regiment. The Master of Sinclair, himself a former soldier, usefully described the process thus:

My Lord Panmure came next into toun [Perth], with a hundred Highlandmen, and tuo hundred Low Countrie men. Auchterhouse,[5] uncle to Strathmore and to the Earle of Aboyne, brought in the Aboyne men. My Lord Nairne and his son brought in their own men, and some of the Duke of Athole's Highlandmen; and now they were in all a great many men, but no such thing as ordor. I did what I could to persuade those who commanded them to pick out such as had served, to make officers and serjeants, and, where they were wanting, to take some of the activest of their folks to supplie; and one day all the guarnisone being drawn out on the South Inch, I told my Lord Panmure there would be no doeing till all that mob was regimented, and accordinglie proposed to him to joyn his men to the Aboyn men, because his Highlandmen of Gleneske and they were neighbours, and it would have a good effect, they having a confidence in one another; that if his Lordship would begin to form a regiment, the others would follow his example. He said, if Auchterhouse was pleased, he desired no better. I went to propose it to Auchterhouse, who was satisfied; and instantlie they formed a regiment, which was called Panmure's Regiment, to which Auchterhouse was Lieutenant-Colonell, and I pointed out to my Lord Panmure one Lesslie, who had served, who he made Major. Barafield[6] and I spoke to Strathmore about joining his Low Countrie men and Southesque's together, being of the same countie. He was satisfied to doe it, but the difficultie was, after they were joined, who should command them; for Strathmore pretended to command the gentlemen of the countie, which it must be owned he had a better title to than Southesque, if either familie or person was to be regarded . . . And that day, Strathmore took the command of Southesque's and his own Low Countriemen joined, and made Barafield his Lieutenant-Colonell, and one Captain Walkinshaw, his Major . . .

My Lord Tullibardine, Lord Charles, and Lord George Murrays formed each of them regiments out of the Athole men and those of Tullibardine, as did their uncle, Lord Nairne, some stronger, and some weaker, as they could get those men to follow them. My Lord Ogilvie, son to the Earle of Earlie, a very younge gentleman, and representative of a verie noble familie, and who was said to be of the first who was engaged, formed a regiment out of the Killiemure [Kirriemuir] and Glenprossen men, and made Sir James Kinloch, who joyn'd him with his follouing, his Lieut.-Colonell. [John] Steuart of Indernitie did the same with the Garntillie [Grantully] men who follued him.

Sinclair then went on to describe how the cavalry were organised:

We, of the horse, were order'd to divide each squadrone in three companies, and name our officers for each company. It was no easie talk to get everie bodie to agree to be commanded by the same officers who were to be named out of the gentlemen; for we had nobodie who had served, and a great manie aspired to a greater or lesser command; and as on all such occasions, these who deserved least, or were good for least, pusht hardest for it. I told those who I was concerned in, That no man must pretend to be Major but one who had served; and till such was found, I'd have none. As to the Captains, Lieutenants, and Cornets, after two days dispute, we at last named them, tho', I can't say, to everie bodies satisfaction; yet we seemed to agree in it better than the other regiments.[7]

The reference to companies (and later to platoons) is odd but probably reflects his own earlier experience as an infantryman, but it will be noted that essentially this was exactly the same organisation as a normal cavalry unit, with three troops to a squadron. The only obvious difference was that the various Jacobite regiments mustered only a single squadron rather than two.

Although not explicitly spelt out, the infantry regiments were intended to be organised like their regular counterparts, with ten companies to a battalion. It did not always work quite so smoothly as this of course, and Sinclair grumbled that:

Tho' orders were given out to form into regiments, everie one did as they pleased. My Lord Drummond, who had got six hundred men together under his name, tho a great part of them belonged to Lord Strathallan, Logie, and his other neighbours, who he teased to follow him, and endeavoured to pass all upon the world as Highlandmen, being extreamlie ambitious to be thought a Highland chief, formed them in three battalions, contrarie to everie bodies advice, who told him they'd make one good, but could not make three. His Lordship laught at those ignorant people, who did not know the mode in France: and being so taken with the sound of the first, second and third battalion of Drummond, there was no persuading him to the contrarie, he imagineing himself a great prince, who had three battalions at his disposal, and the having so many Colonells and Lieut.-Colonells, and other commissions to give, pleased him above all things, and, for the same reason, made the companies as little as possible.[8]

While there is no doubt that Drummond was a law unto himself, in this case Sinclair's animosity proceeded in large part from the fact that the marquis poached a number of Sinclair's men, by offering them commissions in his bloated regiment.

Another similar problem arose with the Earl of Livingston's troop, which was charged with carrying the royal standard. When Mar was joined by the first contingents of men other than his own at Kirkmichael, some twenty or so horsemen were formed into a troop under Livingston and by default charged with carrying the standard. Once the army was properly formed at Perth, however, each of the other squadrons was then milked of two or three men in order to bring the standard troop, as it was by then known, up to a respectable size.

Although Sinclair claimed a great deal of the credit, this sensible process of consolidation and reorganisation of the various contingents to conform with regular practice was otherwise due to the influence of the professional soldiers. One was George Hamilton, a younger brother of the Duke of Hamilton and a career soldier who as a major general had commanded the Dutch Army's Scots Brigade. Although he had served creditably in that capacity under the Duke of Marlborough, it may have been his erratic brother's Jacobite sympathies that brought him back to Scotland with Mar. At Sheriffmuir George Hamilton would be criticised for being unable to adapt to a rapidly changing situation as the hasty advance seemed to dissolve into chaos, but when it came to organising and training the army he may have been exactly what was needed.

The most important of the professionals was probably a man named William Clephane, who had been major of the Laird of Grant's Regiment when it was broken in 1713. When it was then reactivated in July 1715 Argyle seemingly wanted Clephane to organise the Duke of Athole's people, but instead he defected to the rebels, gained a step in rank to lieutenant-colonel and was appointed their adjutant-general. Even the ever-acerbic Sinclair very grudgingly admitted Clephane 'knew the detaile of a regiment', and in the end it may have been Clephane more than any other who succeeded in hammering those raw regiments into shape.[9]

At a lower level too there was a reasonable amount of talent about. Sinclair had himself been a captain under Marlborough,[10] and the widespread redundancies, which followed the end of the war, ensured there were plenty of other half-pay officers prepared to try their luck, as well as former soldiers to serve as NCOs.

Arms and Equipment

Having been formed and officered, those regiments also had to be properly equipped, but perhaps not surprisingly this tended to be patchy. By and large there had been a fair amount of preparation before the rising began. One typical intelligence report in August 1715 claimed for instance that:

> Huntly has been wholly taken up with preparations all this summer, especially in buying of horses and using them to the Drum.[11] He is said to have 600 of them scattered up and down the country well equipped and a great number of foot well appointed. He has employed one Peter McKoul, an old trooper, to list men for the Pretender . . .[12]

At a lesser level, after much argument the Master of Sinclair persuaded his Jacobite neighbours to authorise him to order 'fourscore [80] carbines and carbine belts, and as many pairs of pistols, with a small quantity of pouder and flints' for a troop of horse to be raised in Fife.[13] As gentlemen they would no doubt possess swords as a matter of course and would therefore have been equipped in exactly the same manner as regular cavalry. Alas, thanks to their prevarication his colleagues left it too late for the carbines, but most still managed to find pistols.

Those rebel cavalry raised in Nithsdale and in the borders by Lord Kenmure, and by Forster and Derwentwater in Northumberland, were even worse off, as Sinclair claimed, after speaking with an English courier who turned up at Perth:

> . . . of those few or none were well arm'd, all the greatest part altogether without armes; that their horses were light hunting horses, and hunting saddles and snaffles made up their accoutrements; that there was scarce a cutting sword among them all: in testimonie of which he said, That for such swords as we wore [presumably basket-hilted broadswords] he could change each for a horse of twenty-five guineas . . . I askt him about the Scots who had joyn'd with Kenmure. He said, They were about a hundred, and that they were much better horsed for the purpose, because they had strong ruff horses, and were all very well armed; which I understood, well armed in comparison of the English.[14]

Indeed, all too alive to what was going on, in the months before the rising began the authorities made concerted efforts to seize any stocks of arms and gunpowder they could find. As the crisis approached such seizures were not confined to the houses of 'suspected persons' but extended to any other supplies quite legitimately held in private hands. Thus in Aberdeen on 15 September 1715 the astonishing total of thirty-eight hundredweight of gunpowder – nearly two tons of the stuff – was confiscated from the various merchants of the town.[15]

It thus fell to those powerful enough not to fear the magistrates, to gather the substantial numbers of arms required. When the Jacobites seized Perth, almost by accident, at the beginning of the rising, the young Earl of Strathmore was very quickly able to raise some two hundred Lowland foot, all armed with firelocks to serve as a proper garrison.

A quantity of French muskets had certainly been smuggled in by gunrunners in the years leading up to the rising, but, although a further 20,000 stand of arms were promised, unlike in 1745 few if any were received during the rising. Consequently, while it was relatively easy to provide firelocks and bayonets for most of those men levied out at the very beginning of the rising, finding sufficient arms for the later contingents was a different matter, especially as time went on. Thus we find that on 14 October Mar ordered 150 Lochaber axes to be made at Montrose and another 300 to be made in Aberdeen and delivered to the camp at Perth. Doubtless other burghs received similar demands, and all were destined no doubt for the regiments then assembling there.[17]

Tactics

Nor did the process end with organising and equipping the men, for they then had to be trained in conventional drill and tactics. In this, thanks to George Hamilton and William Clephane, the Jacobites would be reasonably successful, despite their chronic shortage of ammunition. The men who would fight – and in some cases run away – at Sheriffmuir were certainly not a bucolic untrained rabble, and those men carrying Lochaber axes rather than firelocks were almost certainly formed into discrete companies rather than scattered through the ranks.

In terms of training they were at least able to carry out their evolutions tolerably well; that is, they were able to march and carry out basic manoeuvres. Indeed at Sheriffmuir even Argyle's second-in-command, Major-General Wightman, was moved to say: 'I never saw Regular Troops more exactly drawn up in Line of Battle, and that in a moment.'[18] On the other hand, with neither the experienced NCOs to teach it nor the powder to practice it, no attempt was made to train the men in the complicated platoon firing rituals so beloved of the regular army. Instead Clephane very sensibly had the men deliver their fire by ranks, a much simpler method as was practised in the French Army.

An anonymous eyewitness account accordingly noted that at Sheriffmuir: 'They fired by rancks each rank reteering and not in platoons.'[19] Employing this simplified drill turned out to be unexpectedly effective, and, as we shall see, another loyalist volunteer described how sustained Jacobite musketry, probably from Logie Drummond's men, made a sad havoc of Evans's Dragoons.[20]

On the other hand, while many other accounts emphasise a certain degree of disorder. James Keith specifically linked that disorder not to the reasonably well disciplined if raw Lowland units, but to the Highland units who had pushed in amongst them.

The Highland Clans with Sword in Hand

It was Duncan Forbes of Culloden who provided the best definition of a Highland clan when he described them as:

> . . . a set of men all bearing the same surname and believing themselves to be related one to the other and to be descended from the same common stock. In each clan there are several subaltern tribes, who owe their dependence on their own immediate chief, but all agree in owing allegiance to the Supreme Chief of the Clan or Kindred and look upon it to be their duty to support him in all adventures. As those Clans and Kindreds live by themselves, and possess different Straths, Glens or districts, without any considerable mixture of Strangers, it has been for a great many years impracticable (and hardly thought safe to try it) to give the Law its course among the Mountains.

Those described by Forbes were very largely from the western Highlands. Although dignified by the title of regiments, in terms of organisation they resembled regular ones only very superficially. Unlike those units recruited by say Huntly and Panmure, they were in reality tribes large and small, each commanded by their chieftains. In theory raising a clan regiment was very straightforward, since as one of Robert Louis Stevenson's characters remarked: 'When the piper plays the clan must dance.' Companies within these regiments were in turn commanded by their 'near relations' or by their tacksmen.[21] The rank and file were then in turn found from among their subtenants, dependents and anyone else who had an actual or implied obligation to follow them.

On 1 September 1715 Mar sent a letter 'to the Lairds of Glengary, Locheil, Clanranald, Keppoch, Apin, Glenco, McDougal and Glenmoriston' proclaiming that only by restoring James to the throne could the thraldom of the Union settlement be broken, and urging them to raise and arm their men and march immediately to join 'the Gentlemen of Argyllshire in the King's interest'. It is difficult, however, to interpret this other than an appeal to allies rather than to the Jacobites' core supporters. This is underscored both by the lack of visible enthusiasm for the adventure among most of the chiefs, and by Mar's intention that instead of joining him at once they should march on their own against Glasgow.

Notwithstanding this apparent intention to keep them at arm's length, the wild men of the west had always figured prominently in Jacobite planning, because it was assumed that the chiefs could not only raise large numbers of men quickly, but just as importantly they would also neither require to be trained nor equipped.

All three of those easy assumptions were only partly true. As we shall see, bringing the clans out was not as easy as had been hoped. In practice some of those tacksmen and subtenants proved unaccountably backward in obeying the summons of their chief, and at the best of times there was no consistency in the size of regiments or companies, which made it difficult for them to manoeuvre other than as an undisciplined mob.

That they were naturally war-like, trained in arms and already possessed of sufficient weapons to be formidable was true, but only up to a point. Ironically one of the best contemporary descriptions of Highland soldiers comes from a Whig source, talking of Campbell of Mamore's expedition up Loch Lomond, which was joined by a loyalist contingent under Sir Humphrey Colquhoun of Luss and James Grant of Pluscarden:

> . . . follow'd by fourty or fifty stately fellows in their short hose and belted plaids, arm'd each of 'em with a well fix'd gun on his shoulder, a strong handsome target, with a sharp pointed steel, of above half an ell [20in] in length, screw'd into the navel of it on his left arm, a sturdy claymore by his side, and a pistol or two with dirk and knife on his belt.[22]

And very splendid it sounds too, but as with everything else about these clan regiments, it did not quite work that way in the field. In the first place it was generally only the Highland gentlemen, the heads of household, standing in the front rank of the clan regiment who were fully accoutred, with all the awful panoply of broadsword, targe, musket, dirk and pistols displayed by Luss and Pluscarden's contingent. If the whole clan was being levied out, those standing behind them – the ordinary clansmen – were far less well equipped, and, instead of relatively expensive broadswords, at best most made do with Lochaber axes and the like. Indeed the chiefs themselves consistently cited a lack of arms for their followers as one of the impediments to raising them, and complained at length about how badly armed they were when they did join the rebel army.[23]

It is quite true that those able to afford to do so were accustomed to swaggering abroad with swords by their sides and guns on their shoulders, and no doubt they learned how to handle them as well in individual combat, as gentlemen should. However, like everyone else, none of them had been to war since the rout at Cromdale a quarter century before. To all intents and purposes, far from being fearsome warriors they were all of them raw levies quite unaccustomed to anything more than the odd minor scuffle between individuals and were quite incapable of any manoeuvre more complicated than a headlong rush at the enemy.

Although some spoke fondly of the Highlanders' supposed marksmanship there is a whole world of difference between shooting accurately for sport or when out hunting, and shooting at a foe intent on firing back! Not that it actually mattered, for unlike the 'regular' regiments being trained by George Hamilton and William Clephane, the clans had no intention of engaging in a firefight with anyone. Their preferred method of fighting was to fire a single volley with every musket at their disposal, then charge through the smoke sword in hand.

The single, and no doubt quite ragged, volley fired during the famed Highland charge was not of itself decisive, for the success of the business did not depend on laying large numbers of men dead, whether by musket balls or by cold steel, but rather by intimidation. Essentially clansmen tried to rush their opponents and induce them to flinch, break and run before getting in among them. Not only did this tactic work with surprising frequency, but as ever success breeds success and a ferocious reputation helped increase the chances of raw and impressionable troops giving way before them. Conversely, should their opponents not obligingly give way but instead stand firm, there was a real danger that – as at Culloden – the clansmen would themselves stumble to a halt and commence shooting first with muskets, then pistols and then throwing stones. In an unequal contest they were bound to come off worse, unless some hero could get them moving again.

There was also another problem, which became apparent at Sheriffmuir, as James Keith explained:

. . . one must know the habit of the Highlanders and their manner of fighting; their cloaths are composed of two short vests, the one above reaching only to their waste, the other about six inches longer, short stockings which reaches not quite to their knee, and no breeches; but above all they have another piece of the same stuff, of about six yards long, which they tye about them in such a manner that it covers their thighs and all their body when they please, but commonly it's fixed on their left shoulder and leaves their right arm free. This kind of mantel they throw away when they are ready to engage, to be lighter and less encumber'd, and if they are beat it remains on the field, as happen'd to our left wing, who having lost that part of their cloaths which protects them most from the cold, and which likewise serves for bed cloaths . . .[24]

Just as importantly the Highlanders also lost their muskets, which they had discarded before charging. They thus lacked the resilience of more conventional troops. Defeat left them half naked and effectively unarmed, so it is hardly surprising that so many of them returned home after Sheriffmuir and proved even more difficult than before to levy out again.

The fact of the matter was that, on the one hand, a Highland charge could be devastatingly effective. When launched against an uncertain foe it was calculated not just to cause him to break and run, but also to harry him to destruction in the pursuit. On the other hand there was a tendency not press home attacks against an enemy maintaining a resolute front, and this weakness was exacerbated by the fact that clansmen were quite incapable of engaging in a firefight, and once broken tended to be quite useless afterwards. What was more, away from the battlefield Highland troops were notoriously ill-disciplined, much given to plundering friend and foe alike, and very prone to taking themselves off for home or some private venture.

In short it was hardly surprising that, while admitting their bravery and other good qualities, the Jacobite leaders should see them as very useful auxiliaries, but still place their reliance on what were intended to be properly trained and equipped regiments.

As it turned out too, notwithstanding those early assumptions that the clans would provide them with an immediate nucleus of armed and dangerous men, it was those Lowland levies who would take the field first and secure control of their immediate objectives.

Chapter 4

The Rebellion Begins

O N 3 S EPTEMBER , A week after the tinchal, Mar held a more business-like meeting at Aboyne, further down Deeside. According to his own declaration there were eleven other Jacobite leaders present: Alexander Gordon, Marquis of Huntly; William Murray, Marquis of Tullibardine; George Keith, the Earl Marischal;[1] James Carnegie, Earl of Southesk; Alexander MacDonnell of Glengarry; Campbell of Glendaruel, representing the aged Earl of Breadalbane; Patrick Lyon of Auchterhouse; the laird of Auldbar; Lieutenant-General George Hamilton; and Major-General Alexander Gordon of Auchintoul.[2] It was there they formally agreed to 'appear openly in arms' in the name of King James, and so returned to Braemar and raised the standard three days later, on 6 September.[3]

There were only some 600 men present at the ceremony. Some were the nucleus of Mar's own regiment under the command of Lieutenant-Colonel Peter Farquharson of Inverey.[4] Others were no doubt the immediate following of some of the other leaders present and some merely interested spectators. It was certainly not an army, and as soon as the ceremony was over the Jacobite leaders dispersed to raise their people. This did not go as smoothly as they had hoped. As we saw in the previous chapter, some of Mar's own tenants in Kildrummy at first proved unco-operative, and there was some unseemly wrangling with Huntly over others. A considerable amount of time was also spent in writing letters and declarations to those who had not been present. Consequently it was not until 12 September that Mar actually started moving south over the pass known as the Spittal of Glenshee to the village of Kirkmichael. Still short of men, he halted there for a couple of days.

Although Mar had only travelled about twenty-five miles he had effectively come out of the mountains and was joined almost at once by a small battalion raised by Alexander Robertson of Strowan, and enough mounted volunteers to form a small troop of horse under the Earl of Livingston, which was given charge of the standard. Less happily, as it turned out, Mar was also joined by the Marquis of Drummond.

The Curious Affair of the Castle

The marquis, as it happens, was technically on the run, having been distantly involved in organising an abortive attempt to capture Edinburgh Castle a few days earlier. The Edinburgh Castle venture seemed promising enough at the time, but had rapidly descended into something of a comic-opera affair. Most of the regular soldiers in and around the capital had gone up to Stirling, leaving just a tiny garrison in the castle under Lieutenant-Colonel James Steuart:[5] 'only of a hundred men and twenty wanting – all in rags, no proper clothing and never more than one day's provision'.[6]

The key figure in the plot was an Edinburgh gentleman named Thomas Arthur, who had formerly served in the garrison while an ensign in the Scots Guards.[7] Sinclair claimed afterwards that plans for seizing the castle had been laid as long ago as 1708, but if so they must have been tolerably vague. At any event some months before the rising began, Arthur talked to some of the soldiers in the garrison and so with gold and the promise of promotion he induced Sergeant William Ainslie and two of his men to assist. They agreed to attend at a relatively low part of the wall on the north side, near the sally port, in order to assist the conspirators in getting over it. The latter had prepared a number of rope ladders, contrived that they could be drawn up through means of pulleys, by a small rope, which the soldiers were to let down to them. Having completed their arrangements, the rebels fixed on the night of 9 September for the attempt, being the day after the last detachment of the government troops quartered in camp in St Anne's Yards, near Edinburgh, was to set off for Stirling.

The storming party supposedly comprised two groups; forty Highlanders sent from Perthshire by Drummond to infiltrate the capital and another forty or fifty adventurers scraped up in Edinburgh itself from among a miscellaneous rabble of half-pay officers, writers, apprentices and gentlemen's sons. Drummond however was managing the affair from a very safe distance, and there is no evidence that either his deputy, William Drummond (or MacGregor) of Balhaldie, or any of his men were actually present at the débâcle. Instead it was all left to Arthur and to an Aberdeenshire laird named Charles Forbes of Brux, whom Drummond had appointed engineer.

Arthur's brother, William, a physician in Edinburgh, was also to help him with the ladders, but by an unfortunate coincidence William's brother-in-law was none other than Sir Adam Cockburn of Ormiston, the lord justice clerk. Finding what her husband was up to, Dr Arthur's wife sent her brother, Cockburn, an 'anonymous' letter acquainting him with the conspiracy. Sir Adam only received this letter at about ten o'clock that night, but promptly forwarded it to Lieutenant-Colonel Steuart up at the castle. By that time the drawbridge had been raised and the gates shut for the night, so it took some time before the letter was delivered. On reading it, and considering its uncertain origin and the absence of any rebels knocking on his door, Steuart in turn simply ordered the officers to double their guards and make diligent rounds; and then very sensibly went off to bed.

In the meantime, rather than hang around in the streets looking furtive, many of the putative storming party spent the evening drinking in various taverns. The attempt was to be made at 10 p.m., long before Cockburn's warning reached Steuart. Alas, not only were the Jacobites late in assembling in the West Kirk yard, but Forbes of Brux was conspicuous by his absence. So too were the additional ladders he was supposed to be bringing. Not surprisingly there was some dithering at this point, but eventually the conspirators decided to try their luck anyway and scrambled up the rock to the base of the wall. Ainslie and the two sentries, Thomson and Holland, then lowered their rope, and the only available ladder was attached to it. Perhaps inevitably they then discovered when it was hauled up that it was a fathom (six feet) too short. With still no sign of Brux and the additional ladders, dithering turned to consternation 'when the sentrie perceaveing the rounds comeing about, called down to them, "God damn you all! You have ruined both yourselves and me! Here comes the round I have been telling you of this hour, I can serve you no longer." '8

While Ainslie slipped the rope, Thomson fired in the general direction of the Jacobites in an attempt to divert suspicion, but it was too late, for Lieutenant James Lindsay, the officer of the day, had seen them. He and his men also blazed away with rather more deadly intent and then seized Ainslie and Thomson. No one was actually hurt in the affair except an old Jacobite named Captain Allan Maclean, who fell and was injured scrambling down the rock. He and three others were promptly arrested by a patrol from the town guard, who also picked up the ladder and a quantity of muskets and carbines discarded by the conspirators. Inside the castle, Ainslie was eventually given a fair trial and hanged from its wall some time after the rising, while Thomson and Holland escaped with a flogging. The rest of the Jacobites got clean away, and Thomas Arthur next turned up as major to one of Drummond's battalions, while his brother would later serve as a courier between Mar and the English Jacobites.

When Argyle arrived a few days later he decided an immediate example was wanted and had Colonel Steuart imprisoned on suspicion of complicity. He may well have been right, but, as evidence was once again lacking, Steuart was later allowed to retire quietly on half pay. No such doubt attended Lieutenant Lindsay's part in the affair, and when he wrote a brief account of it later that day he signed it as *Captain* Lindsay![9]

Taking Edinburgh Castle would have been a spectacular coup, but keeping it might have been quite another challenge, particularly given the lack of provisions and Argyle's imminent arrival. Notwithstanding, a rather more important Jacobite success occurred just days later, on 12 September.

The Taking of Perth

When news reached them of Jacobite preparations for a rising, the loyalist magistrates in Perth naturally responded by disarming known dissidents and any other suspected persons. The Earl of Rothes, in his capacity as lord lieutenant of Fife, was also asked to call out the shire's fencibles and march to the burgh's assistance. As he had recently taken delivery of 500 stand of arms[10] and a competent supply of ammunition, Rothes readily agreed to help, but the rebels turned up first. Thereupon, on hearing a rumour of the city's capture, Rothes's levies dispersed in confusion. By Sinclair's account this happened before the Jacobites had actually taken the city, but it seems more likely the panic occurred afterwards as the news spread.

As early as 27 July the Duke of Athole had also offered some of his people to assist in the defence of Perth, and after prevaricating for a time the council duly accepted 200 men. However, although Athole was very keen to demonstrate his loyalty to King George, if only to counter rumours he had been offered command of the rebel forces, the rest of his family were otherwise inclined. Discreet enquiries were therefore made by the rebels of the men the duke had sent to defend Perth. Not unexpectedly, the happy discovery was made that they were equally divided in their loyalties and likely to declare for whichever party turned up first. Accordingly on 12 September a message was sent by the local

Jacobites to Colonel John Hay of Cromlix, a son of the Earl of Kinnoull, advising him that the burgh was ripe for revolt if he would only come and take it. Hay, as it happens, was not only an officer in the 1st Footguards but his commission had just been renewed by King George![11] He was also a committed Jacobite, but at such short notice he could only find about forty horsemen, and even they were simply skulking about in order to avoid arrest. Not that it mattered, for – as Sinclair recorded – no sooner did this motley crew appear on the other side of the Tay than the Jacobites in the town 'revolted', seized boats and began to ferry them across. Even though the magistrates had Athole's men drawn up in the marketplace, there was no opposition because they were reluctant to initiate any bloodshed, especially as they were uncertain of the Highlanders' loyalty. There was probably good reason for this uneasiness, for Sinclair claims that one of their leaders, the Laird of Gray, had quietly collected all their flints, rendering their firelocks useless![12] The matter was then quickly decided when Hay and his party confronted them. Notwithstanding their lack of flints, Athole's men very politely enquired of the magistrates whether they should open fire. The provost, unaware that they were bluffing and understandably unwilling to see his own neighbours shot down in the streets, frantically replied 'no blood, no blood'. Very sensibly both sides thereupon came to an agreement whereby the burgh's arms were handed over to the rebels, and those of its defenders who wished to depart were free to do so.

Other burghs north of the Tay, including Aberdeen, Arbroath and Dundee, also fell into Jacobite hands with even less fuss, but the importance of this early seizure of Perth, seemingly without Mar's knowledge, cannot be overstated. It was one of the most substantial towns in pre-industrial Scotland, perfectly situated as a base on which to form an army – both as regards access from other parts of the country, and in being capable of supplying that army with most of its immediate needs in terms of food, clothing and shelter.

Mar immediately responded by confirming Cromlix as governor of the burgh and sending off Strowan's Regiment to serve as a garrison. In the meantime, the young Earl of Strathmore also turned up with 200 foot and the Master of Sinclair with fifty horse, albeit the latter could not resist grumbling:

> We had a hundred gentlemen and servants [horse], without carabines, who could be of no
> use in the defence of a place, and tuo hundred Low Countrie men, with old rustie muskets,
> who had never fired one in their lives, and without pouder and flints, with about fiftie
> Highlandmen no better accoutred.[13]

Sinclair, with his usual happy knack for upsetting people, was also immediately at odds with Cromlix over the state of the burgh's defences. Essentially they comprised a medieval wall, which was not only in a decrepit state, but was also too high and lacking a fire step, especially near the gates, which themselves were flimsy affairs. The circuit of the defences was also too great for the available garrison to cover, and matters were not helped by the fact that Sinclair and a Captain Alexander Urquhart of Newhall were the only officers who had seen any service: Sinclair as a captain of foot under Marlborough, and Newhall in Spain.[14] Although Cromlix was a guardsman, Sinclair loftily claimed, with all the natural disdain of a line officer, that Cromlix was:

> lately come from schoole, and having bought, before the Queen's death, a companie on
> the Footguards, where all the service he had done was to have mounted the guard once
> or twice at St James', was now turned so vaine of his title of Collonell and, and that of
> Gouvernour . . .

Cromlix also took no notice of Urquhart. When Sinclair remonstrated with him as to the state of the defences 'all this was gibberish to him'.

Happily Mar and General Hamilton were also on their way, leaving Kirkmichael on about 18 September and stopping for a few days at a time at Moulinearn and Logierait in their stately progress. At Dunkeld they were joined by a substantial number of the Duke of Atholes's people, under his eldest son and heir, the Marquis of Tullibardine. Eventually no fewer than four battalions were raised from among his tenants and vassals; one by his brother, Lord Nairne, and three more by Tullibardine and two of his younger sons.[15] The duke himself still declined to get involved and loudly protested both his loyalty to King George and his inability to control his family. Whether or not this was genuine or was a matter of posturing to ensure their survival whatever the outcome, this family split had unfortunate consequences.

There was therefore every reason for optimism as Mar rode into Perth on 28 September. Scotland was starting to rise and a whole slew of other units were being levied up and down the lowlands of the east coast and making their way to Perth.

General Gordon in the West

The clans, or at least the western ones, however, were proving surprisingly problematic. In popular imagination, the Highland clans and Jacobitism are virtually synonymous. To a certain extent, given their prominence in the last

Jacobite rising in 1745, this is at the very least an understandable impression, yet at the same time it is an uncertain one. To the clans in 1715, as in previous conflicts, Jacobitism was not primarily a question of supporting the rightful lawful king – whoever he might be – but the pursuit of more localised interests. Lowland magnates such as Mar himself, and Drummond, Strathmore, Panmure and Auchterhouse, might legitimately expect future advancement and influence commensurate with their services should they effect the desired regime change. For those in the west Highlands the potential rewards were more limited, and there must have been an underlying realisation that, whether James or George sat upon the throne, they would be no less marginalised than before. Consequently the Highlanders were slow to commit themselves. Some of the clan chiefs may have attended the tinchal, but only Alexander MacDonnell of Glengarry witnessed the raising of the standard at Braemar, and he was at first the only one to call out his people.

Perhaps anticipating this, Mar had agreed to send a general officer to take charge of the clan levies. This was partly in order to provide experienced leadership but partly to avoid the inevitable wrangling and refusals by the individual chieftains to acknowledge the authority of their rivals. The officer charged with this delicate and ultimately thankless task was an Aberdeenshire man, Major-General Alexander Gordon of Auchintoul. In theory he might have seemed an excellent choice. He had long served in first the French Army and then in the Russian one under Peter the Great, before returning to Scotland on the death of his father in 1711. On the other hand he was now in his fifties and probably getting a little too old for such adventures. His motives for joining in the rebellion are therefore unclear.

While Mar was still at Kirkmichael, Gordon had ridden west with Breadalbane's people to meet with Glengarry and the western clans at Strathfillan on or about 20 September. He was in for a disappointment. Glengarry had indeed brought his own people, together with their traditional allies, the Grants of Glenmoriston and the Glen Urquhart Grants, but no one else turned up.[16] The Camerons were hopefully expected, as were the Stewarts of Appin. Unfortunately both they and the Keppoch MacDonalds professed themselves 'terrified by the garrison of Fort William, who threatens to destroy all the Country how soon ever we leave it'.[17] In reality that garrison was far too weak and isolated to threaten anyone, but the excuse underlines their marked lack of enthusiasm. In the end the Clanranald MacDonalds turned up in some strength along with another Hebridean battalion under Sir John Maclean. Campbell of Glendaruel duly brought in about 200 of

Breadalbane's people, and the MacGregors under Rob Roy and Drummond of Balhaldie may have contributed as many as 300, although it seems doubtful there were so many. It also took far too long to gather them in, and the Camerons and the Appin men had still not turned up by 17 October, when Gordon grimly marched south while Keppoch, still pleading the impossibility of leaving his lands unprotected from the Fort William garrison, contrived not to appear at all.

There is no doubt that Gordon was anxious to get moving when he did before the Highlanders slipped through his fingers again, but his destination proved controversial. The problem was that his instructions from Mar, as repeated on 4 October, were more than tolerably vague:

> The service you are going about, were once the Rest joined you, is of great Consequence; and the more because of the Arms Glenderule writs me are lately put into Inverary; Therefore you are to loose no Time in going about with all Expedition, but you would take Care that you be sufficiently able to execute it, and out of danger of being affronted. I will not begin with burning Houses, so I hope you will have no Occasion of doung that to the House of Inverary, and tho' you may threaten it, you must not put it in Execution till you acquaint me, and have my Return. Let Care also be taken of the Policy (as they call it) about the House, so that it receive no Damage, and every thing else as little as possible.
>
> After you have done the Work at Inverary, which, upon Resistance, I think you had better do by a Blocad than Storm, you may proceed Westward conform to the former Orders; but by Reason of my not marching from hence so soon as I intended, you would not march so far that Way, but that you can join us upon Occasion, nearer than Monteith, if there should be Need for it; tho' I scarce can believe there will, or that we can send you a reinforcement from hence, if they should think of attacking you with any considerable force from Stirling.[18]

When Mar talked of 'proceeding Westward' he evidently envisaged Gordon operating independently out to the west of the main army at Perth, rather than expecting him to march towards the Atlantic. There may have been an idea of seizing Glasgow and perhaps Dumbarton, or even of simply outflanking Argyle's position at Stirling, but it was all very vague and uncertain. Either course could have been effective, if successful, but as the Loch Lomond expedition demonstrated it would certainly not have been a walkover.

Loch Lomond

Alarmed by the appearance of the notorious Rob Roy MacGregor at the north end of Loch Lomond on about 10 October, a variety of loyalist units in the

Glasgow area were assembled to deal with him. The core of the expeditionary force comprised the 120-strong Paisley Volunteers and another 200-odd fencibles from Ayrshire, all under the command of John Campbell of Mamore. A number of longboats were obtained from the navy, together with about 100 seamen to man them, and then brought up the river Leven from Dumbarton on 12 October. Once arrived, most of the loyalist infantry were put aboard, and so off they went.

One of those taking part in the expedition afterwards wrote a splendid little account of the affair, which is worth repeating:

> When the pinnaces and boats, being once got within the mouth of the loch, had spread their sails, and the men on the shore had rang'd themselves in order, marching along the side of the loch for scouring the coast, they made all together so very fine an appearance as had never been seen in that place before, and might have gratified even a curious person. The men on shore marched with the greatest ardour and alacrity. The pinnaces on the water discharging their Pateraroes, and the men their small arms, and made so dreadful a noise thro' the multiply'd rebounding echoes of the vast mountains on both sides of the loch, that perhaps there was never a more lively resemblance of thunder.
>
> Against evening they got to Luss, where they came ashore, and were met and join'd by Sir Humphrey Colquhoun of Luss, Baronet, and the chief of the name, and James Grant of Pluscarden, his son-in-law and brother german to Brigadier Grant, follow'd by fourty or fifty stately fellows in their short hose and belted plaids, arm'd each of 'em with a well fix'd gun on his shoulder, a strong handsome target, with a sharp pointed steel, of above half an ell in length, screwed into the navel of it on his left arm, a sturdy claymore by his side, and a pistol or two with a durk and knife on his belt. Here the whole company rested all night. In the mean time, many reports were brought to them, contrived or at least magnified by the Jacobites in order to discourage them from the attempt; such as, that McDonald of Glengarry, who was indeed lying with his men about Strathfillan, sixteen miles from the head of the loch, had reinforced the Mc greigours, so that they amounted to at least fifteen hundred men, whereas there were not full four hundred on the expedition against them; That the loch being narrow, where the rebels were lying, they might pepper the boats from the shore without any danger to themselves, being shaded by the rocks and woods. In a word, that it was a desperate project, and would be a throwing away of their lives.
>
> But all this could not dishearten these brave men. They knew that the Mc greigours and the Devil are to be dealt with after the same manner, and that if they be resisted they will flee. Wherefor on the morrow morning, being Thursday the 13th they went on in

their expedition, and about noon came to Innersnaat [Inversnaid], the place of danger. In order to rouse those thieves from their dens, Captain Clark loos'd one of his great guns, and drove a ball thro' the roof of a house on the face of the mountain, whereupon an old wife or two came crawling out and scrambled up the hill, but otherwise ther was no appearance of any body of men on the mountains, only some few, standing out of reach on the craggy rocks looking at them.

Whereupon . . . an hundred men in all, with the greatest intrepidity leapt on shore, got up the top of the mountain, and drew up in order, and stood about an hour, their drums beating all the while, but no enemie appearing, they thereupon went in quest of the boats which the rebels had seiz'd, and having casually lighted on some ropes, anchors and oars, hid among the shrubs, at length they found the boats drawn a good way on the land, which they hurled down to the loch; such of 'em as were not damaged they carried off with them, and such as were they sunk or hew'd in pieces. And that same night they return'd to Luss, and thence, next day, without loss or hurt of so much as one man, to Dumbarton, whence they had first set out altogether, bringing along with them the whole boats they found in their way on either side of the loch and in the creeks of the isles, and moor'd them under the cannon of the castle.[19]

It is possible the Jacobites may have been collecting the boats with a view to mounting their own expedition in the opposite direction, towards Dumbarton, but Glendaruel's story about the 1,000 stand of arms brought to Inverary by the Earl of Islay drew them across there instead.

Inverary

By the time the rebels arrived at Inverary on 19 October, Lord Islay, Argyle's younger brother, had put the place in a state of defence. His high-handed behaviour in pulling down outlying houses and barricading the street ends, combined with a barely concealed contempt for all Highlanders including his own clansmen, won him no friends, but his preparations were sufficient to deter Gordon. Just a little more than seventy years earlier, another Highland army led by the Marquis of Montrose and the legendary Alasdair MacCholla had sacked the burgh and burned all the farms and villages for miles around. Ostensibly it was a punitive expedition on behalf of Charles I, but in reality it was the last hurrah of the Clan Donald in its ancient feud with Clan Campbell. Since then the Highlands had mellowed. There might still – as Duncan Forbes complained – be a strong lawless element, but as elsewhere the wanton destruction and loss of life during the Great Civil War had shocked most people into a near-paranoid determination to avoid a repeat of such a breakdown in civil society. There was in short no appetite for it, even discounting Mar's instructions on that score.

The only reason for moving on Inverary in the first place had been to seize those 1,000 stand of arms, and without them the Jacobites themselves lacked the means to mount a serious attack on the burgh. Therefore, finding himself opposed, Gordon, agreeable to his instructions, contented himself with a half-hearted blockade by establishing a camp about a mile outside the burgh and waiting to see what turned up.

Inside Inverary meanwhile the garrison was entertained by various false alarms, such as one night when some horses got loose and the noise of their moving from one pasture to another was mistaken for a Jacobite attack. On another occasion there may have been a genuine raid when a party of Highlanders, popularly supposed to be led by Rob Roy MacGregor, tried to creep into the burgh, only to run off again quickly when they were fired on. A third and yet more spectacular false alarm occurred on the night of 24 October, when the sergeant of the guard forgot the password and was very properly shot at by a sentry. Various others joined in with rather less excuse, and Islay ordered his drummers to beat to arms and turn out the whole garrison. They in turn then managed to shoot up their own sentries as they came running in, before everyone calmed down and remained standing under arms until morning. Afterwards however it was very unkindly claimed that Islay had stayed safely inside the castle all the while and shouted his orders from a window! Not that it mattered, for Mar had already sent instructions for Gordon to join him at Perth, and he accordingly marched eastwards the next morning, without let or hindrance.

Chapter 5

Round the World
and the Kingdom of Fife

WHILE GORDON WAS ENGAGED in his futile expedition in the west, events at Perth were at first looking altogether more promising, albeit there was little actual movement. Instead it was a period of consolidation while individual leaders brought in their men.

Some contingents were large enough to serve as discrete corps. The Marquis of Huntly was said to have arrived with 1,200 foot and a rather improbable 400 horse. This was not without its difficulties. Huntly had to halt most of his followers at Coupar [Angus], to wait while accommodation was arranged for them in Perth. This may in turn account for an otherwise odd report that, when the Earl Marischal also arrived in Perth on 7 October, he had a substantial body of infantry as well as his squadron of horse.[1] As it soon turned out, many of Huntly's cavalry were effectively no more than mounted infantry riding on little garrons. Sinclair's more realistic estimate of 160 cavalry presumably related only to those who were properly mounted, because the rest were soon sent home again, tactfully tasked with patrolling the Banffshire coast.[2]

As discussed earlier, it was more common for the contingents to be relatively small, in which case they would be joined with others to form viable regiments. This often required more than a little tact as we have seen in the case of Southesk's followers, but more awkward was a squabble involving Mar himself.

On 5 October, William Mackintosh of Borlum and the Laird of Mackintosh arrived with a strong regiment from the Inverness area. When Mar first came into north to raise the standard he had become embroiled in a dispute with one of his own vassals, John Farquharson of Invercauld. As Mar at that point had not yet received formal authority for his actions from the would-be King James,

Invercauld was understandably leery of committing himself. Instead he slipped out of his home one night and fled to Aberdeen. Now he and his people turned up after all, but had attached themselves to Borlum's command. Mar not unnaturally expected him to reinforce his own rather small regiment commanded by Peter Farquharson of Inverey, but Invercauld 'was not willing to give over his men to anie bodie, but yet less to submit himself to one of his own name, who was so much his inferiour, That, as he said, he never pretended to put on his bonnet in his presence till he desired him.'[3] Yet since Invercauld had fewer than 200 men there could be no question of his forming a regiment of his own. In the end the matter was settled by making Borlum a brigadier. His regiment formally passed to the Laird of Mackintosh, and Invercauld then became its lieutenant-colonel. Presumably most of his men went with him, although it is quite likely that some prudently opted to transfer after all to Mar's Regiment under Inverey.

The need for such pragmatic arrangements and establishing a proper chain of command was emphasised by a more or less successful raid mounted on the Fife port of Burntisland just a few days earlier.

Burntisland

At 6 a.m. on 2 October, Sinclair was unexpectedly called out to the South Inch of Perth. There he met a friend who had hastened up from Burntisland with news that a ship laden with 3,000 stand of arms had put into the port. This precious cargo was destined for the loyalist Earl of Sutherland, but the ship's master was a local man and had decided to visit his wife and family. Naturally he would not be staying long and apparently intended to leave on the flood tide at midnight. That meant that, if the Jacobites were to have any prospect of snaffling it, they would have to leave Perth by 5 p.m. that evening. Sinclair, by his own admission, was at first uncertain as to how best to proceed. Clearly it was an opportunity not to be missed, but 'not being altogether so well with my Lord Mar, was at a loss how to behave in it'.

Duty soon won out, and he advised Mar of the opportunity. The earl, who was still abed, heard him out but at first declined to commit to anything until he had himself spoken with Sinclair's mysterious friend. Planning the operation then took up most of the day, but eventually, after a couple of consultations, Sinclair was presented with written orders. He was to share command of the expedition with his friend Major Harry Balfour, no doubt because Mar wanted someone diplomatic at his elbow. Unfortunately if Mar hoped that Balfour's moderating influence would restrain Sinclair from upsetting too many people he was to be disappointed.

Like many such operations, once the go-ahead was given it quickly assumed a momentum of its own. Sinclair himself was given some eighty cavalry – presumably all or most of them belonging to his own Fife Squadron. There was however a shortage of pack horses. Therefore he also asked for 100 foot to form a garrison for Burntisland Castle, since it was likely they would be unable to carry all of the arms straight back with them. A counterproposal, to send a couple of boats round the coast to collect the arms, was apparently rejected, and instead Mar agreed that a detachment would be found from his own regiment, under Inverey. However, Mar at first proved reluctant when Sinclair then requested a second detachment to act as a covering force, in case any attempt was made by Argyle's men to intercept the raiding party on its way back. Mar probably felt at this point that things were getting out of hand, but it was a sensible request and eventually he agreed to send Stewart of Invernytie to Kinross with another 500 foot.

So far so good, and at 5 p.m. the cavalry set off, on schedule. From there however it rapidly went downhill, and Sinclair's own very readable account graphically recounts what happened:

Accordingly I set out by five of the clock with fourscore horse. I went out by a wronge gate, and until it was nere dark, rid out of my road a little to amuse. I was not long in finding Malcolme[4] there takeing upon him, for which I gave him such a cheque, that he was like to gone back, but Mar thought nothing could be done without him; houever, I must doe him the justice to say, that, when I call'd for a guide, he offered himself, and did it very well; for I ordered him to shun all villages, which he did so well, that nobodie saw us, and who we met on the road we carried along with us. At last, he who brought the information, met us three miles from Burntisland, and calling for me in the dark, took me aside, and told me the ship was gone out of the harbour. I spoke to Major Balfour, and told him of what my friend said, but that he was in hopes, yea, seem'd sure, the ship was still in the road, and continued our marche. I halted above a mile from the toun, and call'd out such as knew the toun best, and gave command of them to Thomas Hepburn, in all tuelve men, who, after posting tuo sentries on the heads of the harbour, to hinder all boats from going out, I order'd to secure the skipper, if at home, being that toun's man, and rid sloulie after, till that was over, with no noise; which I found done, on my comeing into toun. I found, likewise, my servant there, with a lad come from those boats formerlie mentioned, which I did not expect, my Lord Mar having ordered them without my knowledge, not spoke one word of them in the orders given me; houever they were lying without the harbour. We seized severall boats the minute we came into toun; and, after placing a few sentries about the toun, which, by the by, was no easie task, since nobody cared to stand, we forced some toun's men to goe alonge with ours to bringe in the ship, which was seized with no difficulty; but the wind being contrarie, it was hard enough to get the ship brought into the harbour. I, in the mean time, went out to the point of the quay, with the younge man who came from the boats, to order these boats to goe and help pull in the ship. He went before me, in the dark, and both of us perceived ane armed boat seize them tuo boats; he said it was the man of war's longe boat, and so did I believe. On that I run back to get our people to be silent, and let them land, at the same time run about to get all together; but both was impossible, for the few who stood on the shore made more noise than a thousand men, and the others were separated in the toun, bussie drinking, contrary to my express orders at first comeing in. By this time Major Balfour had taken the alarm on the advertisement I had given, and having got a few together, was goeing straight down the quay, when I intreated him to leave the management of that part to me, and beg'd of him to get out the others, and went doun with eight or nine armed, only with pistols, for that was all the armes we had, and resolved to lye snug to observe their motion, or, if any landed, seize them, which I did not expect they would do, because the noise of our folks thro' the toun continued. While I was goeing nearer with my small peleton [platoon], I met Thomas Hepburn, and found he had come ashore to get help to bringe in the ship, and that it was he, and those with him, who had seized these boats, and that he had stay'd there some time to oblidge them, being large and well manned, to tow in the ship, which was the way I designed to employ them.

Its to be thought, that my sentrie not giving the alarm, I was not to suspect that to me an enemie's boat; but not knowing who he was, or if he had been pleased to stay on his post, I had no trust to give, seeing the whole so irregular. Nor was there sentries to be got to post about the toun, or, if any posted, would others relieve them, nor would anie hold the horses of those who had gone to seize the ship, who went a strouling thro' the toun, and loosed their bridles. Its not to be conceaved how those peaples tongues, and other unruliness, in goeing into alehouses, confounds at all times, but more at night, the unluckie officer who has the command of them, for ther's no want of advisers, sometimes tuentie speaking at once, and all equallie to the purpose, but not one to obey; at same time, I had the toun's men to struggle with about getting them to go aboard, and others to goe home, to avoid confusion; but that was encouraged by our own disorder. At last, those boats brought in the ship by maine force, against the contrairie wind; and those aboard of ours, being seamen, did their duty very well. I stood in the water to the middle of the leg, and with my oun hands, received all the armes from the ship's side, and found, to my great grief, but three hundred, wanting one; we found a bag of flints and tuo little barrels of ball, and tuo or three barrels of pouder, about a hundred ponds each, and some cartridge boxes. But of the fiftie baggage horses, for we had no more, none would load, or, if they did, not above four firelocks; after humblie begging the favour of them fellous to put on more, to no purpose, I gave them round, without distinction, a heartie drubbing, the most persuasive and convinceing argument to those sort of men, and, with my oun hands, tyed on the greatest part of them. We seized the armes of a big ship which lay in the harbour, which were about tuentie-five firelocks, and with them a barrel of pouder; and at the same time the armes of the Toun Guarde, about thirtie. A little before that I received ane account, that Inderie [Inverey], with five hundred Highlandmen, was come to Auchtertoole, a place four miles from Burntisland. I sent orders to him to continue there, and keep his command together. I got on horseback betwixt three and four, and never thought myself happier than when I got out of that toun, being faint and sick with that confusion, and running up and doun working.

We had not marched far when some of the command went off, without leave, to pay their respects to some minister who they had a mind to teaze; and, as those irregular folks generallie contrive it, they returned before break of day with noise. Tho' I had ane avant guarde, hearing a noise on my left, in the dark, I halted and formed; so great is the aversion of those people to regularitie, that was not done without their raisoning strangelie about it; but those who have served know, that from time to time, on a marche, ther's nothing more necessarie to bring a command together. Then I marched to Auchtertoole, where the Highlandmen had orders to halt. I went into the village myselfe, without halting the horse, and found onlie about fortie men, and was some time before I could find ane officer, for all the others were spread up and doun the countrie, plundering. I ordered those to marche who I saw there, but they were so far from obeying, that they pretended they did not understand me, and most cockt their pieces, and presented, to shoot me, and some lay doun on their bellies to take the better aime. If I could have spoke to them, I would have offer'd myself prisoner; had I offered to run away, I was a dead man; but by forceing myself to look pleased, and as a friend, I stopt their furie, till ane officer came, who understood me. I desired him to order his men to marche, which he did, but in vain. Then I told him, to inform them that I was to command them, and tell them I would not waite of them with the horse, and that the Duke of Argyle was within three miles of them; and with that, took off my hat, and bid them adieu, and gallopt off after the horse. Its incredible to believe how them fellous run and overtook the horse, on their being told that, and how soon they gathered from plundering on all hands; for, without making use of that stratagem, they had staid and plundered the countrie at their leisure, on the pretext of being fatigued. By this means I kept them together for some time, but afterwards disbanded again to plunder.

It was needless to complain to those who commanded them, who said, it was not in their pouer to help it. So I made a halt at Kinnaskwood [Kinnesswood], where I laid hold of the occasion of Indernitie's [Invernytie's] comeing from Kinross, whence I desired him to joyn me on the marche; gave out it was the enemie, and put the old stratagem in execution, both to see how the gentlemen would form, as well as the Highlandmen, and to bring them together from plundering the countrie; for they had again broke out. The gentlemen formed prettie well, but the Highlandmen would not by any means, and run together in troops of nine or ten, without taking the least notice of what was desired, except a very few; but it had the last effect, which was the getting them assembled, and leave pillageing, which they did very expeditiously. After meeting Indernitie, with his five hundred, both his men and the other detachment dispersed again. I proposed to him, being one who had a folloúing among them, and who abhorred that manner of theirs as much as I, if he'd goe into it, to stope, before we came to Pearth, and search the whole, and return what they had taken to the poor people of the countrie, who folloúed us, with lamentable complaints; bit, on his assureing me they would not be treated so, and, considering their number, they would destroy himself and me, and the fourscore horse, rather than suffer that, I was forced to be pleased, and let them doe as they would.

We got back to Pearth before five of the clock, and marched nere to fourtie Scots miles in tuentie-four hours; I can say, for my part, without either eating or drinking, or sitting doun, or so much as having my head in a house.[5]

Poor Sinclair's misadventures have been recounted here in full, not just because they paint such a vivid picture of the raid, but also because they illustrate a number of important issues that were to dog the Jacobites throughout the rising.

In the first place the planning was chaotic. Sinclair initiated the process with his early-morning conference with Mar, but thereafter, if his narrative is to be believed, he was only periodically called in to be consulted or instructed on particular points. As a result the command structure was equally fragmented. In the first place, as we have seen, Sinclair found that while he was nominally in charge, not only was his friend Harry Balfour appointed in 'conjunct' command, but he was also saddled with one of Mar's cronies, James Malcolm of Grange, who he suspected was there to keep an eye on him. More seriously Sinclair was only in effective command of the cavalry, and there appears to have been no co-ordination with either the two separate commanders of the infantry detachments, or with whoever commanded the two boats, which turned up so unexpectedly.

This was in turn compounded by the nature of those detachments. Sinclair had asked for 100 foot to serve as a garrison for the castle in the event that he could not carry off all the arms. Mar's own rather small regiment, commanded by Inverey, ought to have been sufficient for that task by itself, but according to Sinclair a very much larger body of 500 Highlanders turned up at Auchtertool. Whether Inverey had deliberately increased the size of his detachment, or whether the additional men had simply tagged along intent on plunder and mischief is unknown. Either way the mob was well-nigh uncontrollable. Similarly the 13 October muster at Perth would reveal just 267 men in Stewart of Invernytie's Regiment, so about half of the men he took to Kinross must also have belonged to other units.

Both Sinclair and Balfour complained bitterly to Mar of these problems and urged that mixed detachments, especially of clansmen should be avoided in future. Mar was at first understandably upset at the criticism of his own regiment, but to his credit he took the lesson to heart. It may therefore not be entirely coincidental that the row over incorporating Farquharson of Monaltrie's men into his regiment took place that very evening. It certainly justified and perhaps hastened the process of consolidation discussed in Chapter 3.

Notwithstanding, the raid had been a qualified success. It was disappointing of course that the anticipated 3,000 stand of arms, which would have quite transformed the army, amounted in the end to just 350 assorted muskets. Nevertheless that was still sufficient to completely equip a battalion. Even more encouragingly, despite Sinclair's troubles, the rebels had marched all the way to Burntisland and back without any opposition. The rich and populous Kingdom of Fife was shown to be wide open to them, and soon more detachments were visiting the other little ports, seizing arms and counting boats.

An Expedition is Planned

There was a cunning plan afoot involving those boats. According to Sinclair, shortly before Mar's arrival in Perth he was taken aside by Hamilton, and asked to recommend a successor to command of his Fife Squadron. Sinclair immediately leapt to the conclusion he was to be left behind in garrison when the army eventually marched. Instead Hamilton told him that it was intended to send him across the Firth of Forth with 1,000 men, to join with the Jacobites in the Lothians and the borders. The men were to include the Earl of Strathmore's Lowland Regiment and the rest were to be Highlanders. However, on Sinclair enquiring how this feat was to be accomplished, Hamilton responded that they were to be shipped across at Queensferry, where the crossing would be shortest. Sinclair immediately expressed his astonishment at this, since by the same token it would be much too easy for the boats to be moved out of their reach. Just as importantly Queensferry was far too close to Stirling for comfort. Instead he recommended crossing much further to the east, but his all-too-evident lack of enthusiasm saw the project dropped, but not forgotten.

Now with free access available to all the Fife ports the Lothian expedition was on again, and it was to be commanded not by Sinclair but by Mackintosh of Borlum. Once again it encapsulates to a degree the rebels' strengths and weaknesses, and this in turn can be attributed almost wholly to the fact that Mar was not, and never pretended to be, a military man. He was a politician engaged in bringing about a revolution in the state, and at this stage in the proceedings he was something of a victim of his own success. Other than the little *coup de théâtre* at Perth, the change from the Hanoverian to the Jacobite regime across most of Scotland above the Forth had been largely uncontested. Local groups of Jacobite activists, sometimes very few in number, had taken control of burghs such as Aberdeen and Dundee simply by appearing in the streets and proclaiming King James with due ceremony. The existing town councils were then replaced with pro-Jacobite ones, and business continued pretty much as usual, with the obvious difference that a high priority was given to supplying the army with the men, the money and the materiel that it required. At Mar's request the Aberdeen town council for example not only organised the manufacture of Lochaber axes, but even forwarded a complete printing press to Perth.

While this revolution in government was not accomplished by fighting, it was certainly facilitated by the existence of the Jacobite Army. Conversely, on the other side of the Forth the presence of Argyle's army obviously inhibited such revolutionary behaviour there. Mar therefore saw the primary purpose of the expedition not to outflank Argyle's position at Stirling, but to provide a solid nucleus of troops around which the southern Jacobites could rise and hopefully assume local control of the civil government, as they had done in the north.

Mar's failure to set clear military objectives when shipping a substantial portion of his army across to the Lothians, although rightly criticised, is therefore explicable in terms of revolutionary politics. While it is easy to identify the lost opportunities for a military solution, the fact of the matter is that Mar as a political gentleman was not thinking in those terms at all. His task, as he saw it, was to prepare the ground for the imminent arrival of his king, rather than to rush into a premature battle, which he rightly doubted his ability to conduct.

That being said, he was at least prepared to hazard a substantial part of his army in order to effect that revolution. When the idea was first broached to Sinclair, mention was made of sending 1,000 men across the Forth. Now double that number were to go with Borlum, comprising the following:

The Laird of Mackintosh's Regiment	
(including Farquharson of Invercauld's contingent)	650
The Earl of Mar's Regiment	150
Marquis of Drummond's Regiment	
(two battalions under Lord Strathallan	
and Logie Drummond)	500
Lord Nairne's Regiment	250
Lord Charles Murray's Regiment	250
Earl of Strathmore's Regiment	250

Some of these very round figures are a little suspect. Sinclair for example consistently rated Mar's own little regiment at little more than a hundred men,[6] but in any case not all of them were to make it across the Forth.

And there was the problem. With the original crossing point at Queensferry rejected, Mar turned to Sinclair for advice as to the availability of boats, but 'all I could tell him was, That what boats were of use were to be found from Wemyss to Creile [Crail], in the touns and villages all along that coast; that there was a great many of them, but could not tell their number'.

Nevertheless off Sinclair went on 5 October, ostensibly to proclaim King James VIII formally in St Andrews and the East Neuk villages of Crail, Easter and Wester Anstruther, Elie, Pittenweem and Kilrenny. He was also instructed to collect up all the arms he could find and to levy the cess, or tax assessment. His real job of course was to count the boats and to make the necessary arrangements with a man named Harry Crawford to have them ready.

From the beginning Sinclair had his usual troubles enforcing discipline, particularly since the legal ritual of proclaiming the king properly required the drinking of substantial toasts! Coupar was the worst, as all of his men insisted on scattering themselves in taverns or going home for the night. Afterwards he took a firmer line, refusing to let them dismount and staying only as long as was necessary to make the proclamation and collect any arms held by the local authorities – which he invariably described as rusty.

All went reasonably well until they reached the little burgh of Pittenweem. There Sinclair managed to pack all his men into the abbey for the night, rather than disperse as they had done at Coupar. Unfortunately he was met there by a letter from Mar, dated 7 October, directing him to send all the boats to Burntisland, as the naval vessel that had hitherto been sitting off the port was safely gone. To say the least this came as something of a surprise. Not only was Sinclair still under the obviously mistaken impression that he had succeeded in dissuading Mar from sending the troops across so far up the Forth, but also the warship in question was still sitting just offshore in plain sight! Worse still, no sooner had he sent off a reply acquainting Mar of his misapprehension than he received another letter – this time from Borlum. The brigadier, as he announced himself to be, was not only already arrived at Burntisland, but was also imminently expecting to be attacked by a detachment of Argyle's men sitting in Dunfermline. Not surprisingly he wanted Sinclair to march at once to his assistance.

What had gone wrong?

Chapter 6
Across the Forth

In one of his regular updates to General Gordon, dated at 10 a.m. on 8 October, Mar advised him: 'I have ordered 2,000 Men to cross the Water from Burntisland to Leith, and most of them will be at Burntisland to Night; so To-morrow, I hope, they will get over without Opposition; there being no Men of War in the Road . . .'[1] This was presumably the gist what he had also written to Sinclair the day before. Not only did the realisation that he had not after all persuaded Mar against using the western passage come as an unwelcome surprise to the master, but the supposition there were no warships in the vicinity was sheer wishful thinking. In any case the necessary boats were not yet secured. Harry Crawford was still reckoning it would take another three days to get the boats ready, yet Sinclair was being asked to send them immediately to Burntisland under the all too watchful eye of the Royal Navy. Little wonder then that he was in a foul mood.

For his part, Borlum's chagrin at turning up at Burntisland to find no boats waiting for him, and first one and then three naval vessels hovering offshore, may easily be imagined. Worse still, Mar had in the meantime got word that Argyle was preparing to attack the detachment with a force of dragoons and some hastily mounted infantry. This was precisely what Sinclair had warned him might happen, and it was this intelligence that somehow got translated to the brigadier as news that the redcoats were already at Dunfermline and preparing to march on him by moonlight. It was at this point that Borlum peremptorily ordered Sinclair to come to his aid.

Sinclair, for his part, responded to the summons by turning petulant. As before, the affair was lacking in any sort of overall co-ordination and until now he was, or at least claimed to be, unaware that Borlum was a brigadier, far less that he was in overall command of the operation. He therefore professed not to recognise him as his superior officer on the slender grounds that his own orders said nothing of his coming under the brigadier's authority. Perhaps aware he was on very shaky ground here, he also justified himself in his memoirs by saying he reckoned cavalry without carbines would be of no use in defending Burntisland castle. Instead of hastening to join Borlum, he therefore wilfully stuck by the letter of his written orders. Having proclaimed King James and secured all the arms he could lay his hands on, Sinclair very pointedly marched straight back to Perth and another falling out with Mar.

Borlum for his part was left breathing fire and accusations of cowardice. However, the threat from Argyle proved illusory; or rather not so urgent as first appeared, and so he turned to the question of getting his men across the Forth. One of the better accounts of what happened next is contained in an anonymous unpublished *Journall of the Proceedings of Army in the Rebbellion under E. of Mar*:[2]

Three or four days thereafter there were seven regiments detached under Borlum's command to Burntisland in order to cross the Forth: the regiments were Marr's men, Invery, Col. Lord Nairn, Lord Charles Murray, Lord Strathmore, Lord Strathallan, Logie Drummond[3] and McIntosh. There was at that time a design to surprise a man of war in the road and for that purpose a detachment out of the said regiments (Invery having the command) was sent off from Kinross, but that attempt miscarried through the ships sailing before they came to the water side.

Having all arrived at Burntisland the Chevalier was proclaimed all the regiments being drawn up about the Croce and the Colonels and other gentlemen and officers as could have room being upon the croce after proclamation Mr Duguid prayed and thereafter some healths were drunk and the men billeted for quarters.

Brigadier McIntosh and some others went to the castle and immediately there was a detachment for Kinghorn [and] Kirkcaldie and so to proceed by the coast in order to uplift the cess and I think one Patrick Smith a brother of Meffans [Methven's] had that command.

Having lyen at Burntisland two or three days one Thomas Arthur Major to Strathallan's Battalion, with a party of horse belonging to Marischall with some foot was ordered to go to Cryll and there secure the boats and men and go to Anstruther Easter and to secure all the boats from that westward to a place Methline [Methil] in order to transport the foresd regiment for the Louthians.

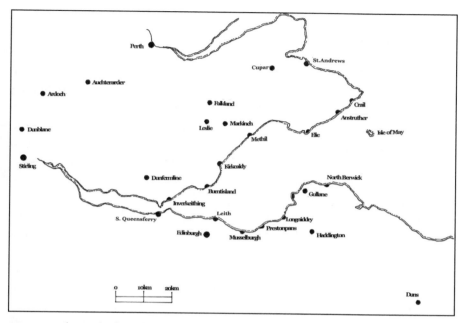

MAP 1: *The Firth of Forth. To all intents and purposes the area covered by this map was the cockpit of the war in Scotland, and the wide dispersion of the various forces engaged in the Forth crossing will be immediately apparent.*

My Lord Strathmore, Strathallan & Logie Drummond's regiments were ordered to embark at Anstruther Easter & the rest to embark at Anstruther Wester & Methline which accordingly was done but the wind proving cross after tossing a night at sea and the men of war appearing in the morning severale of the boats were forced back to the north coast and eleven of them were chased into the May Island and one boat being taken all the rest got over.

The number beat into the island would have been 250 men besides the boats crews. While they were there the Lord Strathmore commanded. They stayed two days on that island and the third day proving muddy and a fresh gale blowing from the west which boar the men of war to the eastward of the island all the men immediately boated and made their escape to Cryll.

While this account appears to suggest that the crossing was made in the course of a single night, it actually appears to have taken place over two successive nights, and was aided by a noisy demonstration laid on by Inverey's detachment in Burntisland. Unfortunately, while the first lift from Anstruther Wester and Methil on the evening of 12 October was successful, the second lift, launched from Anstruther Easter on the following night, was a near-complete failure. Alerted by the earlier crossing, both the Royal Navy and the Revenue service, under an officer named Captain Hamilton, were waiting for them.

Two boats – one with forty-eight very seasick men aboard – were seized by Hamilton, and after the passengers had dropped their arms over the side they were all were carried into Leith.[4] Most of the other boats were chased ashore on the Isle of May, a rather isolated outcrop lying well offshore and more in the North Sea than in the Firth of Forth. In the end only a few boats carrying some of Strathmore's men and a few of Logie Drummond's made it safely across to the other side, but even then they landed so far to the eastward that they were unable to rejoin Borlum and the first lift until several days later.[5]

The 250-odd men stranded on the Isle of May appear for the most part to have belonged to Lord Strathallan's and the greater part of Logie Drummond's battalions. There must also have been at least a part of Lord Strathmore's Regiment as well, since he and his field officers were also included among the castaways. At any rate they all spent a rather tense couple of days on the island. On at least one occasion an attempt was made by the Royal Navy to attempt a landing using longboats, but it was a half-hearted affair and easily beaten off by musketry. Understandably though, Strathmore's assumption of command appears to have been resented by Strathallan's and Logie Drummond's men. However, the wind shifted and, with the naval vessels held offshore, they made a hasty dash for Crail and eventually returned safely to Perth. For many, the ordeal of Sheriffmuir lay before them, but in the end those who survived it no doubt counted themselves lucky by comparison with their comrades who successfully got over the water.

The Brigadier in Leith

On the other side of the Forth, meanwhile, the first lift had landed all the way along the shore between North Berwick and Aberlady and spent their first night in Tranent and Haddington. It was a very much depleted force from the 2,000-odd men who had set off from Perth.

Mackintosh's Regiment had made it across intact. Only half of Mar's Regiment under Major Forbes had actually embarked in the first place, while the rest remained with Inverey at Burntisland. Similarly some of the Athollmen of Nairne's Regiment may also have been part of the force at Burntisland, since Patten only allows that 'a good many of his men' came across. On the other hand it is equally likely that there was simply no room for all of them in the boats when the regiment embarked and they were perforce left behind on the quayside. As to the second lift, Strathallan's regiment is conspicuous by its total absence from Patten's later accounting. Three companies of Logie Drummond's did get across together with four companies of Strathmore's, all commanded by captains; but they had not managed to rendezvous with the brigadier when he counted heads on the morning of 14 October.[6]

Notwithstanding, without waiting to see if anyone else turned up, Borlum boldly commenced marching towards Edinburgh. Afterwards Mar rather uncharitably grumbled that this was a mistake. Instead he insisted that Borlum should have rendezvoused at once with the southern Jacobites. Strangely this ignores the fact that his original instructions intended the brigadier and his men landing even closer to the capital, at Leith. This in turn suggests that the original plan may indeed have contemplated seizing the capital by a *coup de main*, and that when the decision was made to launch the crossing further to the east he shelved the idea, or at least the option, without making that clear to Borlum.

The key figure at this point was, or ought to have been, George Seton, Earl of Wintoun. In preparation for the projected landing and southern uprising, he had already been gathering arms at his home, Seton House, just a short distance to the east of Edinburgh. However, on 15 September he was summonsed to appear before the magistrates in the capital. No doubt correctly anticipating arrest he instead ordered his tenants and vassals to muster next day at Pinkie. As many as 300 men duly turned out and were issued with arms, but to his dismay his erstwhile Jacobite neighbours declined to join him. Instead Argyle despatched two troops of dragoons to deal with the incipient insurrection, and to their great satisfaction they arrived on 18 September to find Wintoun gone and his people dispersed.

He had in fact taken a boat to the other side of the Forth with just twelve companions, all well armed. His immediate movements thereafter are a touch uncertain, but it would appear that he was now cast in the role of go-between. At any rate Mar, in his letter of 21 October, to Lord Kenmure stated he has been told that Wintoun 'was very usefull to our men we sent over' but then went on to 'suppose he is now with your Lordship'.[7] Presumably therefore Wintoun had concerted the arrangements for a rendezvous between Borlum's little army and the southern rebels, and then slipped south again ahead of the crossing in order to acquaint Kenmure and the other southern leaders of the arrangements.

A later government intelligence report, presumably based on the interrogation of prisoners, asserted:

> Mar's plot upon the town [Edinburgh] was thus. He promised to send over 2,000 foot.
> Winton and Kenmore were to have surprised Dumfreece and been in readiness to have
> joynd his foot with 1,000 cavelrie after having garisond Dumfreece and thus to have
> marchd straight to Edinburgh quhich could scarce have misd.[8]

Instead delay had piled upon delay. Wintoun duly joined with the southern
rebel leaders, Lord Kenmure and the Earl of Carnwath, at Moffat on 11 October.
Borlum should have crossed the Forth the day before, but he was seemingly a day
late in leaving Perth and then had to wait three days for the boats to carry him
across the Forth, far later and much further to the east than had been planned.

At all events, only too well aware that he was now running four or five days
late, Borlum reckoned there was a good chance of making up that lost time by
taking the capital at a run. Indeed he may well have decided on this course of
action while still on the Fife shore, waiting impatiently for the boats. A significant
pointer to this is the fact he sent Major Arthur to hurry along their collection,
for that officer was none other than the same Thomas Arthur who had organised
the earlier Jacobite attempt on Edinburgh Castle. Having escaped arrest after
that débâcle, Arthur had then become major to Lord Strathallan's Battalion of
Drummond's Regiment. Unfortunately he had been due to come across with
the second lift and instead was now marooned with the rest of his battalion on
the Isle of May. Whether Arthur could in fact have rallied the capital's Jacobites
in the face of the defensive preparations being made by the Lord Provost, Sir
George Warrender, is a moot point, but it certainly seems possible. At least one
loyalist correspondent in the capital certainly feared so:

> I am afraid at this time of generall consternation the resistance had been but small. One of
> the most defensles ports about this city had a gwaird intirly Jacobits and I ame persweded
> Bristow port had been cast open cheirfuly by them had the enemie come that way. Yow
> can not imagine how miserably things were disposd within and about this city. Our
> associate voluntire companies had the night befor this taken up their station within the
> Nether Bow port and had any attack been made there we had certainly made a vigurouse
> resistance but what else could we have done but falne a sacrefise to the enymy from
> without and the mobbe from within for the good town is still crowded with Jacobites . . .[9]

Nevertheless, when Borlum arrived at Jock's Lodge, that afternoon, just a mile
from Edinburgh's East Port, there was no sign of an uprising, and without
Arthur no reliable means of discovering what was actually going on inside the
walls. Instead he was assured by another local Jacobite – Alexander Malloch of

Moultreehill – that the capital's streets were crowded with armed militia, and that reinforcements were imminently expected from the Duke of Argyle.

Declining to try and force an entrance, without a firm promise of support within the burgh, the brigadier turned aside. By way of a consolation prize he instead seized the adjacent port of Leith. This at least he accomplished without any resistance worth mentioning, and as a bonus he also released most of the men captured by the Revenue service the night before. The officers had already been sent up to the castle, but the rank and file were still locked up in the Leith tolbooth and were promptly broken out again. A no doubt joyful reunion then became decidedly convivial when Borlum next turned his attention to the Customs house and liberated a quantity of wine and brandy. Having done that, the rebels then occupied the citadel, a substantial fortress built during the Cromwellian occupation in the 1650s. Being unwanted afterwards, it was by now superficially in a derelict condition, but the walls and ramparts were still solid enough and so the long-vanished gates were replaced with barricades, ships' cannon were mounted on the walls, and supplies of food and more brandy gathered in.

In the meantime Argyle was indeed racing south to relieve Edinburgh. He had with him a squadron apiece of the Scots Greys and Kerr's Dragoons, and at least two companies of the Earl of Forfar's foot mounted on country horses. On arriving on the morning of 15 October he was joined by 300 men of the newly raised Edinburgh Regiment, 250 Associated Volunteers and 400 men of the Merse Militia. What was more, upon his ordering them to march down to Leith immediately, the fifty-nine veteran soldiers of the city guard insisted on going along too.[10] Alas the bold counterattack then quite literally turned into a damp squib, for, as the volunteer commented, the citadel was 'not so rowinows yet as to be easily attacd withowt bombs or cannon neither of which our armie browght along'.

According to Rae's history, having ostentatiously drawn up his assault columns Argyle summoned the rebels to surrender, whereupon John Stewart of Kynachan, the commander of Nairne's Battalion, retorted 'that as to surrendering, they laughed at it; and as to bringing Cannon and assaulting them, they were ready for him; that they would neither take nor give any Quarter with him; and if he thought he was able to force them he might try his hand'.[11]

Despite the urging of some of the more militant loyalists, Argyle declined to incur irreplaceable casualties among his regulars in a vainglorious assault on the fortress for their entertainment. The volunteers were also gratefully of the same mind, for they 'were sowndly well and hetely wearied for we were long under armes and it was a tempestwows day'. As our chronicler declared:

> My Lord Argyle certenly acted here a very wise parte. They in the citydale were a pack of raskaly Highlenders that cowld not be attacked but at the disadvantage two to one. His men were the flower of the nation and besyds it cowld be no decisive strock had he carryd it and evry man he lost was worth ten of that villanows cannalie.

And so at about 2 p.m. they all turned around again and went back up the hill to Holyrood House to rest and to dry out. No sooner were they gone than so was Borlum. With Argyle in the capital there was no longer any hope that the Edinburgh Jacobites might rise and every expectation that when the duke came back he would bring artillery with him.

The Escape

First Borlum sent off a despatch to Mar, advising him of what had happened. As soon as the boat carrying the message cleared the harbour entrance it was sped on its way by a cannon shot. This successfully convinced the Royal Navy that its occupants were escaping from the rebels, and thus they were allowed to pass unmolested. After those theatricals all was quiet for a time. Then at 9 p.m. that night, taking advantage of the darkness and the ebb tide Borlum slipped out of the citadel unobserved. Marching down to the harbour, he and his men passed around the end of the pier, waded the water of Leith, which was no more than knee deep, and then marched eastwards along the beach for about eight miles.

About forty men were left in Leith. Some accounts, including Patten's, suggest that they were drunk, but he also identifies the men as belonging to Logie Drummond's Battalion. They were more than likely the men captured during the crossing, rescued from the tolbooth and now left behind since they were unarmed and had no officers to lead them. In the circumstances, getting drunk was probably understandable.

That aside it was by various accounts an uncomfortably shambolic progress, which left a number of stragglers in its wake besides those forty-odd men abandoned in Leith. Contact was successfully broken, but approaching Musselburgh there was a brief firefight with some loyalist militia. No one was hurt on either side, and the Jacobites quickly brushed past the town, but it 'occasioned a great Disorder among them'. It also left them very jittery and made them 'suspect all Horsemen for Enemies'. All of them were on foot of course, so when they next spotted a horseman to their front, he was immediately challenged. Inevitably he was shouted at in Gaelic and when he failed to respond was promptly shot dead. Unfortunately he turned out to be their erstwhile friend Alexander Malloch of Moultreehill.[12] That ought have made them more cautious, but instead a short time later the same thing happened again. This time their own advance guard got shot up by those at the head of the column in a brief firefight that left a sergeant of the Earl of Mar's Regiment and a private soldier killed.

At length, at about 2 a.m. in the morning of 16 October, Borlum fetched up at Seton House. This was no coincidence of course, but if he hoped to meet with the Earl of Wintoun there, or at least receive any word of him, he was to be sorely disappointed. The earl was not at home, but somewhere down in the borders with Kenmure and Carnwath. However, Borlum at last linked up with the survivors of the second lift, and learned for the first time what had happened to Strathmore and the others. He was on his own and, with no idea where else to go for the moment, Borlum set to fortifying the place and gathering supplies as he awaited the inevitable countermove.

This time the Duke of Argyle was taking no chances and 'sent an Express to Sterling for four Gunners and two Bombardiers of the small train that was there with the army; and in the meantime, ordered two Pieces of small Cannon and two Mortars to be got ready in Edinburgh Castle in order to dislodge them'.[13] Instead, in reply to his request for gunners, Argyle received three expresses in quick succession from General Whetham, warning that Mar had moved out of Auchterarder and was advancing southwards. By the evening of 17 October the rebels were at Dunblane, just five miles short of Stirling bridge, but by then hard riding saw Argyle safely returned and the crisis evaporated.

Next morning Mar incontinently fell back to Perth, while it fell to General Wightman to deal with Borlum. In the excitement the proposal to bring up some artillery, which would have made short work of the simple stone park wall surrounding Seton House, was evidently forgotten. Argyle had left behind some of Kerr's Dragoons under Lieutenant-Colonel Lord Torphichen, and it was they together with some loyalist horse under the Earl of Rothes and the Lothian militia who were sent off by Wightman to blockade the place. As they mustered only 200 cavalry and 300 infantry in total, they approached their task with a quite understandable marked lack of enthusiasm.

Borlum for his part had no intention of being trapped in Seton House. Later that morning, hearing that the loyalists had followed them as far as Prestonpans, a body of Highlanders marched out and formed up in order of battle to receive them. At that point according to Patten, the loyalists retreated, but as so often in the campaign it was most likely a false alarm. It would have been remarkably swift work for a force to be organised and sent off after them so quickly, and it was most likely no more than a scouting party.

It was not until Monday 16 October, that Rothes and Torpichen turned up in earnest:

> but found the Rebels so strongly posted that it was impossible to dislodge or reduce them without Artillery. This still animated the Rebels and a good Body advanc'd, as if they would charge the Gentlemen, and some Shot were exchanged, but at too great a Distance to do any Harm on either Side; and the King's Troops seeing no Good to be done, retir'd.[14]

So far so good. Borlum continued to gather supplies and 'gave out that they intended to fortify there, and make Seaton-House a Magazine, while they raised an Army, as they pretended also, as well from the Country round about, and from Edinburgh, and from other Friends . . .' By this stage of course he was bluffing, and to his great relief the same boat which he had sent off from Leith now returned with fresh news and orders from Mar. As planned, the rising in the southwest had gone ahead under Lord Kenmure, and the English Jacobites had also risen in Northumberland. The orders to join with them seem to have been tolerably vague, but just three hours later a messenger also arrived from the Northumbrian leader, Thomas Forster, inviting them to meet with him at Kelso.

Accordingly on the Wednesday morning Borlum and his men set out southwards 'seventeen long Scots Miles' to Longformacus. Beyond sending a party to take possession of Seton House and seize the provisions abandoned there, Wightman made no attempt to pursue them. Undisturbed, next morning they pushed on to Duns, where they proclaimed King James and drew up for a time in order of battle, before proceeding on Saturday to Kelso and a fateful meeting with Kenmure and Forster.

Chapter 7
Nithsdale and Northumbria

B Y ALL ACCOUNTS BORLUM was far from impressed by what he found at Kelso, for his new allies turned out to be a pretty sorry crew. Perth, Dundee and Aberdeen had all fallen to the rebels without a fight, largely due to the absence of anyone to stop them, but south of the Forth it was always going to be a different matter. It was recognised by the Jacobite leadership from the very outset that their ability to raise men in the north of Scotland quickly, by drawing upon the Highland clans in an area remote from military garrisons, would not be easily repeated in southern Scotland and in England. There were perhaps would-be rebels enough, but there were also friends to the government and sufficient regular troops to nip any insurrection in the bud. Hence the need for outside help to ensure that, when King James was proclaimed, there were sufficient rebel troops on hand to support and sustain the revolution in government. From the very outset therefore there had been an intention to pass a body of infantry across the Forth to form the nucleus of an insurgent army in southern Scotland and so facilitate that revolution, and ultimately take over Edinburgh itself.

It was a bold plan, but Mar has been castigated first by the Master of Sinclair and then by a succession of historians, for his failure to prescribe how the different parties were to effect a rendezvous, or clearly to define their immediate objectives. This, for once, is a touch unfair to Mar, for, although the plan was prudently not committed to paper, those involved were in no doubt at all as to what was being asked of them. It is also evident that the Earl of Wintoun was tasked with serving as the liaison officer between the Nithsdale rebels and the Highlanders. Mar's letter of 21 October reveals he had a meeting with Borlum shortly before the latter made his crossing, and no doubt advised him of the situation in the

Lothians. However, instead of sailing with the brigadier, Wintoun then rode south in order to meet the southern rebels at Moffat. From what followed there is no doubt that his purpose was then to lead them to a rendezvous either at his home at Seton House, or failing that at Kelso, in the eastern borders. In either event they would be well placed, according to the situation, either to attack Edinburgh or to join with the English Jacobites in Northumberland.

In general terms southwest Scotland, where Wintoun was bound, was traditionally regarded as Whig country, a Presbyterian heartland where the old Covenanters had drawn their strongest support during the Great Civil War and afterwards. Ayrshire and the Galloway Hills had certainly seen the worst excesses of the infamous Killing Times' in the reign of Charles II. Conversely parts of Nithsdale formed an enclave of equally strong support for the Stuarts, thanks to the presence of a number of defiantly Episcopalian and Catholic families.

A prominent Kirkcudbrightshire landowner, William Gordon, Viscount Kenmure, was intended as the leader of the uprising in the southwest, but in reality there was no rising as such. Both he and his colleague Robert Dalziel, the Earl of Carnwath, had irrevocably committed themselves to joining the rebellion at least as far back as May, but like Wintoun they appear to have been rushed into acting before they were ready. The original plan as outlined to Sinclair had envisaged an initial uprising in the Lothians, and they would no doubt have been happy to raise their people and join with that insurrection. Instead, with Wintoun neutralised, it was they who were required to initiate the rising – an unexpected role for which they were patently unprepared, and one which they were perhaps downright reluctant to assume.

Kenmure, despite his supposed leading role, was reputed to have been pushed into the affair through a combination of pressure from his wife and a simple fear of arrest. As a result the process of rebellion was a half-hearted shambles. Like Wintoun, many of the would-be rebels were already comprehended in the warrant attached to the Act for Encouraging Loyalty in Scotland, passed on 30 August. Their subsequent failure to present themselves dutifully before the authorities in Edinburgh was therefore in itself sufficient to excite suspicion and draw unwelcome attention. Yet at the same time they were not yet ready to come 'out' in arms. Instead they 'assembled in Parties at the Houses of some of their Friends, moving secretly from Place to Place in order to put Matters in a Readiness for the speedy Execution of their traitorous Designs'.

As early as 8 October an 'honest contryman' at Lockerbie sent an otherwise anonymous warning of the rebels' intention to surprise Dumfries.[1] At first the magistrates there were inclined to dismiss it as a hoax. Therefore when the local clergy started rousing and arming their parishioners in response to other rumours and more tangible information, the magistrates thanked them for their zeal but assured them it was quite unnecessary. Ironically that was on Monday 10 October, the very day on which the rising was planned to begin.

By contrast, no doubt kept informed by their own sources within the Jacobite camp in Perth, the authorities in Edinburgh were only too well aware of what was going on. They also knew of Borlum's arrival at Burntisland and what that portended. Cockburn, the lord justice clerk, sent off his own warning, which arrived in Dumfries the next day. Finally persuaded things were serious, the magistrates initiated a flurry of frantic activity. The lord lieutenant of Dumfriesshire, the Marquis of Annandale, very properly took charge. The loyalist volunteers, whose services had only just been declined, enthusiastically flocked into Dumfries, led by their parish ministers. They were formidable in nothing but numbers, being poorly armed and obviously quite untrained, but there was no doubting their zeal or the simple fact that there were rather a lot of them.

Rebellion

For their part the Jacobites appear to have been so busy keeping out of sight that they were at first unaware the country was rising against them. Blithely thinking that they could still surprise the burgh, they displayed none of the sense of urgency which was animating the loyalists. Having got themselves on horseback they made their way to Moffat and there, having met with the Earl of Wintoun on 11 October, the next day 'they march'd out of Moffat and took their Rout directly towards Dumfries, and about two a Clock were advanced within a Mile and a Half of that Town, not doubting but in a short time they should be Masters of it'.[2]

If they were hoping to emulate the success at Perth they were sadly disappointed. There a combination of bluff and bluster, and the divided loyalties of the garrison, had seen the burgh fall to the rebels without a fight. At Dumfries the Covenanters were made of sterner stuff, and this time it was the Jacobites who bottled it. Belatedly realising the place was held against them, they halted rather uncertainly. None of them was a soldier, and thus far not a shot had been fired in anger and no one had been hurt. Starting a fight was as yet a step too far for the irresolute Kenmure. In the end he and his would-be insurgents fell back to Lochmaben, where on 12 October they formally set up their standard and proclaimed King James.[3]

Patten describes it thus:

This Standard, supposed to be made by his [Kenmure's] Lady, was very handsome, one side being Blue, with the Scot's Arms done in Gold; the other side a Thistle, with this under, No Union; above the Thistle, the usual Motto, *Nemo Me Impune Lacessit*. This Standard had Penants of white ribbon; upon one of these was written, For our Wronged King, and Oppressed Country; the other Ribbon had thereon, For our Lives and Liberties.

Unfortunately, it was probably the most impressive thing about the rebel army, which according to Rae at this time numbered no more than 153 'horsemen well mounted'. Patten, more charitably, assigned them about 200 horsemen and noted that, on a common near Ecclefechan, they formed themselves into a regiment of two squadrons – one commanded by Wintoun and the other by Carnwath – while Kenmure had 'the chief command'. As we will see, this organisation would undergo some modification, but it was at least a start in the right direction.

At first glance their wanderings over the next few days might seem purposeless. Having failed to raise Nithsdale for the Chevalier and establish a base in Dumfries, the southern rebels had no alternative but to make for Kelso in the hope of a rendezvous with Borlum's forces. With that aim, they moved on to Ecclefechan, where they rather unwisely spread themselves pretty widely around the village in order to find billets for themselves and stables for their horses. They also very conscientiously locked their arms in the local jail for safe-keeping! This of course was exactly the sort of amateurish behaviour that the Master of Sinclair had been at such pains to put a stop to, during his perambulations in Fife, and it led to their getting a considerable fright. The rebels were not long settled in when there was a report of a body of horsemen moving towards the place. A trumpeter duly sounded the alarm, but not surprisingly it took a dangerously long time to turn everyone out. Fortunately the newcomers transpired to be a party of fourteen local Jacobites under Sir William Maxwell of Springkell. They had been trying for some time to locate Kenmure and his people, but rallying to King James's standard was not easy when it was constantly on the move. The incident might have ended well, but not surprisingly the whole business left the rebels 'very uneasy and much out of Humour'. Continuing by way of Langholm they reached the border town of Hawick on 16 October, and there they received some very unwelcome news indeed.

Their intended rendezvous at Kelso had not only been leaked by someone, but it was also sufficiently well known for the government's supporters to take the appropriate measures to frustrate it. A prominent local loyalist – Sir William Bennet of Grubbet – had been serving with Argyle's army at Stirling. However, as early as 11 October, while Kenmure and Wintoun were still raising the standard at Moffat, he was summoned to return. Grubbet did not come back alone of course 'and having an Order to get Arms out of the Castle of Edinburgh, he came to Kelso on the thirteenth and made it as tenable as the Shortness of the Time and Situation of the Place would allow'.[4]

Makeshift though Grubbet's garrison and his barricades might have been, the merest show of opposition was once again sufficient to dismay the all too easily discouraged Kenmure. There was no sign of Borlum, who at this point was still barricading himself into Seton House, and so the Jacobites immediately turned around to retreat back to Langholm. Left to their own devices after what had been a discouraging week, they may soon have started dispersing and individually making their peace with the authorities. King James's standard might still be bravely carried by Carnwath's brother, John Dalziel, but precious few men were rallying to it; and nor were they likely to while the rebels continued their peripatetic existence.

The Northumbrians

Hardly had they wearily set off, than two miles south of Hawick they were met by a noted borderer named Robert Douglas. He was carrying a message from the Northumberland Jacobite leader, Thomas Forster, which changed the situation completely. Forster and his colleagues, they read, had taken up arms as long ago as 6 October and now invited the Scots to come over the border and join them. Grasping eagerly at the invitation, Kenmure and his sorry crew spent the night of 17 October at Jedburgh. Here they also heard for the first time that Borlum was over the Forth, but, after some debate, the news that he was being hard pressed by Argyle probably confirmed their decision to cross the border into England. Thus, instead of marching north to Borlum's assistance, they instead trekked forty miles over the hills to the little market town of Rothbury, in Northumberland. It was 'perhaps such a March', commented Patten feelingly, 'as few people are acquainted with, being very mountainous, long, tedious, and marshy'.[5]

Unfortunately the uprising that they were expecting to join was just as much a shambles as their own – and for much the same reasons. The Chevalier's agents, including a number of Irish officers, such as Colonel Henry Oxburgh, had been active on Tyneside for some time. Many of the local Jacobites were consequently privy to the Earl of Mar's plans for a general uprising in August and fully intended to play their part. There were, as it happened, two leaders or at least potential leaders in Northumberland.

One was James Radcliffe, 3rd Earl of Derwentwater, an affluent young gentleman of twenty-six, resident at Dilston Hall, near Hexham in the Tyne Valley. In considering his suitability as a figurehead for the enterprise, his complete lack of any military knowledge or experience might have been offset by the fact of his being a cousin and childhood companion of the would-be King James. Unfortunately the natural consequence of this close relationship was that he was an openly practising Roman Catholic. Ironically this meant that his leadership of a rebellion aimed at setting a Catholic monarch on the English throne was considered politically unacceptable.

Thus command fell to a quite different gentleman – Thomas Forster. As Patten noted: 'He was no soldier; nor was the command given him as such, but as he was the only Protestant who could give credit to their Undertaking, being of Note in Northumberland, of an ancient Family, and having for several years been Member of Parliament for that County: and therefore very popular.'[6] Afterwards it would be alleged he was a pompous fool, though it is hard to avoid the impression this might be an instance of being wise after the event. If it was so, he was in good company. More seriously, although the Earl of Mar was himself equally unversed in the art of war, he at least had some proper military advisers and was prepared to listen to them and to delegate the conduct of operations into their hands. Those attending on Forster and Derwentwater on the other hand were men of little discernible talent or influence, and indeed Patten commented that the most senior of them, Colonel Oxburgh, was more fitted to be a priest than a soldier.

Not surprisingly, although there had been a lot of talk and correspondence flying to and fro in the preceding months, no real preparations were taken in hand to effect an uprising, and neither arms nor ammunition were stockpiled in readiness. The whole affair was once again fatally compromised not only by a lack of competent or even vigorous leadership, but also by the unrealistic expectation that at the outset the Chevalier would land with the Duke of Berwick by his side and French soldiers at his back. Willing as they were to rally to the Stuart standard, the Northumbrians simply had no real notion of fighting to secure their position.

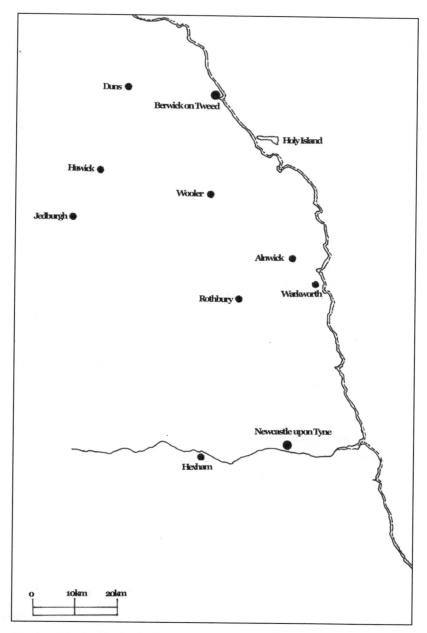

MAP 2: *Northumberland. Once again it can be seen how widely the rebels travelled in an effort to avoid confrontation – and what ought to have been their primary objective of Newcastle upon Tyne.*

As it was, the whole business came dangerously close to collapsing before it even began. In Scotland, as we have seen, suspected Jacobites were genteelly summoned to present themselves for examination by the authorities, but little serious attempt was made to secure the persons of those who declined the invitation. In England, on the other hand, the secretary of state rather more robustly sent his officers out to bring them in. Thus 'at about the latter end of September' both Derwentwater and Forster, who also lived near Hexham, were effectively forced to go on the run – moving about from house to house in order to avoid arrest. Eventually Forster narrowly avoided being taken by a messenger near Bywell in the Tyne valley, by a matter of mere minutes. Thoroughly shaken by his narrow escape, he agreed with Derwentwater that they should appear in arms without further delay:

> There was no Safety any longer in shifting from Place to Place; that in a few Days they should all be secur'd, and clapp'd up in several Prisons, or hurried away to London; that as they should be severally confin'd, so they would be severally examin'd, and none could say what the other should answer: so that for fear of betraying one another, they should be readily brought to do it; That now was the time to show their loyalty to their King (Pretender) and that if this opportunity was lost, they had no room to hope for another.[7]

It was hardly an auspicious start. Nevertheless, on 6 October, four days before the Scottish rising was scheduled to begin, both leaders assembled with about fifty servants and other followers on Green Rig, near Corbridge. Almost immediately they then moved some twenty miles north to the relatively remote market town of Rothbury. Why they did so is unclear, since it was too early to join with the Scots, but no doubt it was felt to be safer than lingering in the Tyne valley. At any rate Forster wrote that night to Mar, advising him the Northumbrians had risen with 160 horse and had every expectation of taking both the city of Newcastle upon Tyne and Tynemouth Castle. He also asked for the assistance of 2,000 foot and 500 horse from Scotland – a request that was to have important consequences.

In the meantime the rebels next moved down the valley of the Coquet to the much more congenial but equally remote surroundings of the small coastal town of Warkworth. There they were joined by another prominent local Catholic, Lord Widdrington, and it is hard to avoid the suspicion that plain Mr Forster's sudden elevation to General Forster came about next day in order not to be upstaged by the nobility. For the first time in England too, on 9 October King James was proclaimed at Warkworth with 'the Sound of Trumpet, and all the Formality that the Circumstances and Place would admit'.[8]

Exactly why they had fetched up at Warkworth is not discovered in any of the narratives of the time, but there does seem to have been some sort of expectation of a French blockade-runner arriving off the Northumberland coast at about this time. This was certainly the background to an odd little incident, which occurred next day on Holy Island, just a short distance south of Berwick on Tweed. The island is dominated by the castle of Lindisfarne. It was maintained as an outpost by the garrison of Berwick, which rotated out a few men under a sergeant on a weekly basis. It was all very casual, and an equally small party of Jacobites led by Lancelot Errington managed to surprise them and take possession of the castle without a fight. Indeed one version of the story very plausibly claims that Errington and his men simply got the garrison drunk. Alas their enterprise went unrewarded, because the governor of Berwick immediately sent out a party of thirty men to retake the place, which they did with the enthusiastic assistance of fifty local volunteers. At low tide they all marched across the sands and briskly retook Lindisfarne Castle 'sword in hand'. There was no resistance. Errington was wounded while trying to escape, and he and his men were carried off in triumph to Berwick.[9]

Completely oblivious to this little drama, Forster and Derwentwater's Jacobites were also on the move again that morning, retracing their steps a short distance to the county town of Alnwick. Then on the following day they headed south along the high road towards Newcastle. Encouragingly they were joined on the road by as many as seventy mounted Scots Jacobites under the Honourable James Hume, a brother of the Earl of Hume. However, a good many would-be recruits were turned away:

> for they would entertain no Foot, else their Number would have been very large, but as they neither had nor could provide Arms for those they had mounted, they gave the common People good Words, and told them they would soon be furnish'd with Arms and Ammunition, and that then they would list Regiments to form an Army. This was upon the Expectation they had of surprising Newcastle, in which Case they did not question to have had as many Foot as they pleased.[10]

Indeed capture of one of the largest and most important cities in the north by the Jacobites would have been a considerable coup. Aside from the political significance of such a step, it would obviously have provided the rebels with a firm base in which to raise a proper army. Furthermore its possession would also have offered considerable leverage outside the area in cutting off the coal supply to London just at the outset of winter.

Instead and quite predictably it all went wrong. In the first place it was nonsense to suppose, as they themselves seemed to believe, that after all their bluster and activity they could take Newcastle by surprise. It might just conceivably have been possible if they had ridden straight to the city rather than fled to Rothbury on the very first day of the rising, but in retrospect even that seems doubtful. A prominent Newcastle merchant – Sir William Blackett – had promised to muster sufficient of the colliers and keelmen[11] in his employ to seize control of the city from within. Working through his overseer, some attempt was in fact made to arm them and to organise them in companies in readiness. However the local loyalists, led by another prominent merchant – William Cotesworth – and the mayor, John Johnson, were equally active. The city's trained bands were called out and mustered on nearby Killingworth Moor, along with other local militia and volunteers. The city's gates were barricaded, and Blackett himself was placed under house arrest long before the rebels arrived. Thereupon most of his people, including his overseer, promptly enlisted as loyalist volunteers! They were no doubt encouraged in their zeal by the prompt arrival of regular troops in the form of Colonel Charles Hotham's Foot and Lord Cobham's Dragoons on 9 and 12 October respectively. What was more, Lieutenant-General George Carpenter was following close behind with two further regiments of dragoons: Molesworth's and Churchill's. With the exception of Cobham's, all of these regular units were freshly raised or at least reraised. Some were neither properly equipped nor trained, but they were nevertheless stronger, better equipped, better officered and ultimately a good deal more determined than the rebels.

Consequently, on arriving at Morpeth and finding no word of an uprising in Newcastle, Forster and Derwentwater made for Hexham – not too far away from where they had started out. They then remained there for three days, proclaiming their king and seizing any arms and horses they could find. Some attempt was also made to organise themselves into proper troops of horse, but no one had any enthusiasm for an attempt to seize Newcastle. It was also only a matter of time before Carpenter came looking for them. The news of Kenmure's insurgents arriving at Rothbury was therefore all the excuse they needed to evacuate Hexham on 18 October and head north once again.

The two contingents duly met at Rothbury on 19 October, and after a convivial evening they next day moved on together to Wooler. There they halted for some much needed rest, and there received the happy news that Mackintosh of Borlum was just across the border at Duns with his little army.

The Border Fells

At long last, on 22 October, they all converged on Kelso. Kenmure and Forster arrived first, and were greeted by the happy news that Grubbet and his loyalist garrison had abandoned the burgh the night before. Then at about 3 p.m. they moved out to Ednam bridge to greet the Highlanders, who 'came in with their Bag-pipes playing, led by old Mackintosh; but they made a very indifferent Figure; for the Rain and their long Marches had extremely fatigued them, tho' their old Brigadier, who march'd at the Head of them appear'd very well.'[12]

The following day was a Sunday, but on the Monday the whole army was paraded in the market square in order to proclaim King James, and Robert Patten took the opportunity to enumerate them.

The infantry were of course entirely composed of Borlum's men, now comprising six battalions of varying size:

The Foot design'd to cross the Forth, were regimented under these Colonels, being Six Regiments in all.

The First, the Earl of Strathmore's; but he and his Lieutenant-Colonel Walkinshaw of Barrowfield were forced back in their Passage by the King's Men of War, with several others, and obliged to go on shore in the Isle of May. This Regiment was not in Highland Dress, as the others were . . .

The Second Regiment was the Earl of Mar's. . . His Regiment came not entire over the Forth, for at Preston there were only these Officers taken Prisoners, viz. Nathanael Forbes, Major, a Man singularly brave, of pleasant Discourse . . . He was very strong, and by the Help thereof forced his way out of the Marshalsea. The other Officers were three Captains and three Lieutenants . . . the rest were driven back by the King's Men of War upon the Coast of Fife.

The Third, Logie Drummond's. This Regiment came not entire over the Forth, being driven back on the Fife-side, with many more; for of the 2,500 designed to cross the Firth, the better Half were prevented.[13]

The Fourth, the Lord Nairn's, Brother to the Duke of Athol; but by marrying an Heiress, according to the Custom of Scotland, chang'd his own Name for hers: He came over the Firth with a good many of his Men. He is a Gentleman well belov'd in his Country, and by all that had the Advantage to be acquainted with him: He had formerly been at Sea, and gave signal Instances of his Bravery: He was a mighty Stickler against the Union. His Son, who was Lieutenant-Colonel to Lord Charles, took a great deal of Pains to encourage the Highlanders, by his own Experience, in their hard Marches, and always went with them on Foot through the worst and deepest Ways, and in Highland dress.

The Fifth Regiment was commanded by Lord Charles Murray, a younger Son of the Duke of Athol: He had been a Cornet of Horse beyond Sea, and had gained a mighty good Character for his Bravery, even Temper, and graceful Deportment. Upon all the Marches, he could never be prevailed with to ride, but kept at the Head of his Regiment on foot, in his Highland dress without Breeches . . .

The Sixth Regiment was called Mackintosh's Battalion, a Relation of the Brigadier's, who is chief of that clan . . . This regiment came entire over the Forth.[14]

In addition there was also what Patten claimed was a sizeable body of 'gentlemen volunteers' commanded by a Captain Skene and a Captain Maclean, who had presumably joined with Borlum after he crossed the Forth.

The cavalry on the other hand were effectively formed in two bodies, of which the Scots under Kenmure numbered five troops. The first, which was Kenmure's own, was commanded by the Hon. Basil Hamilton, a nephew of the late duke. The second, known as the Merse Troop,[15] was led by the Earl of Hume's brother, the Hon. James Hume. The earl himself had sensibly answered a warrant issued against him and was comfortably languishing in very genteel captivity in Edinburgh Castle. The third troop, Wintoun's, was actually commanded by a Captain James Dalziel, and the fourth, nominally belonging to the Earl of Carnwath, was led by their uncle, also named James Dalziel. All four troops were pointed described as being made up of gentlemen, but there was also a fifth troop commanded by a half-pay officer named Lockhart, largely made up of their servants: 'These Troops were well mann'd, and indifferently arm'd; but many of the Horses small, and in mean Condition', noted Patten. 'Besides these Troops, there were a great many Gentlemen Voluntiers, who were not formed into any regular Troop . . .'

For their part the English Jacobites also mustered five troops of horse, though not, according to Patten, 'altogether so well regulated, nor so well armed as the Scots'. They were however double officered 'to oblige the several Gentlemen that were among them'. Forster himself did not have a troop of his own, and the first troop was notionally commanded by the Earl of Derwentwater, but actually led by his brother, the Hon. Charles Radcliffe, and Captain John Shaftoe. The second troop was Lord Widdrington's, commanded for him by Thomas Errington of Beaufront, who had at one time been an officer in the French service. The third belonged to a noted smuggler and reputed horse thief – Captain John Hunter – whose motives were opportunistic rather than a matter of conviction, while the fourth troop was raised by Hunter's colleague Robert Douglas, who was chiefly employed as a courier between Forster and Mar. 'He was indefatigable', said Patten, 'in searching for Arms and Horses, a Trade, some were pleased to say, he had follow'd out of the rebellion as well as in it.' The fifth troop was commanded by an Irish officer, Captain Nicholas Wogan, and as with the Scots there were in addition 'a great many' gentlemen volunteers not formed into troops.

All in all, according to Patten, they numbered about 1,400 men, although he made no attempt to break down that number and may indeed have underestimated them. Borlum, as we have seen, managed to get about 1,200 men over the Forth, and despite a very high level of desertion 712 out of the 1,026 Scots who eventually surrendered at Preston can be identified as belonging to Borlum's command. The remainder must therefore represent Kenmure's cavalrymen, which might suggest they had numbered as many as 300 at Kelso. Most likely therefore Patten's estimate of 1,400 men referred only to the Scots and did not include Forster's English Jacobites, who appear to have accounted for another 300.

Be that as it may, and however indifferently armed, at long last the Jacobite rebels were combined into a fairly respectable body of horse and foot and even had a couple of small cannon, abandoned by Grubbet.

The question was what to do next.

Chapter 8
Into England

THE QUESTION OF WHAT to do next proved surprisingly problematic and reflected deep splits in both the Jacobite leadership and the rank and file. The original plan was for Kenmure and Borlum to combine and then move north, either to take Edinburgh or at the very least threaten Argyle's rear. Mar was evidently still expecting them to do so as late as 24 October, when he wrote some further instructions 'to the King's friends besouth the Forth'.[1] As always, this letter simply took the form of a situation report rather than a setting out of positive commands.

The problem, once again stemmed from the fact that Mar was not a military commander and was all too ready to defer to those who knew or at least pretended to know what they were doing. Furthermore Mar's messengers, such as Dr William Arthur, were always liable to interception and delay. At the best of times co-ordinating movements over such a distance, with an imperfect appreciation of the situation on the ground, was always going to be difficult, if not impossible. Therefore, while making his wishes known in general terms, Mar as always left the execution of the wishes to those on the spot and so 'left it to themselves to do what was thought most expedient for the service'. Unfortunately, although the delegation of operational flexibility might ordinarily be accounted a good thing, in this case it was a recipe for disaster.

Not only were most of the Jacobite leaders in question manifestly unfit to mount a guard on a privy, but they were also quite unable to agree on a sensible course of action. Wintoun, who had of course been involved in the initial planning, advocated doing exactly as Mar asked. More particularly, since Edinburgh was clearly no longer vulnerable to a *coup de main*, he favoured marching west again to take Dumfries, as they had originally intended. From there they could then move northwards to Glasgow, in order to open up communications with the Highlands and so threaten Argyle's rear.

There is no doubting that Wintoun was correct in advocating a march on Glasgow, for only that course offered a definite possibility of a prompt and decisive victory in Scotland. Had the rebels taken or even bypassed Glasgow and appeared in his rear, Argyle would certainly have been in a considerable amount of trouble, and his narrow victory at Sheriffmuir might well have been impossible. Politically and militarily, however, the more ambitious course of first seizing Dumfries seems much more problematic, for a swift conquest of the southwest was by no means a foregone conclusion.

At first glance the addition of Borlum's infantry to the original rabble of ill-equipped horsemen offered an obvious and potentially significant advantage. Conversely the very fact of their mostly being Highlanders – and Patten made a point of noting that only Strathmore's men were not in Highland dress – would inevitably have roused memories of the infamous Highland Host in 1678. As part of the then government's campaign against the Covenanters, several thousand Highlanders had been called out for the traditional forty days Scottish service and had been unleashed upon Glasgow and the southwest. Living at free quarters they were employed in levying fines, seizing arms and arresting the refractory. Ominously, in the manner of Louis XIV's infamous dragonnades against the French Huguenots, before commencing their work they were given a blanket indemnity for any criminal acts they might commit in the course of carrying out this patriotic duty. Memories linger long, and, as we shall see, the advent of a second Highland Host in 1715 was to rouse the countryside against them.

Such an outcome may well have been in the back of Borlum's mind when he proposed as an alternative plan – immediately seeking out and defeating General Carpenter. Having secured Newcastle upon Tyne, the general very properly had no intention of sitting quietly there. Leaving behind Hotham's Foot and the militia as a sufficient garrison for the city, he was now rapidly moving north in pursuit of the rebels, with his three regiments of dragoons.

When Borlum suggested offering battle, he was already reported to be at Wooler, just a short distance away. Exactly how many men Carpenter actually had under his command at this point is uncertain. The official establishment of each of his three regiments was about 250 officers and men apiece, but it is most unlikely that any of them were fully up to strength. Those cavalry units serving with Argyle at the end of October had an average strength of just 168 troopers besides officers, so Patten's estimate that Carpenter had a total of just 500 men is probably fairly accurate.[2] That meant he was badly outnumbered by the rebels, now that Borlum had joined them. Furthermore, although regulars, his men were of course virtually untrained and their ill-managed horses consequently rather jaded.

The Jacobite cavalry were arguably no better, and indeed probably a good deal worse. The English Jacobites in particular were not only very poorly armed, but also mounted on light hunting horses, saddled and bridled for speed, leading the Scots to be afraid 'when they should come to action, of the English running away from them on their fleet horses'.[3] However, despite being short of ammunition, the Highlanders alone would have caused Carpenter some real problems. With good management, a Jacobite victory in battle was not only a real possibility, but would also completely transform both the military and the political situation on both sides of the border.

The contrary view was held by Forster and the other English leaders. Disappointed of their hopes in Northumberland, and with absolutely no desire to fight anyone, let alone regular troops, they flatly rejected the idea of taking Dumfries and then swinging north. Instead they should head south, into Lancashire, which was portrayed as ripe for rebellion.

In fairness, it is entirely possible to sympathise with their viewpoint. At this date Scotland was still in a very real sense a foreign country. Furthermore the Scots themselves were very overtly intent on bringing about a revolution that would restore their country's political independence from England. Whatever Forster and his colleagues' views on such a separation, following the Scots now would mean their marching into a strange country to fight in a war that was not their own. Ultimately a victory over the Duke of Argyle would not put King James on the throne of England – only an English revolution could accomplish that.

Inevitably, in these circumstances agreement was impossible and so the leaders settled for the shallow compromise of moving further down along the border to Jedburgh. Thus they put off for the moment the decision as to whether to march north into Scotland or south into England, and yet at the same time still allowed for the possibility of running into Carpenter somewhere on the road. It was only a short journey of some nine miles, but even that was not accomplished without incident.

Most of the cavalry pushed ahead in their usual disorderly fashion to secure the best quarters for themselves, and were then thoroughly alarmed by a false report that Carpenter had fallen on the infantry. Once again it was down to two parties of Jacobites each mistaking the other for the enemy. In this case, espying a strange body of horse, one of the Irish officers, Captain Nicholas Wogan, rode out to have a look at the newcomers. He told Patten that he would fire a pistol as a signal if they were hostile or toss his hat in the air if they were friendly. Quite naturally, as he approached the party one of them also rode out to meet him with the same object. Wogan thereupon took fright and promptly shot at him. Happily he missed, for they were indeed fellow Jacobites, but the report of the shooting preceded them to Jedburgh, where the single pistol shot was magnified into General Carpenter attacking the Highlanders' rear!

Not surprisingly, the rest of the Jacobite cavalry were put into 'the utmost consternation' at this news, and Patten made a point of commenting on the pale faces of their leaders. Allegedly some even tore off the white cockades identifying them as Jacobites. Nevertheless in the end Charles Radcliffe got a body pulled together and rode out to assist the foot. By the time he got out there of course it was all over, and so they returned to Jedburgh 'worse frightened than hurt'.

Unfortunately dissention soon broke out once again, and this time it provoked a full-scale mutiny. Thoroughly demoralised by the day's débâcle, Forster and his Northumbrians announced that they wanted to turn southwards, into England. Their intention was to head down into North Tynedale, and from there make their way back once again to Hexham, before then striking westwards for the promised land of Lancashire. To that end they even sent Captain John Hunter ahead of them, as he knew the road, to organise quarters for them *en route*. However, the Highlanders, who were as reluctant to go to England as the English were to stay in Scotland, flatly refused to cross the border. Initially they seemed to be pacified by the issue of a generous ration of oatmeal, requisitioned in Jedburgh, but Wintoun was still stirring them up, and on approaching Hawick on 29 October the mutiny broke out in full flood.

According to Patten, the Highlanders:

> separated themselves, and went to the top of a rising Ground, there rested their Arms, and declared that they would fight if they would lead them onto the Enemy, but they would not go to England; adhering to the Lord Wintoun's Advice, that they would go through the West of Scotland, join the clans there, and either cross the Forth some Miles above Stirling, or send word to the Earl of Mar that they would fall upon the Duke of Argyle's Rear, while he fell on his Front, his Number then being very small.

Rae on the other hand portrayed the mutiny in even more dramatic terms, describing how 'the Horse surrounded the Foot, in order to force them to march South; whereupon the Highlanders cocked their Firelocks and said, if they were to be made a Sacrifice, they would choose to have it done in their own country.'[4]

The armed stand-off lasted about two hours:

> While this Humour lasted among them, they would allow none to come and speak with them but the Earl of Wintoun, who had tutor'd them in this Project; assuring them, that if they went for England, they would be all cut in pieces, or taken and sold for Slaves; one part of which has proved too true.[5]

At length it was agreed that the Highlanders would continue to march with the army only for so long as it remained in Scotland, but would then be free go their own way if it was later resolved to march into England.

So far so good, but later that night there was a curious sequel to the day's alarms. Not only had the cavalry secured all the best billets, but somehow without any discussion all the guards and outpost duties were also being delegated to the infantry. Sometime after dark there was another false alarm – this time supposedly taking the form of a body of horse patrolling in front of the advanced posts. By moonlight all the Highlanders promptly turned out and formed up in a very soldier-like fashion, but it soon transpired there was no one out there. Afterwards, according to Patten, there was a rumour that the alarm had been arranged by some of the English officers as a test to see whether the Scots would fight. It is probably rather more likely however that the cause was simply some wandering cattle, disturbed by all the unwonted activity.

In a thoroughly bad humour, next day the Jacobites made a longish march to Langholm. There they rested up while Carnwath took 400 horse forward with the avowed intention of 'blocking up' Dumfries, prior to a formal attempt on the place. It was essentially a show of strength, but, reaching Ecclefechan a little before daylight, the party halted briefly, presumably while Carnwath tried to contact the local Jacobites. Not far beyond the town, he was told by 'friends' that Dumfries was still resolutely held by the militia and other Whig volunteers. Thereupon he decided to go no further and sent back word to the main body, which by this time had only just left Langholm. Predictably, instead of hastening forward to back him up, the leaders all fell once more to arguing.

The Decision

There was no denying that at this moment the capture of Dumfries would have been invaluable to the rebels. They very badly needed a victory of some kind, and, while a rabble of poorly armed horsemen could scarcely be expected to storm a resolutely defended town, 1,000-odd Highlanders were a different matter entirely. Moreover the place was reputedly stuffed with arms and ammunition, as well as other supplies. Whether it would have served as a base is perhaps more questionable, given the local antipathy towards Highlanders, but in the short term that might not have mattered.

This was all to prove academic because from the very first days of the rising both Kenmure and Forster had been shy of fighting. The merest show of resistance was sufficient to discourage them. Just as Kenmure had backed away from Dumfries, and Forster from Newcastle at the outset, so they now did so again. The real question animating the Jacobite leaders was not whether and how they should attempt to seize Dumfries, but rather what they should do instead. The proper course was still to head north towards Glasgow.

The English Jacobites, under Forster, were naturally opposed and argued in favour of marching for Lancashire. There was no reason at all why the two parties, distrustful of each other as they were, should not have separated at this point. Kenmure might then have led the Scots northwards in obedience to Mar's instructions, while Forster would have marched the English southwards to Lancashire. However according to Patten:

> The English Gentlemen were positive for an Attempt upon their own Country, pretending to have Letters from their Friends in Lancashire, inviting them thither, assuring them that there would be a general Insurrection upon their appearing; that 20,000 Men would immediately join them; and promising the Mountains which they were to perform by Molehills. Whether they had any such Expresses or no, is to this Day a Question; but they affirm'd it to their Army, and urged the Advantages of a speedy March into England with such Vehemence, that they turn'd the Scale.[6]

In retrospect both Forster and Kenmure were obviously again clutching at straws. They were prepared to seize on any possible excuse to avoid a confrontation with Argyle or Carpenter or anyone else – reckoning it far better to march down into England in the hope of raising those supposed thousands of eager volunteers, rather than go north to an uncertain fate in Scotland. Whether or not those letters existed or were genuine, the widespread pro-Jacobite, or rather anti-government, rioting earlier in the year at least gave some shallow substance to the supposed invitations. They were of course deluding themselves and perhaps at bottom they knew this, but what is much less clear is how they carried Borlum and some of the other Scottish officers with them.

Patten, who is unfailingly hostile towards Borlum, roundly declared that he was actuated by avarice. Throughout his narrative he cited or invented a number of instances of the brigadier stooping to outright robbery as well as playing the old soldier in presenting false pay musters. Not dissimilarly, an anonymous letter about the Occurrences quoted Borlum as declaring 'why the devil not to go into England, where there is . . . meat, men and money'.[7] They were not the brigadier's only critics as it happens. Sinclair in particular was extremely hostile towards him and claimed that Strathmore and other of his officers also resented Borlum's high-handed behaviour. Clearly he was one of those strong-willed characters who fitted Clarendon's description of the civil war commander Sir Arthur Aston, who 'had the fortune to be very much esteemed where he was not known, and very much detested where he was'. However, while admitting the possibility that Borlum may have had an eye to his own advantage, that does not explain why Murray and Nairne acquiesced in the move. The most likely explanation is that they simply found themselves too deep in the business and, being young and wilful, reckoned that it was easier to go forward than to ignominiously turn back.

Wintoun and many other of the Scots were of course violently opposed to the proposal. Therefore when Kenmure agreed – apparently without demur – to go south with Forster; they again broke out in mutiny:

> . . . the Highlanders, whether dealt with underhand by the Earl of Wintoun, or whether being convinced of the Advantages they were going to throw away, and the Uncertainties they were bringing upon themselves, halted a second time, and would march no further. It is true, they did again prevail with their Leaders to march, making great Promises, and giving Money to the Men: But many of the Men were still positive, and that to such an extremity, that they separated, and about 500 of them went off in Bodies, chusing rather, as they said, to surrender themselves Prisoners, than go forward to certain Destruction.[8]

By any reckoning this was a serious blow. There is general agreement that some 1,200 men belonging to six different battalions had made it across the Forth. However men had been deserting singly and in parties ever since they landed. When they subsequently surrendered at Preston the two Athole battalions – Nairne's and Lord Charles Murray's – mustered only 122 officers and men and

137 officers and men respectively, which means that both had lost about half their strength to desertion between crossing the Forth and crossing the border – it is unlikely that many slipped away after entering England. Even more dramatically Mackintosh's Regiment, despite coming over the Forth 'entire', was down to 295 officers and men at Preston – less than half its original strength. Mar's Regiment mustered just eight officers and twenty-eight men, although oddly enough they still included those very reluctant recruits from his Kildrummy estates. Strathmore's Lowlanders, by contrast, appear to have been pretty well unaffected, for the regiment counted 158 officers and men at Preston. As to the remaining unit – Logie Drummond's Battalion – no figures are available, and although Patten listed seven officers by name, if the same proportion of officers to men applied as in the other units, it cannot have had much more than about twenty men.[9] In all there can hardly have been more than about 750 men remaining, and the brigade was effectively crippled by the refusal by so many to cross the border.

'All imaginable Means were used to have prevented this Desertion', said Patten, 'but nothing could prevail on these Men to alter their Resolutions, neither fair Promises, nor any Arguments; so they went their ways in Parties over the Tops of the Mountains.'

Alas the local people did indeed remember 1678, and they rose up against the Scottish rebels as they straggled northwards through Moffat and into south Lanarkshire. At Crawford the Highlanders split up, with some heading east towards Lamington and the others west towards Douglas. The choice no doubt depended on whether they were trying to swing around by Stirling and rejoin the army, or simply escape across the Clyde and into the hills. Few of them can have made it in either direction, because at least 300 of them were captured and sent to Edinburgh.[10] Had Wintoun's arguments carried the day it is moot whether the rest of the army might have fared better, but once again those prisoners eventually taken to Edinburgh may have considered themselves the lucky ones.

Initially Wintoun and a number of his own troop of horse also went off with the Highlanders, but the earl himself was eventually persuaded to return and to march south with the army after all, rather than desert his friends. He did so very pessimistically however, and thereafter was very pointedly excluded from councils and more informal discussions by the rest of the leadership.

Over the Border

As for the rest of the rebels, having spiked and abandoned their now redundant cannon, they set off southwards from Langholm on Monday 31 October. By that evening were at Longtown in Cumberland, where they were rejoined by Carnwath's party. They were obviously much depleted in number from the army that had assembled at Kelso and were a far cry from the near 5,000 men who would march south with the Young Pretender thirty years later. There could be no question of trying to take Carlisle, as their successors did in 1745.

Happily the Carlisle garrison were just as anxious to avoid the rebels as they were to avoid the old border fortress. The governor, Brigadier-General Thomas Stanwix, had ventured out to Longtown with a party of horse earlier in the day, but, after snaffling a Highland gentleman named Patrick Graham of Inchbrackie, he hastily retired again on the news of the rebels' approach. Thus, undisturbed, they all marched next day to Brampton, proclaimed King James and collected sufficient excise money to keep the Highlanders quiet by paying them sixpence a day.

Then, as now, the Cumbrian Fells were sparsely populated and thereafter the rebels' progress was virtually unopposed and almost without incident. At Penrith, it is true, there was a general levy of the country called out by Lord Lonsdale and the bishop of Carlisle. This bucolic body was rather improbably reputed to be 14,000 strong, but, as Patten recorded, as soon as the rebels came in sight they promptly bolted. Not surprisingly, he commented:

> Some were pleased to reflect upon him [Lonsdale] for his Retreat from Penrith; but those
> that know how naked and unprepar'd that Multitude were of all warlike Arms and Stores,
> justly commended his wide conduct, to retreat and prevent the Effusion of so much Blood
> and innocent Lives.[11]

Happily, many of the arms they did have were thrown away in their flight and scooped by the Jacobites together with a number of horses and other useful things. Cheered up by their uncovenanted 'victory ' the Jacobites then drew up in order of battle, 'that they might enter the Town in a good Figure'.

Appleby was next, where the rebels halted for a day's rest until 5 November, oblivious to the presence nearby of two companies of Invalids bound for Carlisle. In those days the army's provision for wounded servicemen was sympathetic but robust. If too old or too badly injured to support themselves they might be admitted as pensioners to one of a limited number of spaces in the famous Chelsea Hospital or discharged with an 'Out' pension calculated to reflect the extent of their disability. If however they were still willing to serve as soldiers, they were transferred to an Invalid Company. These companies were then used to provide garrisons and other permanent staff for castles such as Carlisle, for

PLATE I : *John Campbell, 2nd Duke of Argyle (1678–1743), after a portrait by William Aikman.*

PLATE 2 LEFT: *Artillerymen, as depicted by Herbert Knotel. Prior to the formation of the first permanent companies in 1716, gunners were dressed in red.*

PLATE 3 BELOW: *Scottish fisherman after Burt. Although the original was sketched in the Inverness area in about 1730 his appearance is typical of the men serving in the Lowland regiments of the Jacobite army.*

PLATE 4 RIGHT: *Charles, 8th Baron Cathcart (1686–1740), commander of the Scots Greys, after a portrait by Allan Ramsay.*

PLATE 5 BELOW: *A Victorian depiction of the body of John Graham of Claverhouse being carried from the field of Killiecrankie – a Jacobite victory in 1689 which created an exaggerated impression of the effectiveness of Highland clansmen in battle.*

PLATE 6: *James, 3rd Earl of Derwentwater (1689–1716)*
after a portrait by Sir Godfrey Kneller.

PLATE 7 RIGHT: *King George I (1660–1727) after Sir Godfrey Kneller.*

PLATE 8 BELOW: *John Erskine, 11th Earl of Mar (1675–1732) after a portrait by Sir Godfrey Kneller.*

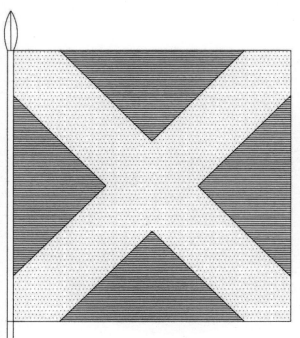

PLATE 9 LEFT: *Colours of the Appin regiment; a yellow saltire on a blue ground. This flag was brought away from the field of Culloden in 1746, but is referenced in a contemporary account of the muster at Dalcomera in 1689, so there is every reason to suppose it was carried at Sheriffmuir.*

PLATE 10 BELOW: *Dragoon, after a contemporary sketch.*

PLATE 11 BELOW: *Dutch infantryman.*

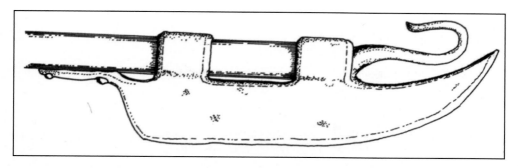

PLATE 12 ABOVE: *Lacking sufficient muskets, the Jacobites had to resort to instructing the authorities in Aberdeen, Montrose and other burghs to make large numbers of Lochaber axes.*

PLATE 13 BELOW: *Highlander riding a garron, as depicted by McIan in his* Costume of the Clans *and providing a splendid illustration of one of Huntly's 'light horse'.*

PLATE 14: *Edinburgh Castle, as viewed from the Grassmarket. Tom Arthur's attempt to seize the castle was made on the other side of the rock, but this illustration well conveys both the strength of the castle — and how it dominated the burgh.*

PLATE 15 LEFT: *Tom Forster (1675–1738) after a portrait by Rosalba Carriera.*

PLATE 16 RIGHT: *John Gordon of Glenbuchat (1673–1750); a Victorian illustration based on a contemporary portrait.*

PLATE 17 ABOVE: *One of the trophies recorded at Culloden in 1746 was a blue silk colours bearing the motto* Sursum Tendo *— peculiar to the Kinloch family and in this case to Sir James Kinloch, who joined his men with those of Lord Ogilvy.*

PLATE 20 ABOVE: *This surviving colour, white bearing the Gordon arms, was carried by Glenbuchat's Regiment in the '45 and presumably in the '15 as well.*

PLATE 18 CENTRE RIGHT: *The surviving blue colours of Lord Ogilvy's Regiment as carried during the '45 and no doubt during the '15 as well.*

PLATE 19 BELOW: *Cameron of Glendessary's 'ruddy banner', as described in 1689 and preserved at Achnacarry. Red with a green central panel bearing the Cameron arms.*

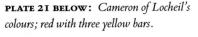

PLATE 21 BELOW: *Cameron of Locheil's colours; red with three yellow bars.*

PLATE 22 RIGHT: *Highland swordsman in trews; based on one of a number of sketches by an artist in the Penicuik area in 1745, this provides a splendid illustration of a typical Jacobite officer.*

PLATE 23 LEFT: *Grenadier. By 1715 grenadiers had largely given up furred caps in favour of mitre-shaped cloth ones, but this illustration based on an earlier image still provides a fair rendering of these elite soldiers.*

PLATE 24 ABOVE: *James Stuart; otherwise the Chevalier St George, King James VIII of Scotoland or III of Great Britain, or the Pretender, according to viewpoint.*

PLATE 27 RIGHT: *Simon Fraser of Beaufort, the once and future Lord Lovat, as sketched shortly before his eventual execution in 1746, having changed sides once too often.*

PLATE 25 ABOVE: *Brigadier Alexander Grant of Grant [1679–1719]; an experienced soldier, he was appointed governor of Edinburgh Castle by Argyle in place of the hapless Colonel Steuart, yet appears to have commanded a brigade at Sheriffmuir.*

PLATE 26 ABOVE: *Lord George Murray, the youngest son of the Duke of Athole and in 1715 a lukewarm Jacobite, whose regiment did not take part in the Sheriffmuir campaign.*

PLATE 28 ABOVE: *Jacobite soldier with Lochaber axe, as depicted in 1745 but very typical of all too many of Mar's men in 1715.*

PLATE 29 RIGHT: *A loyalist volunteer from Penicuik as depicted in 1745 but providing an equally good picture of a loyalist or Jacobite volunteer from the Scottish lowlands.*

PLATE 30 BELOW: *Highland clansmen, after the Penicuik artist 1745.*

PLATE 31 RIGHT: *Civic militia, as depicted by Herbert Knotel and typical of loyalist volunteers in Edinburgh.*

PLATE 32 BELOW: *The MacRae monument on Sheriffmuir.*

Musketier. Fähnrich Tieleman Franciskus   Fähnrich. Grenadier.
Hoynek van Papendrecht.

PLATE 33: *Dutch infantry by Knotel. All are wearing the ordinary Dutch uniform of the day with grey coats and blue facings. The colours carried by the* fanrich *(ensign) date from William of Orange's time, and the garter reflects his being king of England.*

PLATE 34: *Inverness marketplace, as sketched by Edward Burt in the 1720s.*

royal dockyards, barracks and any other military establishments. Clearly they were no longer up to the rigours of ordinary campaigning, but by all accounts they were generally regarded as a pretty hard-bitten crew. If the Jacobites were unaware of their proximity, they for their part certainly knew that the rebels were in Appleby and were 'resolv'd to make a vigorous Defence, if assaulted, by forming themselves into a hollow Square, under the Conduct of undaunted Officers, whom they assured they would live and die by'.[12]

Whether the Jacobites were oblivious to their proximity or simply chose to ignore them is unclear, but at Kendal their fortunes at least appeared to improve. Thus far very few volunteers had joined them since they crossed the border, and certainly no one of any stature. However, on the road to Kendal, a Furness gentleman named John Dalton of Thurnham came to them, and likewise at Kendal itself 'some Lancashire Papists with their Servants came and joined them'.

By 7 November they were at the town of Lancaster and three days later at Preston. An encouraging number of recruits were now starting to come in, led by men such as Edward Tyldesley of Myerscough, whose grandfather Sir Thomas was a major-general under Charles I. Establishing just how many of them there actually were is difficult. Although no fewer than 396 Lancashire men were numbered among the prisoners taken at Preston, easily as many more are reckoned to have made their escape before the surrender. Like the Northumbrian rebels they were of course virtually unarmed and of negligible value as soldiers, but there was also another problem. Most if not all of them were Catholics. Thus far, as we have seen, the Jacobites had bent over backwards to avoid being stigmatised as such, but there was no disguising the affiliations of the Lancashire men. And nor was there any way of avoiding the uneasiness this aroused in the Presbyterian Scots' ranks.

The rebels' progress through England had until then been unopposed. The Cumberland militia had fled without a fight at Penrith, and so too did the Lancashire militia at Lancaster. There Sir Henry Houghton had mustered as many as 600 men, and command of them was assumed by a regular officer, Colonel Francis Charteris of nearby Hornby Castle.[13] Charteris planned to blow up the bridge that carried the main road over the river Lune, but the town's inhabitants refused to allow him to do so. Similarly a Quaker merchant named Lawson flatly refused either to hand over six small cannon in a ship he owned or to send the ship safely out to sea. Frustrated at every turn, Houghton and Charteris gave over any hope of blocking the road, but, instead of dispersing their followers as Lonsdale had done, they retired first to Preston and then to Wigan. Their retreat from

Preston was covered by two troops of Colonel William Stanhope's Dragoons, who then in turn evacuated the town in haste, well ahead of the rebel advance guard. Vastly encouraging as all this was, no one at first thought to wonder what that small detachment of regulars was doing there in the first place.

The fact of the matter was that the British Army was closing in at last. Hampered by the fact his raw dragoons were insufficiently well trained to carry out any aggressive form of reconnaissance, General Carpenter lost contact with the rebels after they left Jedburgh. Not unreasonably he assumed they were intending to join with Mar, and as he did not come under the authority of the commander-in-chief Scotland – and had no desire to either – he felt justified in dropping back down to Newcastle to rest and refit. There, however, he was met by a messenger from Houghton and Charteris, advising that the rebels were in fact on the point of invading Lancashire. To his credit, Carpenter acted at once and with considerable speed. Notwithstanding his men were already exhausted and his horses in poor condition, he left Durham on 7 November, and by 12 November was approaching Clitheroe, just a dozen miles from Preston.

By then, however, General Forster had even more to worry about.

Chapter 9

The Battle of Preston, 12 November 1715

WHILE STILL ON THE road to Lancaster, the Jacobites were joined by Lord Widdrington's brother Charles, bringing the encouraging news that King James had been proclaimed in Manchester. Indeed it was said a troop of horse was already being raised and equipped there at public expense, while other volunteers were appearing on every hand. Lancashire was rising in force for King James, just as Forster and the other English Jacobite leaders had promised.

Unfortunately Widdrington's happy news was completely untrue. There had been some pro-Jacobite rioting in Manchester, but that was away back in May and June, and the trouble was quickly quelled. Would-be Jacobite leaders such as Thomas Syddall (a 'mob captain' sneered Patten) were imprisoned, and there had been little if any trouble there since.[1] Instead, in response to the present crisis, a substantial body of regular troops now stood squarely in the rebels' path.

First to arrive was Colonel George Preston's Regiment of Foot, otherwise known as the Cameronians, which had been recalled from Ireland. Landing at Chester the regiment was immediately placed under the command of Major-General Charles Wills, together with four new regiments of dragoons – Wynn's, Honeywood's, Munden's and Dormer's – while a fifth regiment, Newton's Dragoons, was left behind as a police force in Manchester to prevent any further unrest. Moving forward to Wigan, Wills was then joined by two more cavalry regiments – Colonel Philip Stanhope's Dragoons and Colonel Thomas Pitt's Horse – and by the Lancashire militia under Charteris and Houghton. All in all, that gave him something in the region of just over 2,000 men. The militia might be of negligible value and all of his dragoon regiments were newly raised and barely trained, but both Pitt's Horse and Preston's Cameronians were seasoned veterans and so Wills was spoiling for a fight.

Not so General Forster.

Since entering Lancashire the Jacobites had been moving relatively slowly. Simple fatigue aside, their constant wanderings earlier in the rising had made it difficult for would-be volunteers to find them, let alone rally to King James's standard. Now that recruits were at last starting to appear in appreciable numbers it was only sensible when the Jacobites arrived in Preston on 10 November to pause, gather the volunteers in and make a start on organising them into companies, troops and even regiments. Yet at the same time, as Patten admitted, something went very badly wrong with the rebels' intelligence gathering:

> All this while they had not the least Intimation of the Forces that were preparing to oppose them, much less of the near approach of the King's Army: And as it is a Question often asked, and which very few can answer, viz. How they came to be so utterly void of Intelligence at that time, as to be so ignorant of the March of the King's Forces, and to know nothing of them 'till they were within sight of Preston, and ready almost to fall upon them? It may be very proper to give a plain and direct Answer to it, which will in short be this, viz. That in all their Marches Mr Forster spared neither Pains nor Cost to be acquainted with all General Carpenter's Motions, of which he had constant and particular Accounts every Day, and sometimes twice a Day; but the Lancashire Gentlemen gave him such Assurances that no Force could come near them by Forty Miles but they could inform him thereof, this made him perfectly easy on that side, relying entirely on the Intelligence he expected from them: And therefore, when on the Saturday Morning he had given Orders for his whole Army to march from Preston towards Manchester, it was extremely surprising, and he could scarce credit the reports that General Wills was advancing from Wigan to attack them: But he was soon satisfied of the Truth of it by Messengers on all hands.[2]

There is some suggestion that the news of General Wills's approach actually arrived on the Friday afternoon. Be that as it may; it was early on the morning of Saturday 12 November 1715 that the Jacobites scrambled to receive him. A party of 100 foot from Mackintosh's Regiment under Lieutenant-Colonel John Farquharson of Invercauld was hastily posted on the Ribble bridge, while Forster himself rode out along the Wigan road with a party of horse to reconnoitre. He did not need to go far, for no sooner had he crossed the bridge and climbed the steep bank on the other side of the river than he bumped straight

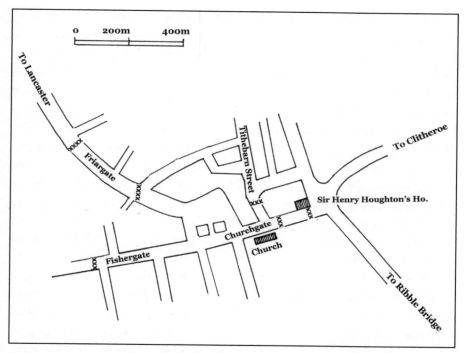

MAP 3: *This rough sketch, largely based on work by Mike Lawson, provides a useful indication of the approximate locations of the Jacobite barricades and the areas of most serious fighting in Preston.*

into Wills's vanguard in the village of Walton-le-Dale, less than two miles from Preston marketplace.

General Wills, as it happens, was also proceeding very cautiously, and it is a measure of just how raw his cavalry were that his vanguard comprised a single company of the Cameronians, with the rest of the regiment following a little distance behind and then Wills's cavalry very much in the rear. This reversal of the normal procedure was probably only sensible in the circumstances, but it enabled the Jacobites to disengage easily. More importantly they were afforded more precious time in which to barricade themselves into the town.

Preston in 1715 was a prosperous market town of about 6,000 inhabitants, largely occupying a low bluff above the river Ribble, which flowed more or less from east to west a little distance away on its south side. The bridge occupied by Invercauld's detachment consequently lay outside the town itself, and, as soon as the decision was made to stand and fight, Borlum insisted on its being withdrawn.

Patten and generations of historians after him have condemned this decision, arguing that the crossing ought to have been contested, but the fact of the matter was that the river was fordable at a number of points above and below the bridge, and especially at low tide. Not only was the bridge easily outflanked, but as a fighting position it was quite untenable since it was effectively in a hole overlooked both by the town to the north and by the high ground at Walton-le-Dale to the south. Significantly, during an earlier battle at Preston in 1648, Colonel George Keith's Scots infantry brigade had been badly cut up trying to defend that very same bridge, precisely because it was so exposed to fire from the higher ground.[3] Indeed the approaches to the bridge were so swept by fire from Cromwell's men that it was impossible either to withdraw or reinforce the brigade before it was overrun. Notwithstanding that later criticism, Borlum's immediate abandonment of the bridge was unquestionably the correct decision. Instead the Jacobites were to concentrate on defending the town itself.

There were four principal approaches to it. From the southeast, the Wigan road rose up the bank from the Ribble bridge to turn slightly where the Clitheroe road also came in from the east and then become an east–west thoroughfare called Churchgate. The other end of this thoroughfare, which first became Fishergate beyond the marketplace and then the Liverpool road, eventually bent down the hill to a ford over the Ribble at Penwortham, about a mile downstream from the bridge. Another principal approach was the Lancaster road, which curved down from the northwest to enter the top end of the marketplace by the Mitre Inn.

There were obviously a considerable number of other minor lanes entering the town of Preston, but an abundance of thick hedgerows lining the main roads hampered deployment into the fields beyond them, just as it had done in 1648, and consequently channelled the assaults accordingly.

Deployments

Just how many men the Jacobites actually had available to defend Preston is far from clear. Contemporary estimates ranged from 2,000 men all the way up to 4,000 – and even, in at least one letter, 5,000 men. Against that only some 1,500 officers and men were afterwards numbered as prisoners, albeit a considerable number had succeeded in escaping from the town before the surrender.[4] Most of those who got away, obviously enough, were English and in particular the largely unarmed local recruits. The fact of the matter was that, while there were certainly a considerable number of rebels stuffed into Preston at the outset of the battle, the fighting strength of the army was for all practical purposes largely confined to the 750 Scots infantry.

It took no great military genius to foresee that the principal assault would come straight up the Wigan road. Therefore at the point where it entered the town proper, Sir Henry Houghton's relatively tall, flat-roofed town house was turned into a strongpoint and a barricade was thrown across Churchgate. However, the main position was another barricade slightly further up the street by the church itself, covered by another around the back, in adjacent Tithebarn Street.

Borlum took personal command at this point, placing the thirty-odd men of Mar's Regiment in the house itself, while Lord Charles Murray's men held the Tithebarn Street barricade and the adjacent barn. The Churchgate barricades may therefore have been manned by Nairne's Regiment, while the gentlemen volunteers, most of them mounted, were drawn up in the nearby churchyard under the Earl of Derwentwater and the other noble lords, in order to serve as a reserve. In addition Borlum had the dubious assistance of two of the small ships' cannon brought down from Lancaster, but their fire was seemingly quite ineffective.[5]

On the northwest side of the town, the Lancaster road was covered by Mackintosh's Regiment, with a barricade situated by a prominent windmill and a fallback position further up the street, where it becomes Friargate, just before entering the marketplace. The Fishergate position, covering the Liverpool road up from the ford at Penwortham, was manned by Strathmore's Regiment under Major William Miller and Captain William Douglas.[6] Where the remnant of Logie Drummond's little battalion was deployed is not stated, but it was most likely with Borlum on Churchgate.

As to the rest of the rebel army, the likelihood is that most of them were scattered around the perimeter covering the various minor lanes, alleyways and other entrances. In effect they were little more than unhappy spectators to the drama, and many of the local men would soon begin slipping away along those otherwise unguarded lanes and footpaths.

On the other side, General Wills mingled surprise and relief on discovering the Ribble bridge was unguarded. The Cameronians, under Lieutenant-Colonel Lord Forrester, once again led the way, crossing the bridge at about 1 p.m. and feeling their way up the road, expecting at any time to be ambushed from the hedgerows. At the top of the bank they halted, and Wills came up to have a look before calling the rest of his men forward.

As a first step he intended that a cordon should be thrown around the town. The militia and volunteers under Colonel Charteris and Sir Henry Houghton were posted along the river, guarding the bridge and covering the fords. North of the town Colonel Richard Munden's Brigade, comprising Pitt's Horse, his own regiment of dragoons and half of Stanhope's Dragoons, were to be deployed in an arc between the Lancaster and Clitheroe roads. The principal attack – on Borlum's position on Churchgate – was to be carried out by another of Wills's brigadiers, Colonel Philip Honeywood. For this purpose he was assigned the whole of the Cameronians and a second *ad hoc* infantry battalion comprising detachments of fifty men apiece dismounted from each dragoon regiment, while the remainder of his own regiment remained mounted as a reserve. The third of Wills's brigadiers, Colonel James Dormer, was then given the task of attacking directly down the Lancaster road, for which purpose he was assigned his own and Colonel Wynn's regiments of dragoons, both of which were to fight dismounted as infantry, while a mounted squadron of Stanhope's Dragoons was to be a reserve. No attempt was to be made to attack up the Liverpool road from Penwortham, simply because Wills was already overstretched and had no troops to spare.

The Battle

Judging by events, the first attack went in before either Munden or Dormer were properly in position. This was a probing attack on Borlum's forward barricade, led by Lord Forrester of the Cameronians and was speedily repulsed by a very heavy musketry.

However, while the Cameronians fell back to regroup for a proper attempt, Borlum also took advantage of the lull to evacuate Sir Henry Houghton's house and retire to his fallback position close by the church. Once again he was fiercely criticised for this, especially as Houghton's house provided a very useful vantage point. However given that he was so short of men and ammunition, Borlum probably intended from the first to hold a relatively tight perimeter around the town centre, and Houghton's house was only ever intended as a forward outpost.

This decision was also no doubt heavily influenced by the difficulty of covering all the lanes and passageways off Church Street, and was vindicated by the inevitable discovery by some Cameronians of an unguarded lane which emerged on the south side of Churchgate behind the first barricade. It appears that some of the volunteers under Douglas and Hunter had been tasked with covering these lanes, but as they were only armed with pistols their effectiveness was limited.

Be that as it may, Borlum pulled back Mar's and Nairne's little battalions, and, as they were now short of ammunition, may have manned the main barricade with Strathmore's Regiment under Miller and Douglas instead. This was timely, because Lord Forrester was about to try again, rather more forcefully this time and:

> ... came out into the open Street with his drawn Sword in his Hand, and faced Macintosh's Barrier, looking up the Street and down the Street, and viewing how they were posted. There were many Shots fired at him, but he returned to his Men, and came up again at the Head of them into the middle of the Street, where he caused some to face the Barricade where the Brigadier was posted, and ply them with their Shot, at the same time commanding another Party to march cross the Streets, to take Possession of those Houses [i.e. Sir Henry Houghton's and one opposite owned by a Mr Ayres]. It was a desperate Attempt and shows him an Officer of an undaunted Courage. While this was doing, the Rebels from the Barrier, and from the Houses on both sides, made a terrible Fire upon them, and a great many of that old and gallant Regiment were kill'd and wounded: The Lord Forrester received several Wounds himself. Besides the Damage they received on that side, they were sore galled by some Windows below them, by Captain Douglass and Captain Hunter's Men. Preston's Foot fired smartly upon the Rebels, but did little Execution, the Men being generally cover'd from the Shot, and delivering their own Shot securely, and with good Aim.[7]

Another Jacobite volunteer – Peter Clarke – described the scene more laconically, noting that: 'About 2 a clock this afternoone, 200 of General Wills men entred the Churchgate street, and the Highlanders, firing out of the cellers and windows, in 10 minnits time killed 120 of them.'[8] His estimate of the casualties was obviously more enthusiastic than accurate, but there is no doubting that the attack was stopped cold. All in all ninety-two officers and men, out of the total of fifty-six killed and eighty-six wounded returned by General Wills, belonged to the Cameronians and most if not all of them must have fallen during this attack rather than in the earlier probing one.

A detailed breakdown of their losses is not available, but the known casualties certainly included Lord Forrester, shot at least twice, the second-in-command Major James Lawson also wounded and the colonel's son, Captain Robert Preston, dead of his wounds. An ensign who was killed and four other ensigns returned as wounded must also have belonged to the regiment.[9]

Be that as it may, there is no disguising the severity of the Cameronians' losses, which must have accounted for a third or more of their strength.[10] Thus crippled they fell back, leaving some of their wounded, including Captain Preston, to be captured by the rebels. However, they still clung onto their foothold at the edge of town, including Sir Henry Houghton's house. Colonel Honeywood moreover had no intention of giving up, so he launched a second attack – this time with his *ad hoc* battalion of dismounted dragoons, against the Tithebarn Street barricade.

Unfortunately the Jacobites had established an observation post in the church tower, which spotted them moving into position. Being forewarned, fifty of the volunteers were sent forward to reinforce the defenders. Once again few of them can have had muskets, but, while pistols alone would have been of limited use in holding off an attack, they very effectively supplemented the Highlanders' musketry.

For his part Honeywood not only had to contend with an enemy securely posted behind a substantial barricade, and well-directed crossfire from the flanking buildings, but his men were also almost certainly not trained for such fighting. Dragoons were of course mounted infantry, and a little paradoxically perhaps – being newly raised – were probably more at home on foot than they would have been if mounted. However, while they may have mastered the rudiments of infantry drill and musketry, it is most unlikely that they would have been trained in specialist tactics such as street firing.

Instead of firing by platoons in a linear fashion, a deep formation was adopted and each rank fired in turn, dropping back to the rear as soon as it had done so in order to reload in the expectation that by the time the last rank had discharged their muskets the first rank would have reloaded and be standing ready to repeat the cycle. The Cameronians' heavy losses were probably attributable to this drill, rather than to the Highlanders' supposed marksmanship, for while their fire was very 'regular', in order to deliver it they were tightly packed in the middle of the street, forming a target that was very difficult to miss.

Not knowing the trick, as the saying went, Honeywood's raw dragoons advanced straight down Tithebarn Street and on coming under a fierce fire let off a volley or two in return. However, they then very sensibly fell back again without incurring much loss, although Honeywood himself received a bruise in the shoulder from a spent musket ball and Major Humphrey Bland was wounded in the arm.[11]

Wills's greatest fault at this point was his abject failure to co-ordinate his assaults. Forrester and then Honeywood had attacked and been repulsed one after the other. Some of the blame obviously falls to Honeywood as brigade commander, but it is also quite likely there was a deliberate lack of co-operation on the part of the Cameronians, who may have been unwilling to take orders from a cavalry officer. Be that as it may it was only after Honeywood had been halted, that Colonel Dormer attacked down the Lancaster road sometime around 4 p.m.

Supposedly it was dismounted dragoons who first attempted a frontal assault on the windmill barricade, but Colonel Mackintosh's men 'made a dreadful Fire upon the King's Forces, killing many on the spot, and obliging them to make a Retreat; which, however, they did very handsomely. This was owing to the common Men, who were but new listed; though the Officers and old Soldiers behav'd themselves with great Bravery.'[12]

In fact Dormer may initially have attempted to go in dismounted. His regiment subsequently returned just three men killed and four wounded besides himself (he had a contusion on the knee) and Wynne's had six killed and three officers and twenty-one men wounded. The two regiments also returned a total of thirty-one horses killed and fifteen wounded.[13]

A subsequent attempt to outflank the barricade as Lord Forrester had done on Churchgate was similarly seen off in just as peremptory a fashion. With that, the steadily failing light brought an effective end to operations, although both sides maintained their positions and occasionally shot at each other through the night.

Carpenter arrives

On an immediate tactical level the Jacobites appeared at first sight to have done well. They had after all handsomely beaten off all of the attacks launched against them. On deeper reflection, their situation was much less favourable. While they had largely succeeded in holding their positions, that was not the same thing as defeating their attackers. Wills had very effectively pinned them down; he was still surrounding them and obviously had no intention of leaving. For their part, the Jacobites had neither the food nor the ammunition to withstand a blockade, particularly when there were no friendly forces outside to lift that blockade. Realistically there were already no more than two stark and unpalatable choices open to the Jacobites. They could attempt to break out or they could open negotiations for surrender.

The first option was apparently canvassed by Forster during the afternoon of 12 November, when he proposed to Borlum that his Highlanders should launch a counterattack, sallying out sword in hand. Borlum however flatly refused, no doubt rightly suspecting that the horse would then take the opportunity to escape, leaving the Scots in the lurch – a topic that he revisited in captivity:

> That Lord [Widdrington] continued to demand of him, Why he did not sally out himself with his Men? Or why he would not obey Mr Forster, who would have had the horse to have sallied out? To this he gave Answer, That if his Foot had sallied out, they might by that means have been parted from the horse, and so left naked to have been cut off: Besides, nothing more frightens the Highlanders than horse and Cannon. As for obeying Mr Forster, in letting the horse sally out, he said. If the horse had attempted any such Thing, they would have gone through the Fire of his Men; for they were afraid the Horse design'd such a Thing, and would have been able to have made a Retreat, and left them pent up in the Town.[14]

Borlum was quite correct in that any attempt to break out was doomed to fail. There was no way that the infantry could win clear, and successfully fight their way home to Scotland. However their sacrifice was the only way to give the cavalry at least a chance of doing so. But there was more. When the prisoners taken by the Jacobites were interrogated, they revealed that General Carpenter was also at hand and closing in fast. As we have seen, by 12 November, just as the battle for Preston was getting underway, he was approaching Clitheroe. Joined by the Earl of Carlisle and Lord Lumley he pushed on next morning and reached the embattled town of Preston by about 10 a.m. on 13 November, at which point the rebels' fate was sealed.

Carpenter, as the senior commander, greeted Wills warmly and congratulated him on his success. With a very proper magnaminity, he began by assuring his subordinate that as 'you have begun the affair so well, you ought to have the glory of finishing it'. Unfortunately the two officers knew each other of old, having served together and quarrelled in Spain during Queen Anne's War. Very soon the old animosities resurfaced. Riding around the town to inspect Wills's dispositions, Carpenter quickly began finding fault. Out by the Lancaster road he found the troops packed too closely together, with many crowded in 'a deep narrow lane' and ordered them spread out, in separate parties. 'Also going to view the Ground towards the River, he found, to his great Surprise, that no Troops were posted at the End of Fishergate Street, to block up that part of the Town; and that for want of it, several of the Rebels had escaped there, and more rid off that Way even before his Face.'[15] Pitt's Horse were promptly ordered to seal off this particular escape route, but after that Carpenter largely refrained from interfering, especially as the first approaches were now being made by the rebels as to a proposed surrender.

Surrender

Seemingly it came about after a discussion between Forster, Lord Widdrington and Colonel Oxburgh. The day before, Forster had behaved bravely enough, riding about and encouraging the defenders, but his advisers were a different matter. Patten alleged Widdrington was an alcoholic coward, who sat out the battle claiming to be incapacitated by an attack of gout. Similarly, although Oxburgh was reputed a good soldier 'he either wanted Conduct or Courage, or perhaps both; He was better at his Beads and Prayers than at his business as a Soldier; and we all thought him fitter for a Priest than a Field Officer.'[16] At any rate the upshot was that at about 2 p.m. Oxburgh rode out to seek terms.

Wills was in a bullish mood and refused to negotiate. The Jacobites were rebels who had slain the King's subjects and would be treated accordingly. The most he was prepared to offer was that, if they laid down their arms within the hour, they would not be executed out of hand. In the meantime, suspecting that their English colleagues might be about to sell them down the river, the Scots sent out an emissary of their own in the shape of Captain Dalziel. He was offered essentially the same stark terms, but requested time to consult properly with his colleagues. While Oxburgh had received short shrift, Wills evidently recognised Dalziel as a gentleman and agreed to consider the matter.

In the meantime, one of the general's staff, Colonel Stanhope Cotton, rode up to the Mitre Inn with a drummer beating a chamade as a signal of truce. The original one hour allowed to Colonel Oxburgh was up, and Cotton required to know their intentions. Learning that the Scots wanted more time he agreed to extend the ceasefire while he sought clarification from his general, but to the mortification of all concerned his drummer was shot dead outside Sir Henry Houghton's house. Notwithstanding this, Wills eventually agreed to give the rebels until 7 a.m. the next morning, providing they neither strengthened their fortifications nor made any attempt to escape. He also demanded hostages, and eventually at about 8 p.m. Borlum and Derwentwater went out and surrendered themselves.

There could be no doubt as to the outcome, and, in view of their efforts, the Cameronians, under Lord Forrester, were given the job of supervising the capitulation next morning. All in all the rebels reckoned to have lost seventeen killed and twenty-five wounded, against Wills's admitted fifty-six killed and eighty-six wounded. Something in the region of 1,500 Jacobites then surrendered on the morning of 14 November.[17]

The Jacobite officers duly handed over their swords while the rank and file were disarmed in the marketplace. Rank still had its privileges in these circumstances, and, while the common soldiers were packed into the church, the officers and noblemen were more agreeably accommodated in the various inns. Rank however also had its perils. Wills had offered no guarantees and proceeded to demonstrate the fact by very quickly identifying six of the prisoners as men holding the king's commission. A summary court martial duly followed on 28 November, and of the six only Captain Dalziel could show that he had resigned before the rising began. Another, Lord Charles Murray, was reprieved through the influence of his father, the Duke of Athole, but the remaining four – Major Nairne, Major Erskine, Captain Lockhart and Captain Shaftoe – were put against a wall and shot long before the civil courts dealt with the ordinary prisoners.

That lay in the future. By a curious coincidence much remarked upon at the time, on the same day that the Jacobites surrendered at Preston, bringing the English uprising to an end, a similar crisis was reached in Scotland and to there we must now return.

Chapter 10

A Time to Dance

HAVING SUCCESSFULLY SENT A substantial detachment across the Forth and into Argyle's rear, Mar has been criticised for not following up the operation with an immediate offensive against Argyle. The latter could not after all be in two places at once. If he elected to stand fast at Stirling then Borlum might take Edinburgh and then move on his rear. Conversely if he fell back to deal with Borlum, the crossing at Stirling might be uncovered. In either event Mar needed to move quickly, either to pin Argyle in place or take advantage of his absence. Instead Mar's movements were tardy, quite ineffectual and soon abandoned. Nevertheless, while there is no denying his hesitation and lack of determination, he did face a number of practical difficulties.

Not the least of these was the problem of communications. The rebel army had obviously been very substantially weakened, not just by sending away 2,000 men under Borlum, but also through scattering a number of smaller detachments to Burntisland and elsewhere in order to cover the crossing. Mar was therefore understandably wary of rushing into a general engagement, before Borlum and the southern rebels were in a position to threaten Argyle's rear simultaneously. However, the forces with which he was to co-operate were not only separated from him by a considerable distance, but were also physically cut off from him by the Firth of Forth. Thus what should have been a cunning plan quickly unravelled. The timetable was thrown off by the various delays at the beginning, and when the crossing did get underway it was intercepted and Mar was left for some time in complete ignorance of its success or failure.

In the meantime as we have seen, once across the Forth, rather than seek a prompt rendezvous with Wintoun and the Nithsdale rebels, Borlum took it into his head to try and capture Edinburgh all on his own.

The upshot was that Mar did not receive confirmation that Borlum and at least a part of his men were over the Forth until sometime on the night of 15 October.[1] Even then the news was bad. Nevertheless, with a commendable promptness which for once belies his lethargic reputation, the army was assembled and made ready to march early next morning. Before setting out, however, he called a hasty council of war:

> My Lord, with a most dejected countenance, and a sad voice, told us, He was sorrie to give us the bad neus of Mackintoshes being invested in the Citadell of Leith, and that his goeing there, contrary to his Lordshipp's last orders, would, in all appearances prove a fatall mistake to him; and next read us tuo dismall letters, where Mackintosh, appearing disheartened, said that a few hours would determine his fate, in these words, but that he'd doe his best; tho' he mentioned the preparations of cannon and bombs with terrour, which, he said, would soon doe his work.[2]

There was seemingly no mention in the letters of Borlum's plans for a breakout, and unsurprisingly Mar opined that he should be given up as lost. General Hamilton, however, being made of sterner stuff suggested that an immediate advance on Stirling could do no harm and might yet prove an effective diversion to relieve pressure on Borlum. Accordingly they marched immediately to Auchterarder, and from there on 17 October to Ardoch. By now it was extremely cold and wet, but the cavalry pushed on to seize Dunblane, and Glenbuchat's battalion went with them to provide security.

That alas was the limit of their enterprise. While Mar himself remained behind with the main body of the army, the Marquis of Drummond was placed in command of the advance guard at Dunblane. There he very sensibly went to bed, leaving Sinclair and some of the other officers to fret over the likelihood of being surprised by General Whetham and the forces still in Stirling. Glenbuchat for his part helpfully pointed out that his ammunition was soaked by the rain, and that his men could neither sound the alarm nor fight off an attack. When some of his men were nevertheless detailed to go back out into the rain to guard a bridge, they retaliated by refusing to let some of the cavalry pass to fetch their horses. Sinclair sulked of course and then congratulated himself on persuading them all to mount and form up before dawn.

Meanwhile Whetham very properly made no attempt to disturb them. Instead he sat securely behind Stirling bridge and sent off a succession of urgent messages to recall Argyle from Edinburgh.

Time was soon running out for Mar. Even if all his forces had been closed up at Dunblane it would have been difficult, if not well-nigh impossible, to take Stirling bridge before Argyle returned. By way of a compromise Hamilton proposed to seize Causewayhead and so lock the northern end of the crossing. From a tactical point of view this happy notion would have had much to commend it, but only as a means of covering an immediate turning movement towards the fords further upriver.

Maintaining a garrison there was wholly impractical. Unless the rest of the army was impotently closed up behind it, the outpost would have been difficult to maintain and far too vulnerable to a counterattack. As for a turning movement, that might have been possible if Mar had marched westwards with all his forces from the outset. Yet he would still have to fight Argyle and without the assistance of those 2,000 men sent off with Borlum. Consequently he seems to have reasoned that it would be folly to risk such a move when substantial reinforcements from the west under General Gordon and from the north under the Earl of Seaforth would arrive within days. As he was also still awaiting the arrival of King James and perhaps the Duke of Berwick, it must have seemed that he had far too much to lose by rushing things. Better then to wait, especially as there was trouble in the north.

The Rising in the North

In the popular imagination there is always something of a tendency to see the Jacobite risings as synonymous with Highland uprisings. This is true up to a point in as much as a substantial proportion of the rebels were indeed Highland clansman, but it is also misleading. The Highlands and the Highland clans were by no means united in their support of the Stuarts and this was particularly so in the north. This was in large part due to the influence of the Earl of Sutherland and his neighbours, Lord Reay and Robert Monroe of Foulis. Nearer to Inverness, Brigadier Alexander Grant was of course a serving officer and his brother Colonel William Grant already had a strong Independent Company.

On 19 August the *London Gazette* formally announced the appointment of the Earl of Sutherland to serve as lord lieutenant of the counties of Ross and Cromarty, Moray, Nairn, Caithness and Sutherland, while Brigadier Grant of Grant likewise became lord lieutenant of Inverness and Banff. Both were empowered to name and appoint deputies and to raise fencible battalions, and, if expedient, troops of horse. In Grant's case the appointment was necessarily a nominal one, but, after conferring with the king on 9 September, Sutherland sailed for the north by way of Leith. There he collected 300 stand of arms and a further shipment was then seized by Sinclair, as we have seen in Chapter 5. In the meantime however there was a more serious setback when the Mackintoshes declared for the Pretender, and with the connivance or rather the acquiescence of the magistrates took control of Inverness.

An odd little campaign then followed in which the principal objective of either side was to avoid any unnecessary unpleasantness. Whatever their political affiliations they were still very conscious that they were friends and neighbours.[3]

On or about 26 September William Mackenzie, 5th Earl of Seaforth, declared for King James and began mustering his clansmen and followers at Brahan Castle. Sutherland landed at Dunrobin a couple of days later and responded by mustering a similar number of loyalists at Alness, just five miles from Seaforth's camp at Brahan. Although the two forces were evenly matched in numbers, Sutherland probably had the edge in that his men were almost certainly better armed.

Then more rebel reinforcements arrived: the MacDonalds of Sleat and some other clans, totalling about 1,200 men. Finding himself badly outnumbered, Sutherland immediately sent for help. With commendable promptness 500 men were raised by the Grant lairds in Strathspey and another 120 by Duncan Forbes of Culloden and Hugh Rose of Kilravock. The intention was to embark them at Findhorn, and a large number of boats were accordingly assembled by Kilravock to carry them all across the Moray Firth. Unfortunately Seaforth forestalled them by advancing on Alness on 9 October. Sutherland at that point appears to have lost his nerve and promptly fell back to the river Bonar, whereupon most of his followers simply went home.

The Jacobites celebrated with a brief orgy of plundering, but Seaforth had already received two messages from Mar, urging him to march south at once. Accordingly he moved to Inverness on 15 October, which was co-incidentally the same day Mar received word that Borlum was at Leith. An attempt by Seaforth to seize arms from Culloden House was rather peremptorily seen off, but by way of consolation he was joined by a large body of Frasers. As a result, when he eventually marched out of Inverness on Monday 24 October, Seaforth was able to leave behind a strong garrison of some 400 men under Sir John Mackenzie of Coull. In order to reach Perth however he would still need to pass through Strathspey, which being Grant country ought to have been accounted hostile.

Instead it seems that Seaforth went to an alehouse at Kirk of Duthal 'to adjust matters with the principal gentlemen of the name of Grant'. Supposedly those present included Seaforth and Lord Duffus, William Sutherland and his brothers, Sir Donald MacDonald and a Colonel William Grant. The upshot was that, rather than fight each other to no good purpose, it was agreed Seaforth would be allowed free passage out of the area and that both parties would peaceably refrain from plundering either on the march or by invading the rebels' lands in their absence.[4]

There matters might have remained but for the advent of a Highland gentleman named Simon Fraser of Beaufort. Once a captain of grenadiers in Dutch William's army, he was now the head of the Clan Fraser and would-be Lord Lovat. Through the failure of the original Lovat line he had come to that position through grim determination and a good deal of largely discreditable manoeuvring. The sordid details need not detain us here, but in the process he made some powerful enemies and by 1702 had seemingly lost everything. The Lovat estates passed by marriage to a gentleman named Alexander Mackenzie, son of Lord Prestonhall, who thereafter variously styled himself Mackenzie, or Fraser, of Fraserdale. Despite the patronage and protection of the Duke of Argyle himself, Simon Fraser found it expedient to take himself abroad. A surprisingly inept career as a double agent soon ended with imprisonment in France, but in November 1714 he escaped and saw an opportunity to recover his estates and title. As he travelled north an offer to command the loyalist militia at Dumfries against Kenmure's insurgents was politely declined by the Marquis of Annandale, but his arrival home coincided with Seaforth's departure.

It might be shrewdly suspected that the timing of this homecoming was planned all too neatly. Although his honesty and loyalties might be suspect, no one could ever doubt Simon Fraser's energy, intelligence or sense of purpose. As many as 400 of his erstwhile clansmen had marched off under Seaforth and Mackenzie of Fraserdale, but a well-timed letter of recall would secure their immediate withdrawal. In the meantime, abrogating the style if not the title of Lord Lovat,[5] he publicly declared for King George. Having advertised his credentials, he then cajoled the other loyalist leaders into planning the recapture of Inverness. Sutherland accordingly called a meeting of the deputy lieutenants at Invergordon on 1 November.

At the meeting a not very elaborate plan was agreed. All of them, including Lovat, were to raise their people and march upon the Highland capital, but little attempt was made to co-ordinate operations. Consequently it was all over before Sutherland managed to march down from Dunrobin in the far north of Scotland.

Inverness

In the meantime there was an odd little incident involving Coll MacDonald of Keppoch. Being a notorious bandit, his loyalties were straightforward, insofar as he had none. At the beginning of October he had declined a kind invitation from General Gordon to join the rebels, disingenuously claiming that he was hindered from doing so by the garrison of Fort William.[6]

In reality the governor, Sir Robert Pollock, literally had his hands full just holding the fort and preventing it from falling down of its own accord. He had two regular battalions, but a return of 15 June revealed that Hill's Regiment had just 162 effectives and Hamilton's 178, besides various detachments in remote outposts.[7] Worse, Hill's (which became Edward Montagu's on 30 July) was in process of being recalled to Stirling.[8] Those actually left on duty at the Fort William garrison were sickly, underfed, poorly clothed and equipped and understandably apt to consider themselves forgotten. What was more, the place was literally crumbling, and one of the bastions actually collapsed. In short, the fort was to all intents and purposes indefensible. However, it is hard to say whether the reluctance of the Jacobites to attack it stemmed from an unwillingness to incur pointless casualties in taking the place, or whether it provided an all too convenient excuse for inaction not just by Keppoch, but also by the Camerons and other local clans as well.

Therefore it comes as something of a surprise on 5 November to find Keppoch marching towards Inverness with about 250 men, ostensibly in order to reinforce the Jacobite garrison under Mackenzie of Coull! A more unlikely scenario is hard to imagine, but Simon Fraser immediately sprang into action, and marched at once at the head of 120 of his clansmen. Evidently taken by surprise, Hugh Rose of Kilravock and Duncan Forbes of Culloden scrambled to follow him with another 300-odd men and thirty horse. Thereupon, on 7 November Keppoch, who was probably playing his part in a non-too subtle pantomime, turned about and headed south by way of Glen Urquhart. With consummate timing he eventually turned up at Perth after the Battle of Sheriffmuir had been fought.

Having seen off this chimerical threat, all three loyalist leaders then turned again on Inverness. Lovat crossed the river with his 120 Frasers and set up camp on the west side, while Culloden and Kilravock established themselves to the east and awaited the arrival of Colonel William Grant with his regular Independent

Company from Strathspey. If there appeared to be a suggestion of rivalry in such busy activity, Culloden and Kilravock were less concerned with taking the town before Sutherland arrived than they were in forestalling Lovat. As the Jacobite commander, Sir John Mackenzie of Coull, was Kilravock's son-in-law, a suitably genteel correspondence ensued, but at first Coull proved obdurate. And so a raid was determined on to demonstrate that the loyalists were in earnest:

> Arthur Ross [*sic*], Brother to the Laird of Kilravock; a young Gentleman that had been Captive in Turkey for many Years before, and but just come home, was order'd to cover Mr Forbes's passing the River with a Party: He finding the Rebels Guard relieving their Centinels by the Riverside, pursued them so close to the heart of the Town, that entering the Tolbooth Door, where the Governor had lodged himself with his Main Guard, he was by the Centinel within shot through the Body, and thereafter he discharged two Pistols he had under his Sash, among the Guard, and had they not crushed his Sword-Hand in forcing the Door close, he might have lived some time longer than he did, which was but about ten Hours.[9]

Nevertheless Arthur Rose's death proved to be a catalyst. His brother, Kilravock, reputedly threatened to burn Inverness from end to end. The magistrates were duly terrified and clamoured for a prompt surrender. Equally sickened by the death of his young relative, Mackenzie of Coull had no stomach for a fight either, and so on the night of 12 November the Jacobite garrison was allowed to slip out quietly.

Next morning the loyalists marched in unopposed, and no doubt to Lovat's disappointment Colonel Robert Monroe of Foulis installed himself as governor by virtue of waving a proper military commission. Rather less tactfully, and with their tongues firmly in their cheeks, they:

> now found it convenient to let the Earl of Sutherland know that they had the town: and his lordship receiving my Lord Lovat's Letter, returned him a very kind Letter, wherein he was glad his Lordship, by his Conduct and Diligence, was sufficiently intitled to the King's Favour and that none would more truly represent it than he.[10]

That fact of the matter of course was that Sutherland was far from glad that his thunder had been stolen. He had, in his view, done all of the work in mobilising support for the king, delaying Seaforth's departure for as long as he could and making it possible for his ungrateful subordinates to recapture Inverness in the first place. Not even an empty promotion to lieutenant-general and a royal letter of thanks could assuage the sense of injustice. All he could do was play down their efforts and petulantly criticise those concerned for allowing the Jacobite garrison to escape. Even there he probably missed his mark.

As we have seen, although there was a certain amount of breaking and entering, and outright robbery going on from time to time, both rebels and loyalists did their level best to avoid actually fighting each other. It is true that young Rose got himself killed, but that was through his own rashness and ultimately seen as a family matter. Real unpleasantness was scrupulously avoided and with it any requirement for gaols and the awful penalty of the law.

To anticipate matters a little, the wisdom of this sensible attitude was seen a few weeks later. Seaforth reached Perth just in time to be precipitated into the débâcle of Sheriffmuir. It was all too evidently a chastening experience for him and just a few weeks later, at the beginning of December, he returned home again, giving as his excuse the need to protect his lands from Sutherland. No sooner had he done so and made threatening noises about retaking Inverness than Sutherland marched up with 1,800 loyalists at his back and received his prompt submission.

Huntly had also followed Seaforth's lead in this, deserting the rebel army in order to protect his estates from the Grants – and equally promptly submitting. The point was that not only was no personal retribution visited on those who confessed the error of their ways at an early date, but as now loyal subjects their lands and goods would be protected. It was of course a very strong incentive indeed for others to follow their lead, and the timing as it turned out was to be extremely fortuitous.

Fife Again

In the meantime Mar's principal concern as to the north was the fact that the Highland clans, on which so much of the original planning had depended, were proving extremely problematic. Hopes of effecting a political revolution by scattering troops far and wide to bring about a general uprising had largely failed, and at long last Mar was starting to appreciate the necessity of concentrating his forces. The problem was achieving that concentration speedily, for neither Gordon nor Seaforth appeared to possess a sense of urgency. As much for the sake of retaining his increasingly precarious initiative as for the sake of the money, Mar therefore issued orders for uplifting the 'cess' or assessment on the counties of Perth, Fife and Clackmannan on 21 October.

Fife traditionally was regarded as Whig country, and, since the local authorities were unlikely to produce the money without compulsion, an expedition was necessary. While two battalions of Athollmen under Lord George Murray and Colonel John Stewart of Invernytie proceeded into the interior, a third battalion of 300 Highland foot and eighty horse was assigned to serve as a covering force while the money was being collected. Unfortunately the relative success of Borlum's operation and the various diversions laid on to cover it had inspired an inflated spirit of overconfidence and the whole business was botched from the start.

No harm befell the two battalions of Athollmen, but the so-called covering force came to grief almost immediately. The senior officer present was John Gordon of Glenbuchat, one of the Marquis of Huntly's two battalion commanders, who 'tho' a Colonnell was to be under Major Grahame's command'. This seemingly was on the strength of Grahame being an old soldier who had served under Claverhouse a quarter-century before. As such he was arguably getting more than a little past it. Yet in the circumstances the decision was reasonable enough. Glenbuchat in his lifetime had a formidable reputation as a fierce soldier, and according to an improbable legend gave George II nightmares, from which he awoke crying 'De great Glenboggit is coming!' In fact, having been born in about 1673 he was only sixteen or seventeen at the time of Claverhouse's rising, and his actual military experience prior to 1715 was negligible. As it was, neither officer was to distinguish himself, and Sinclair's unhelpful verdict that Grahame's appointment was made 'in the same manner as most of our commissions were given of late for want of officers' was equally applicable to both.

In fairness, their orders did not help for they were instructed not to take the direct route from Perth to Dunfermline, but instead to swing around by Castle Campbell, just a few miles east of Stirling. This was presumably in order to advertise their presence to Argyle and so discourage any attempt to interfere with the collections. James Keith in fact specifically referred to their needing 'to cover some convoys which were coming up from that country to the army'. Rather predictably it had quite the opposite effect.[11]

On arriving in Dunfermline, Glenbuchat's men were very sensibly quartered in the sprawling abbey buildings, which were at once large enough to accommodate them and also served as a good defensive position. The horse, meanwhile, 'who were almost all gentlemen, for conveniency, quarter'd themselves separately in the toun'. Some, perhaps most, went to bed, but others as so often before sat down 'to take a heartie bottle'. Equally predictably, even while Grahame was fobbing off suggestions that the single sentry posted to cover the Stirling road should be reinforced, Lieutenant-Colonel Charles Cathcart of the Scots Greys was deploying his men just outside the burgh. As soon as it grew quiet he sent in scouts or spies to discover where the rebels were quartered, and then at 5 a.m. on the morning of Monday 24 October, the Greys struck.

Cathcart had split his force in two. One squadron galloped straight down the main road, killing first the 'poor solitarie horse sentrie' on the Tower Burn bridge and another man whom Glenbuchat had posted outside the abbey, before getting into the burgh by the West Port. The movements of the second squadron are unknown, but in accordance with best practice on such occasions they had presumably used the time to swing right around and enter by the East Port.

While the details are lacking in contemporary accounts of the affair it is not difficult to work out what happened next since it was very much a textbook operation. Having crashed into the burgh as noisily as possible, the first squadron contented themselves with securing the West Port and covering Glenbuchat's men barricaded in the abbey. They for their part very sensibly sat tight. Not so those scattered in the inns and alehouses. As always seems to happen in raids of this kind, those who thought themselves alert or at least more or less awake stumbled out into the street and were promptly scooped up by the dragoons scouring along it from the East Port. Within a bare matter of minutes it was all over. The snatch squadron would have passed through the security squadron and out by the West Port. The whole lot then returned safely to Stirling with eighteen prisoners, the two unlucky Jacobite sentries being the only men reported killed on either side. As for the rest, as Sinclair recalled in one of his more sardonic passages:

> No wonder if, after this ruffle, everie one run a different way; some left their horses sticking in dunghills, in the streets, and others, when their horses fell in anie narrow lane with jostling or making too great hast to get away, left them on the spot, and came to Pearth on countrie horses, and said they had their horses shot under them; others ran to Burntisland, some to different places of the countrie, some got under beds, others up to garrets, and most of this when the ennemie was gone, who, knowing of the Highlandmen's being in the abbey, did not stay to dalley in the town, and beat their retreat very quicklie after their comeing in, for they seised nobodie in homes.[12]

In terms of casualties the Dunfermline raid was pretty inconsequential, but there is no doubt the rebels were a very good deal more frightened than hurt. All in all it was a sorry affair, but, worse still, an unnecessary one. Far from protecting the expedition it was the covering force that was hit. It is hard to avoid the suspicion that, had it not been dangled so temptingly, Argyle would not have risked sending one of his cavalry regiments deep into Fife in search of the main body. Indeed, despite Grahame's defeat, Murray and Invernytie blithely continued with their tax gathering, and so failed to rejoin the army in time for what promised to be the long-awaited climactic battle.

Chapter 11
Approach March

IF THE DUKE OF Argyle had good reason to be pleased at the successful outcome of Colonel Cathcart's raid on Dunfermline, even better news was soon to follow. Not only was there welcome confirmation from London that the Dutch government had at last authorised the embarkation of the promised 6,000 troops on 18 October, but there was also an infantry brigade from Ireland. Commanded by Colonel Jasper Clayton, it had already arrived in the Clyde, along with the first of two squadrons of Evans's Dragoons.

The Irish reinforcement may still not quite have been what Argyle was hoping for. Apart from the cavalry, it comprised only two battalions: Morrison's; and Clayton's regiments of foot. As we have seen, regiments carried on the Irish establishment in peacetime were invariably maintained at a significantly lower strength than comparable units on the British establishment. Ordinarily this meant that, whenever an Irish battalion was ordered on service, it had to be hastily brought up to strength by drafts taken from other units. In this case, however, such was the urgency of the emergency that few if any additional men were rounded up for Clayton's battalions before embarking. They could therefore only muster about 240 men apiece. Providentially a third battalion, Montagu's, was available to complete the brigade, but as Hill's Regiment it had mustered only 162 effectives at Fort William back in June. Even allowing for locally raised recruits being funnelled into Montagu's to bring it up to a respectable strength, Clayton's brigade comprised the weakest battalions on the field at Sheriffmuir.[1] Nevertheless beggars cannot be choosers. Weak as it was, the brigade – together with Evans's veteran cavalrymen – represented a comparatively significant accession of strength. It was sufficient for Argyle to embark upon a much more aggressive strategy than before.

The Plan

The Earl of Mar, for his part, was also heartened and perhaps a little embarrassed by a sudden and rapid accession of reinforcements. First, Lieutenant-General Alexander Gordon of Auchintoul finally arrived from the west Highlands. He turned up at Auchterarder on or about 5 November with around 2,500 reasonably well-armed if unruly clansmen. Then, within just a day or two the Earl of Seaforth followed him with as many as another 2,000 men from the north, including the Frasers, and 700 MacDonalds raised by Sir Donald MacDonald of Sleat, as well as his own people.[2] Even more men, seemingly, had been expected under Lord Duffus, who in fact turned up with no one. Whether Mar or anyone else was disappointed by Duffus is not known, but the arrival of nearly 5,000 men within a matter of days did mean that the earl had neither reason nor excuse to linger any longer at Perth.

Therein lay the problem, for Mar had done all that could humanly have been asked of him – and more – in raising and assembling a fine army for his master, but it had never been contemplated by the earl or by anyone else that he should actually lead it into battle. The Duke of Berwick was still the preferred choice of commander if he could only have been released from the French service, and then there was the Chevalier, the would-be King James himself, expected almost daily. Left to his own devices there is no doubt that Mar would have preferred to sit tight at Perth until he could hand over the army to his king. The arrival of Gordon and Seaforth had been long and anxiously anticipated, but now they were actually with the army further inaction was out of the question since it would be impossible to keep it concentrated over the winter. Logistics aside, inactivity would soon wither its strength. Mar could no longer afford to wait for King James. Now he had such a substantial army at his disposal he had to use it, but how to break through the barrier of the Forth?

Sinclair mordantly summed up the difficulties facing the Jacobites thus:

> To pass at Stirveling was impossible; the Foords of Forth was the common storie, but I never heard of anie man of our armie who knew anything of those foords except Rob Roy, who, they themselves said, they could not trust . . . Nor was it to be expected that the Duke of Argyle, who had surveyed those foords and passages narroulie, and spoilt the foords by digging and putting great beams in them with iron pikes, would let us pass them

undisturb'd without disputing the matter, having it always in his pouer to be there before us after we had gone higher than Stirveling, where he had nothing to fear if he left tuo hundred men to defend the bridge: Besides it was said he had made lines on all the foords, which is not to be doubted he did if he found them practicable for we gave him time enough to take all his precautions.; or, if the ground was such that there was no passing but by force of fire, and attacking, and being repulsed and attacking again, we were not to expect that of our Highlandmen, whose business, all know, is not to stand fire, and if the first were repulsed, the others, without further enquirie, would goe to the divill, eventho' they had not been in want of armes. Most seem'd to agree that these foords were onlie passable when the river was low, which we could not expect to find in that season of the year. Another obvious difficultie arose, the enimie having cut the bridge of Doun, not far from Stirveling, our onlie way to the Foords of Forth; nor could we pretend to pass that river which is called the Teith, and rather worse to pass than the Forth, as all who knew it said.[3]

The truth of this appeared self-evident to the Jacobite leaders, although no one seems to have thought to verify the reports of Argyle fortifying the fords. As a result the Jacobites remained obsessed with devising cunning plans to outwit him – all of them involving elaborate deceptions.

At a council of war held on 9 November it was agreed that, since there was no question of forcing Stirling bridge, they should indeed swing around to the west of Stirling. This first meant crossing the river Teith, which ran from north to south directly in their path and was no mean obstacle in itself. Indeed Sinclair reckoned with some justice that it was probably a bigger obstacle than the upper Forth at this point. Once over the Teith they would then need to carry on further west for some distance before turning south to the Heads of Forth, well above Stirling. Therein of course lay a problem, for while Perth made an admirable base for the army from an administrative viewpoint, it lay at such a distance from their intended objective that it was inevitable Argyle would have ample warning. For the troops quartered in Perth this would require a march of some thirty-five to forty miles. Providing all went well, it would need about three days simply in order to reach their jumping-off point. Moreover, for this move they had minimal logistic support, and no tents to shelter them at night, despite the fact they would be lying out of doors in mid-November!

In order to mislead the duke as to their real intentions and so have a chance of getting to the crossings before him, it was proposed to make a number of ostentatious demonstrations. The first was to be mounted against the outpost at Causewayhead, thus appearing to threaten Stirling bridge itself. The second demonstration was to be directed at the ferry crossing by Cambuskenneth Abbey, a little further downstream. The third one was then to take place upstream at Drip, near the confluence of the Teith and the Forth, closely covering the actual passage of the army to the Fords of Forth.

Whether this complicated scheme might have worked had it actually been put into execution is obviously open to question. Predictably enough, however, Argyle was appraised of its general outlines almost at once and so made his own plans accordingly.

The Blind leading the Blind

Blissfully unaware they were betrayed, the rebels finally left Perth on the morning of 10 November: 'A la bonne aventure, the blind leading the blind, not knowing whither we were going or what we were to do', as Sinclair so cynically put it. Leaving behind three battalions under the elderly Colonel John Balfour to serve as a garrison for the city,[4] the Lowland infantry marched thirteen miles to a rendezvous with Gordon's contingent at Auchterarder that evening, while the horse were quartered nearby at Dunning.

In an inauspicious start to the operation, a whole battalion incontinently deserted later that night. Seaforth's newly arrived contingent had included some 400 Frasers under Mackenzie of Fraserdale. As we saw in the previous chapter, by ill-luck their true clan chief, Simon Fraser, the soi-disant Lord Lovat, had returned from exile and now recalled them in a calculated demonstration of loyalty to the government. Sinclair also claimed that most of Gordon of Glenbuchat's battalion deserted as well, wearied with constantly being called upon for any service that was required. Huntly certainly still had two battalions in the battle, including Glenbuchat's, but significantly the 1,200 men counted on 13 October had become just 400 men on the day of the battle.[5]

Brushing aside that little local difficulty, next morning, 11 November, Mar reviewed his whole army at Auchterarder. This was no vainglorious indulgence, but rather the first opportunity there had been to sort the newly combined force out into a proper order of battle and appoint brigade commanders. The necessity for doing this was seemingly underscored by a series of squabbles as to precedence among the horse in particular, and 'the posts of our squadrons, which were never so constant in any thing as our being disorderlie'.[6] Mar evidently had a very shrewd suspicion that Sinclair was at the bottom of this. The charge was of course denied by the master, albeit with a quite unconvincing display of injured innocence. Unfortunately it is hard to avoid a suspicion that, although seemingly resolved, the squabbling contributed in no small measure to the confusion among the cavalry in the coming battle. What was more by the time everything had been sorted out there was clearly no point in commencing the march late in the afternoon. Instead they all settled down again to spend a second night at Auchterarder, giving Argyle yet more precious time to call in his outposts and detachments.

Next day, the Jacobites ought to have been marching as hard and fast as possible to secure the crossing points. Instead they continued to dawdle along in the same lackadaisical fashion. Only Gordon and his Highlanders, together with three squadrons of horse under Sinclair, were actually to make for Dunblane. From there they were presumably intended to split up and mount those elaborate demonstrations called for in the deception plan. Rob Roy and his people in the meantime went directly towards the Fords of Forth, either to secure them or at least to mark the way. The rest of the army was follow `them westwards along the other side of Allan Water, but only as far as Ardoch, where it was intended to halt for the night. Of itself, if they were still making for the Teith and then the Heads of Forth, this route was sensible enough and avoided crossing Allan Water twice to no purpose. However, not only did it mean a greater degree of dispersal than might be thought prudent when moving into contact, but Mar himself, as he admitted in his official report, chose to absent himself for much of the day:

> The Earl of Mar order'd Lieutenant-General Gordon, and Brigadier Ogilvie, with three squadrons of the Marquis of Huntley, and the Master of Sinclair's five squadrons of horse and all the Clans, to March and take Possession of Dumblain, which was order'd to be done two Days before, but was delayed by some Interruptions; and all the rest of the Army was order'd at the same time, to parade upon the Moor of Tullibardine very early and to march after General Gordon. The Earl of Mar went to Drummond Castle to meet with my Lord Broadalbin, and order'd General Hamilton to march the Army.[7]

Not only does the report disingenuously imply that Hamilton was supposed to follow after Gordon towards Dunblane, rather than continue westwards to Ardoch, but no explanation is offered as to why Mar chose to ride seven miles in the opposite direction. There had been ample opportunity for a conference during the long weeks of inactivity at Perth. In any case, as two battalions of Breadalbane's people were already marching with the rebel army, it is hard to see what else might be gained at this juncture. Perhaps, now that the long-heralded advance had finally got underway, Mar was keen to have Breadalbane seen to be riding by his side. However politic that might have been it was still an extraordinary dereliction at a crucial moment in the campaign. The only explanation can be that Mar thought himself to be perfectly secure in scattering his forces, in the naive assumption that Argyle would sit supinely behind the Forth while the rebels manoeuvred around him.

Alas Argyle was in fact already in the process of making a sad havoc of Mar's cunning plans. The crucial factors not taken into account by the rebels were not only the timing but also the deteriorating weather. Below Stirling bridge the Forth was completely impassable without boats at any time of the year. Above the bridge the chief strength of the river as a barrier lay not in the watercourse itself, but in the great Flanders Moss, a vast expanse of bog which surrounded and drained into it. Ordinarily movement over the moss was restricted to just a few ill-defined tracks, unsuitable for wheeled vehicles or cannon. However, it was now mid-November and the temperature, especially at night-time, was falling fast. As Argyle recognised only too well, frost and ultimately ice would soon form a hard crust, rendering both moss and river passable almost everywhere above Stirling. As his official account explained:

> . . . [the duke] found he was obliged either to engage them on the Grounds near Dumblain or to decamp and wait their coming to the Head of Forth. He chose the first on many Accounts, and among others, that the Grounds near Dumblain were much more advantageous for his Horse, than those at the Head of the River; and besides this by the Frost then beginning, the Forth might become passable in several Places, which the small number of his Troops did not enable him to guard sufficiently.[8]

Returning from Edinburgh, where he had been overseeing the erection of barricades and other defensive works, General Wightman found the preparations for a move well underway on 11 November. Clayton's brigade had been called forward from Glasgow, arriving just that morning, and other detachments were also recalled from their quarters in Kilsyth and Falkirk. Argyle was already anticipating the Jacobite move and only awaiting confirmation of Mar's intentions before putting his plans into execution.

The addition of Clayton's infantry brigade and Evans's Dragoons had changed the situation completely, because while the duke was still badly outnumbered he now had sufficient men to risk moving out from behind his lines to fight the rebels in the open. There, discipline, training and firepower ought to give him the advantage, or at least compensate for the disparity in numbers. He had determined, as he confided to Townshend, to meet the rebels 'on the rising grounds on the other side Dumblain, where we are sure of both provisions and forage. When we are there where the ground is good, if the enemy should advance we can have no better ground to receive them in.'[9]

This sounds very much as if he intended from the outset to take up a position on the Sheriffmuir. Once there, depending on the rebels' intentions he could either squarely block any direct advance on Dunblane and Stirling, or interdict a westward march towards the Heads of Forth. Accordingly, on the morning of 12 November, the defence of Stirling was confided to just two loyalist units: a fencible battalion raised in the Stirling area itself by the Earl of Buchan; and the Glasgow Regiment of Volunteers under the redoubtable Lieutenant-Colonel John Blackadder. In total there may have been about 1,000 of them. Otherwise with every man he could muster, Argyle led his army across Stirling bridge and up along the narrow causeway where Hugh de Cressingham and his army had been slaughtered by Moray and Wallace four centuries before. Then he turned northwards to Dunblane, where he intended to quarter that night before taking up his battle position.

Contact

Oblivious to this unforeseen development, the Jacobites were still straggling southwestwards with the same object, or at least the advance guard was. Sinclair and his cavalry were evidently marching a little way ahead of the clans. Otherwise only the regimental quartermasters had been sent on ahead to organise the reception and billeting of the troops when they reached Dunblane. It is perhaps worth emphasising at this point that, in the eighteenth-century, quartermasters were not responsible for stores and supplies as such, but rather their primary function was to arrange the quartering or accommodation of the troops. As this entailed scouting well ahead of the army it was not a job for the faint-hearted. Unexpectedly, at about 3 p.m., they came hurrying back to Sinclair with unwelcome news: Argyle was marching through Dunblane with his whole army!

Admittedly the quartermasters had not actually seen the redcoats for themselves, but had picked up a 'lame boy' sent to warn them by Lady Kippendavie. Since her husband, Charles Stirling of Kippendavie, was riding with the rebel cavalry, Sinclair had no reason to doubt the boy. He immediately passed him back to General Gordon, who in turn promptly hurried to the front. Sinclair and Gordon were obviously in something of a quandary at this point, hesitating to halt an army in full march on the strength of a single as yet unsubstantiated report.

Yet at the same time they were very properly mindful of the danger of blindly continuing the advance and perhaps bringing on an engagement prematurely. In the end Gordon sensibly decided that some prudence was called for. Sinclair was ordered to deploy his squadrons, and the clans likewise were instructed to halt and form a battle line. Sinclair then ordered out half a dozen more scouts to try and verify the information, while Gordon sent back an express to find Mar and acquaint him of what was happening.

So far so good, but Mar of course was nowhere to be found, having taken himself off on that jaunt to dine with Breadalbane at Drummond Castle. In the meantime the quartermaster-general, Peter Smith, turned up, and at this point the situation turned into a black comedy. In Mar's absence Smith insisted on their continuing the march in accordance with their orders, saying that it would be 'a shame to halt'. Sinclair had an unfortunate knack of treating anyone who disagreed with him as an idiot, and thereupon turned sarcastic:

> I always lookt upon him as ane out of the way, ignorant, noisie fellow, but was stunned at his impudence, having been nothing but a surgeon, to pretend to speak to a Generall after that manner; and askt him, Why he did not put those orders in execution, and what hindered him from takeing up the quarters at Dumblain?

Nevertheless Smith insisted, and so Gordon reluctantly ordered the advance to continue. His uneasiness was soon increased as he was met by numbers of country people coming up with the same news of Argyle's being at Dunblane. By now dusk was falling and so after just a mile Gordon decided enough was enough and called a halt again rather than run the risk of blundering into Argyle's men in the dark. This time he formed a battle line on some rising ground, which must have been Kinbuck Moor, and waited there until Sinclair's scouts returned.

As it happened they were not long in coming back. Once again neither they, nor Peter Smith who had accompanied them, had actually seen the enemy. Nevertheless they had heard or thought they had heard sufficient of them to be wary of venturing too close, and getting snaffled. Thoroughly convinced by now that Argyle must indeed be within two miles of them, Gordon decided to find a strong ground and have the men lie on their arms until morning, or until Mar came. Sinclair, properly concerned about finding forage for his horses then had the bright idea of taking possession of some large barnyards which he could see on the other side of Allan Water. Gordon quite rightly refused because 'it would ruine the foot, who were to lie out on a whole frostie night, to make them pass a river'.

Turning down a further suggestion that the horse might lift them across at the fords, Gordon went off to see if there was any other accommodation nearby. Eventually he led them all down to what Sinclair called a 'little hollow, hard by, on the riverside, where there were tuo little farme-houses and corn yards'. This was evidently what is now the small village of Kinbuck. While the horses were all very tightly packed together into the two stone-walled yards, Sinclair and the 'gentlemen' of the cavalry crammed themselves into one house and Gordon, Huntly and the 'heads of the clans' into the other. The ordinary troopers and clansmen were left to bed down as best they could on the already frosty ground, save for a few 'horse guards' scattered as picquets on the higher ground around them.

It was an awful position. The present village of Kinbuck has obviously grown a little since 1715, but it still remains wedged in a narrow piece of ground in a bend of the river with a steep hillock at the back. As Sinclair sourly described it:

> All the ground about had a sudden rise from the houses and yards, for tuo hundred paces, except toward the north, where we were hard upon the river, which was behind us; for it can't be properlie said we had front or rear, more than it can be said of a barrel of herrings . . . I believe eight thousand men, for we were about that number, were never pakt up so close together since the invention of pouder; and I can take it upon me to defie the most ingenious ingeneer, after a month's thinking to contrive a place so fit for the destruction of men, without being in the least capable to help themselves.

No sooner had they begun to settle down than the Earl of Southesk turned up with the Angus Squadron and news that Mar himself was on his way with the rest of the army. Then, at about 9 p.m. the great man himself actually turned up. Obviously irritated at having been dragged away from an agreeable dining table at Drummond Castle, he walked in on an argument between Sinclair and Southesk as to the relieving of the picquets and demanded to know 'what intelligence we had got'.

Although Sinclair and Gordon were in no doubt at all that Argyle was out there, they had to admit that neither they nor any of their scouts had actually seen, far less counted, the redcoats. Mar was therefore not too unjustified in treating what Sinclair told him 'with ane air of neglect, as if he had a mind to accuse us of fear; and said, he'd lay anie money it was not true'. Gordon himself and Huntly were then sent for and on their likewise asserting they believed Argyle was at Dunblane, Mar flatly said he knew otherwise. To this fatuous bravado, as Sinclair commented, 'there was no answer to be made'. Leaving the house to

Mar, Sinclair decided to take a last look around, but, after falling flat on his face in the icy mud, he thought better of it and moved in next door for the night.

There is a tendency to think of eighteenth-century campaigns as being genteel affairs conducted by well-bred officers whose first priority was ensuring their own creature comforts. It is sobering therefore to find Sinclair eventually lying down in the straw on the floor squeezed between Sir John Maclean and the Captain of Clanranald. At least they had the straw, and a roof over their heads; for most of their men there was just the cold hard ground below and the stars above. What was more, many of them were lying down with wet feet, for, although Gordon had declined to cross to the far side of the river, Mar and Hamilton evidently had no such scruples when bringing the Lowland division down from Ardoch. They had made their men cross the river and bivouac on the more exposed Kinbuck Moor.

Morning

At about 6 a.m., long before dawn on 13 November, the clans and Sinclair's cavalry moved stiffly out of the hollow and rejoined Hamilton's division on Kinbuck Moor. They all then formed up in order of battle, probably somewhere near the steadings at Upper and Lower Whitestone, with the dark mass of the Sheriffmuir proper rising up above them. According to Mar's official account they were then standing on the left-hand side of the road, by which he presumably meant what is now the B8033, and were facing towards Dunblane, that is more or less towards the southwest. No one mentioned having eaten any breakfast, and at first there was a notable lack of enthusiasm for doing anything remotely exciting.

Nor were their opponents in much better condition. According to General Wightman, the previous night the loyalists had discovered that the rebels were camped three miles to the north of them. However, beyond establishing that useful fact, they made no attempt to interfere with them. Instead, notwithstanding the plunging temperature, Argyle resisted the temptation to occupy Dunblane itself and moved his men out onto his chosen battlefield, on the high ground to the east, with his left towards the town and his right towards the Sheriffmuir. At this stage he was positioning his men in order to block a direct advance on Dunblane and Stirling bridge. It did not occur to him that the Jacobites might be so enterprising as to attempt to outflank him and so he neither moved up onto the moor proper, nor even posted any scouts up there.

After thus drawing up his men, Argyle issued orders that no tent should be pitched during the night by officer or private soldier; that all the officers without distinction should remain at their posts; and that the troops should rest upon their arms in the exact order in which they had been formed. Though the night was extremely cold, the troops lay down upon the bare ground, and snatched a few hours' repose. Argyle himself retired to a sheep pen at the foot of a hill on the right of the army, where he passed the night sitting on a bundle of straw.[10]

It is unlikely though that he or anybody else had much real 'repose' in the bitter cold, which very soon turned into a hard frost. Eventually, like their opponents, the loyalists all very properly stood-to shortly before first light. At this point Argyle's scouts came in and reported that the rebels were also forming, and so they all waited while the duke rode forward with Major-General Wightman and a cavalry escort to discover just exactly what the rebels were doing and where.

Chapter 12
Come Ye Here the Fight Tae Shun?
Sheriffmuir Part 1

The SUN FINALLY CAME up over what was to be the battlefield at about 8 a.m. on 13 November and revealed to the shivering Jacobites 'a command of horse on the high ground to the south of us'. This was of course Argyle reconnoitring, and so the rebels hurriedly sent out some scouts of their own, 'who came back and told us the enemie were all about the enclosures of Kippendavie'.

Up until that point Mar may still have been deluding himself that the reports about Argyle being in the vicinity were false or exaggerated. Sinclair is positive that when they assembled that morning 'even then we pretended to pass the river of Teith in order to try the heads of Forth or the Foords'. Perhaps it was thought that, with Argyle in Dunblane rather than Stirling, there was an opportunity to dodge past him and get over the river. However, as Sinclair disgustedly observed, that would still have entailed a further march of three or four miles with every prospect of finding the crossing places impassable. Nevertheless Mar still remained reluctant to commit himself to a battle he did not want to fight and had not anticipated fighting so soon. Consequently, as Sinclair continued:

> . . . it was past eleven of the clock before it seems our Generall took his resolution, and I, as well as everie bodie at this moment, admire what he could be thinking of all that time, for it was not his part to make the disposition, which was done soon; but there he was out of his element. Had he been scribbling in his chamber at Pearth, his resolution had been soon taken, and orders sent to the commanding officer to attack, right or wronge, without further consideration.[1]

Instead, an *ad hoc* council of war was convened 'in front of the horse on the left', because, if Mar was no general, he at least had the good sense to be aware

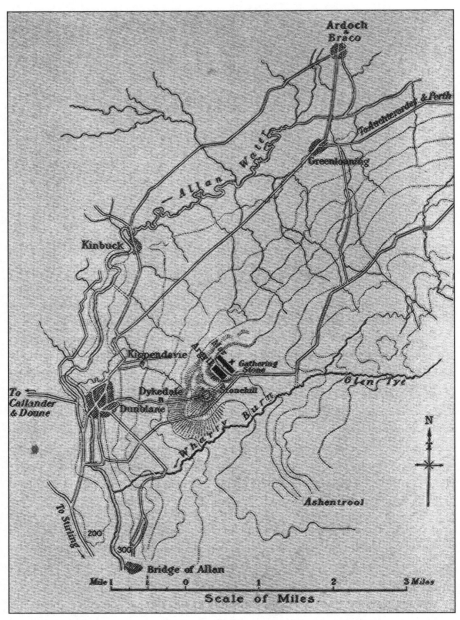

MAP 4: *Sheriffmuir and the immediate vicinity. Although topographically accurate, this plan places the two armies on the wrong alignment and occupying far too narrow a frontage. It is useful nevertheless in providing a proper context for their movements on to the battlefield.*

of his limitations as a commander. After making a very spirited speech, which impressed even Sinclair,[2] he then deferred to his assembled officers as to whether they should retire to Perth to await the imminent arrival of the Chevalier, or whether they should attack at once. All accounts later agreed that the latter course was agreed unanimously and almost without comment, and so it was determined to fight.[3]

So far so good, but those redcoated cavalry were still sitting at top of the Sheriffmuir watching them. Accordingly the Marischal with his own squadron and Sir Donald MacDonald's Regiment[4] were sent up to deal with them. Unsurprisingly, by the time they reached the top somewhere near the Gathering Stone,[5] they found Argyle gone but then as James Keith related, discovered to their dismay:

> their whole body, marching without beat of drum, about two musket shot from us. It was now too late to retrait; we therefore form'd on top of the hill, and the Earl Marischal sent an aid de camp to advertise the Earl of Mar that he was fall'n in with the enemies army, that it was impossible for him to bring off the foot, and therefore desired he wou'd march up to his assistance as quick as possible . . .[6]

Argyle Deploys for Battle

As it happens, Argyle was having troubles of his own. Alerted first by the sound of bagpipes and then finding the rebels standing on Kinbuck Moor rather further to the east than they had been reported the previous night, Argyle not unreasonably concluded they were intending to outflank him. Originally he had thought his right was secured by the boggy ground of the moor. Unfortunately the overnight frost had hardened it, and so to frustrate any attempt at a turning movement he sent Wightman to bring up the army, intending to 'stretch' to the right along the trackway now known as Sheriffmuir Road.

As originally drawn up the night before, Argyle's army was perfectly symmetrical. The infantry, commanded by Wightman, were formed in two lines, of which the first was organised in two wings or brigades, each comprising three battalions:[7]

Left wing (Brigadier Jasper Clayton)[8]

Clayton's foot	240
Montagu's foot	240(?)
Morrison's foot	240

Right wing (Brigadier Archibald Douglas, Earl of Forfar)

Shannon's Foot	340
Wightman's Foot	250
Forfar's Foot (the Buffs)	320

Behind them was a third, smaller brigade of just two battalions under Brigadier Alexander Grant:[9]

Orrery's Royal Scots Fusiliers	320
Egerton's Foot	250

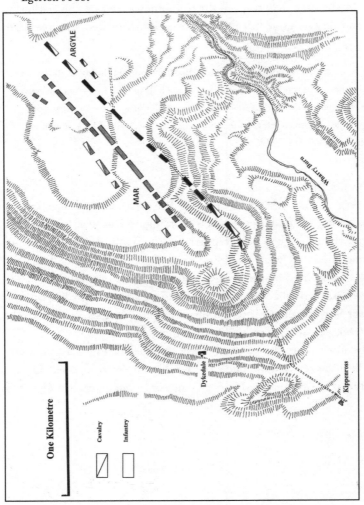

MAP 5: *Tactical map for the battle of Sheriffmuir; although the precise position of certain units is speculative (see text) the frontages occupied by both armies is to scale although the depth of units is slightly exaggerated for the sake of clarity. Jacobite infantry units are assumed to be four deep and regular ones three deep with one metre allowed for each man in the front rank. Cavalry units, identified by gyrony rather than solid colour, occupy a frontage of two metres per horse and rider.*

To the right of the foot, under Lieutenant-General William Evans, stood Evans's own regiment of dragoons (180) and Portmore's Scots Greys (180), commanded by lieutenant-colonels Henry Hawley and Charles Cathcart respectively. Both regiments comprised two squadrons together with a squadron belonging to Stair's Dragoons posted behind the right of the foot, and a little troop of about sixty loyalist volunteers under the Earl of Rothes standing behind Evans's Dragoons.[10]

Similarly, on the left under Lieutenant-General Thomas Whetham, were Kerr's and Carpenter's Dragoons, again each nominally mustering 180 men and drawn up in similar fashion, with three squadrons in front and two behind, including the second squadron of Stair's Dragoons. In total, therefore, Argyle may have had something in the region of 2,200 foot and 960 dragoons, albeit the figures presented are rounded ones. Very neat they might have looked too, had they been deployed as the duke intended, but it all went very badly wrong very quickly.

Having ordered his men to lie on their arms all night, which essentially means that once drawn up in order of battle they were expected to lie down to sleep exactly as they stood, he not unreasonably anticipated them to be ready to move off at a moment's notice. In this he was badly disappointed. To his anger and dismay it was not until 'About Twelve before they were ready to March' fully two to three hours after he had sent for them – and four hours after sunrise.[11] Unsurprisingly he expressed himself about this inexplicable dereliction, but there was no time to take it further at that point.[12] What should have been an orderly advance to take the high ground in good time instead developed into an undignified scramble, which saw the army effectively stretched along the road into a single line with large gaps between the brigades.

Jacobite Deployments

Meanwhile the rebels were experiencing exactly the same problems. When they first formed up on Kinbuck Moor early that morning their front line, commanded by Lieutenant-General Alexander Gordon of Auchintoul, supposedly comprised some 3,185 men belonging to all the recently arrived western clans, viz from right to left:[13]

Sir Donald MacDonald of Sleat's Regiment	700
McDonnell of Glengarry's Regiment	
(including the Glen Urquhart	
and Glenmoriston Grants)	460

MacDonald of Clanranald's Regiment	565
Sir John Maclean's Regiment	350
MacDonald of Glencoe's Regiment	150
Earl of Breadalbane's Regiment	
(two battalions under Campbell of Glenlyon)	400
Stewart of Appin's Regiment	260
Cameron of Locheil's Regiment	300

Behind it stood a second line, commanded by Lieutenant-General George Hamilton, and to all intents and purposes corresponding to what remained of Mar's original army. Largely raised in the northeast of Scotland, in the hills of Perthshire and the broad farming country of Angus and the Mearns, this second line amounted to some 2,600 men, again numbered here from right to left:

Earl of Seaforth's Regiment[14]	400
Marquis of Huntly's Regiment	
(two battalions led by Ogilvie of Boyne	
and Gordon of Glenbuchat)	400
Lord Panmure's Regiment	415
Earl of Tullibardine's Regiment	
(under the Earl of Strathmore)	300
Marquis of Drummond's Regiment	
(two battalions under Lord Strathallan	
and Logie Drummond)[15]	500
Robertson of Strowan's Regiment	203

The actual command structure is a good deal less clear than it is for Argyle's army. It would be reasonable, however, to suppose that when Hamilton subsequently formed the two lines into four columns, each of those columns corresponded to a brigade. Clanranald, as we will see, went into battle on horseback and may therefore have been acting as one of the two brigadiers in the front line. The other was probably Sir John Maclean. In the second line, Tullibardine was certainly acting as a brigadier and so too was Panmure's uncle, Patrick Maule of Auchterhouse. However, in the confusion that followed it is difficult to establish the extents of their respective commands once battle was actually joined.

As with Argyle's army, some of the figures quoted for each regiment are obviously very rounded and are more likely to be optimistic than accurate. Nevertheless, taking them as a guide, Mar should have had something like just over

5,800 infantry. In addition there was also a body of about 800 cavalry, nominally under the overall command of the Marquis of Drummond as lieutenant-general of the horse. Initially the cavalry were split more or less evenly on either wing. There were also five cannon, but they never came into action – Sinclair making the curious allegation that in any case there was neither powder nor ball for them. That aside, the Jacobites had a respectable little army, in numbers at least, but rather less than the 9,000 men Argyle afterwards boasted of beating.[16]

Given that the long slope from Kinbuck up onto the Sheriffmuir is relatively even and was then clear of trees, marching the army straight up to the top in order of battle ought to have been perfectly feasible. Instead Sinclair described how:

> [General] Hamiltone broke our lines each in tuo colloms, and order'd the four squadrons of horse on the right with tuo thousand Highland men who compos'd the collom of the right of the first line, to marche and take possession of that high ground where the enemies horse appear'd . . . The second colome on the left of the first line marched likewise by the right, and followed the other at a great distance; then the first colome of the second line march'd by the right as did the second colume of the second line.

Taking into account the time lost in redeploying the two lines into four columns it seems more likely that Hamilton may have already formed, or was forming them thus, in anticipation of marching westwards to the river Teith and beyond. This would certainly help explain what happened next. As Mar himself (and indeed everybody else present) candidly admitted: 'They fell in some confusion in the forming, and some of the second line jumbled into the first on or near the left.'

James Keith, watching in bemusement from the top of the hill with the Marischal's squadron, explained in slightly more detail:

> . . . the army, which marched in four columns, arrived in such confusion that it was impossible to form them according to the line of battle projected, every one posted himself as he found ground, and one column of foot enclining to the right and another to the left of the Earl Marischal's squadron of horse, that regiment which should have been on the right, found itself in the centre, separated from the rest of the horse and opposed to the enemies foot; our foot formed all in one line, except on the left, where a bog hunder'd them from extending themselves, and encreased the confusion.

There was in fact good reason for the confusion. Since Argyle was hurriedly extending his army eastwards, it was necessary for the Jacobites to do likewise in order to avoid being outflanked in turn. Hamilton must therefore have ordered the second line to move up and prolong the front line in that direction. The hurry of doing so was then sufficient to throw them into disorder, given their relative lack of training. This was doubly unfortunate. Although an old and experienced officer from the Dutch service, Hamilton not only lacked 'natural genious', according to Keith, but 'having been always used to the regularity of the Dutch, thought all lost when he saw the first sign of confusion among the Highlanders'.[17]

There were two major factors in this. Unlike the Lowlanders, who had been drilled by Hamilton and Clephane, the newly arrived clansmen were totally unpractised in manoeuvring. They were incapable of undertaking rapid changes of formation and direction without falling into confusion. The immediate result was that, amid all the excitement, the actual order of battle became jumbled. Judging by Mar's account, most of the right wing survived intact but its order of battle may have been reversed and Huntly's two battalions from the second line seemed to have come up to form the extreme right flank alongside Breadalbane's men, while the Appin Stewarts and Locheil's Camerons drifted east to join what was now the left wing.

For their part the Lowland troops who made up the greater part of what had originally been the second line, were as reasonably well trained as could be expected in the circumstances. What no one seems to have realised was just what poor physical condition the men were in. Having halted at Ardoch the previous night as originally planned, they had then been roused to close up on the advance guard at Kinbuck. Although the distance was not great, this unexpected move in the darkness would no doubt have been 'extremely fatiguing and accompanied with confusion and disorder'. Worse, the men would have had to ford the icy Allan Water, and then spend the freezing night with no prospect of getting properly dry. Many must not only have been hungry and exhausted, but already suffering from exposure and consequently lacking in both the alertness and fortitude which the situation demanded.

The Battle Begins

At any rate as each regiment came up at its own best speed Hamilton was forced to form it on the left of the preceding one without regard to order, and the confusion appears to have been compounded by the presence of a bog. This, as James Keith, noted hindered their deployment, leaving some regiments stacked up, still struggling to form, when the battle began, as Sinclair explained:

In what manner our three colums run away, none of those among them could tell, nor where the flight begun, everie corps putting it off themselves on each other, as is usuall. Most agreed that few of them had ever formed, and those who did, begun to fire at a great distance; that the three colums fell in with one another in that running up the hill, and when they came in sight of the Duke of Argyle's right wing, which was already formed, they were in disorder; and the last confusion when his dragoons made a mine [a cock-fighting term] to attack them through the morass, which happened to be betwixt them . . .[18]

He was also emphatic that when the 'huzza', or cheer, was raised from the centre to commence the attack, a good few of those on the left promptly bolted straight back down the hill again. Others were at first more resolute, and General Wightman, standing with Forfar's Brigade on Argyle's right, wrote that they 'gave us fire and a great many came up to our Noses, Sword in Hand'.

Some thirty years later Lieutenant-Colonel Henry Hawley of Evans's Dragoons, by then commander-in-chief Scotland, penned a remarkable set of fighting instructions for his troops, which reflected what he saw that day as the overhasty Jacobite advance rapidly turned into a shambles:

They commonly form their front rank of what they call their best men, or true Highlanders, the number of which being always but few, when they form in battalions they commonly form four deep, and these Highlanders form the front of the four, the rest being lowlanders and arrant scum.

When these battalions come down within a large musket shot, or three score yards, this front rank gives their fire, and immediately throw down their firelocks and come down in a cluster with their swords and targets making a noise and endeavouring to pierce the body, or battalions before them, becoming 12 or 14 deep by the time they come up to the people they attack.

Hawley would go on to propose that the best way to 'demolish' such an attack was to fire by ranks. On this occasion at least, Wightman was clear that the charge was stopped in its tracks by 'the constant Fire of the Plattoons of Foot' before they could close with their broadswords.[19] Consequently the losses in Forfar's Brigade were minimal. Shannon's Regiment afterwards reported only Captain Alexander Arnott killed and five or six men killed or wounded, while Wightman's Regiment had only Ensign Mark wounded and two grenadiers and two or three other men killed. For their part Forfar's Buffs similarly returned Ensign Branch and eight men as killed, but more significantly Forfar himself was shot in the knee, resulting in Wightman taking personal command of the brigade to the detriment of his wider duties.[20]

At the same time Argyle had ordered his cavalry forward, intending to take the rebels in flank, but his deployment appears to have foundered in the same morass that hindered the Jacobite deployment. An unknown volunteer in Rothes's troop described what happened:

> After the duke had been upon the side of the hill to reconnoitre the enemy, he ordered the Greys to advance against the enemy, and at the same time to incline to the right as far as they could, which was uphill. Next to them marched Evans's regiment and after them the volunteers. The Greys were upon the right of all, next them Evans's, next them Forfars, Whitmans on their left, and Shanons on the left of them. The volunteers were drawn up in the second line behind Evans's, and one of the squadrons of Stairs to the left of us behind the foot. I can give no account of what passed on the left of Shanons . . . the Rebells had only foot upon their left in the first line, and some horse in the second line, but the horse did not stay till we came up with them, and we saw them only flying. The Clans, with the body of their horse, were upon their right, where my L. Mar commanded . . .
>
> When we came up the hill, we were surprised to find the enemy formed, and so close upon us, so that the dragoons and we had only time enough to draw up, and the three regiments of foot were attacked when they were forming. The action began upon the right, and the enemy kept up their fire longer than could have been expected. The fire was very hot upon Evans's regiment for a quarter of an hour. They had a deep stripe before them which they could well pass, which made them turn about upon us and they were in some disorder, but immediately they inclined to the right, and got in among the enemy, but the Greys, who are never backward upon these occasions, were the first that cut them to pieces; and whenever we got among them, they fled in the utmost disorder . . .
>
> At the time that Evans's came among us, my horse got on end, and his hind feet sunk in the marshy ground we were formed in, which made him fall back on me, and I concluded he had been killed dead, but he immediately got of me. I kept the reins, and got him mounted again with great difficulty for the balls were flying so thick that the horse did not stand long in one posture, and I had the good fortune to escape with some bruises occasioned chiefly by the fall.[21]

Oddly enough, although no one identified the Jacobite units responsible for this withering fire, there is an otherwise unsubstantiated family tradition that Logie Drummond 'unseated' many dragoons. At any rate, not only was Lieutenant-Colonel Hawley shot through the shoulder, but Evans himself was also unhorsed and received a nasty wound on the head. Just as Wightman had stepped in to take command of Forfar's Brigade, so too Argyle threw caution to the wind. Heedless of his duty as commander-in-chief Scotland, he placed himself at the head of the cavalry brigade and helped Hawley rally Evans's regiment.[22] This repulse of Evans's Regiment afforded Hamilton a brief respite and, according to Sinclair, encouraged him to frantically call for cavalry support of his own.

The Collapse of the Jacobite Left

Hamilton called in vain. In the rush to deploy on the ridge the Jacobite cavalry had become even more tangled than the infantry. As originally drawn up earlier that morning, the right wing of horse under the Marquis of Drummond had comprised: the Earl Marischal's squadron, some 180 strong; a single troop of seventy-seven men from Stirlingshire under the Earl of Linlithgow, designated as the Standard Squadron; two squadrons of Huntly's men, totalling about 160; and some forty 'scrub horse' belonging to Seaforth. The left comprised: Southesk's Angus Squadron, mustering 100 troopers; Sinclair's Fife Squadron, with ninety; and Rollo's Perthshire Squadron, with another seventy. This would have made a total of some 330 or 340 horse.[23]

Mar's printed account of the battle placed the Marquis of Huntly on the right of the front line when the army was first drawn up, together with his own two squadrons and Linlithgow's Stirlingshire troop, while the Earl Marischal's squadron flanked the right of the second line. Similarly on the left under Sinclair, his own and Rollo's squadrons flanked the front line and Southesk's squadron the second.

So far so good but first the Marischal's squadron was ordered up onto the ridge. When the rest of the army hastened up the hill, the Marquis of Drummond took Huntly's and Linlithgow's squadrons to join them. Thus, as Sinclair remembered:

> Drummond and Marischall, instead of forming on the right of that colume with their four squadrons, formed on the left, which made the centre of the foot, it seems not knowing their left hand from their right, thought themselves well there. We observing them form so quicklie, and all the other three colums who were marching most irregularlie at some distance, the three squadrons continuing according to order, to follow the last colum of foot, who kept us at a gallop, inclining towards the ground our left designed to take up. When we had advanc'd prittie well that way with the haste we made, ane Aide-de-Camp of Kilseyths came to Rollo, who, being nixt the foot, was on the front of the three squadrons of horse, and order'd the three squadrons to the right of the whole army with all possible expedition, as did with the same breath some one from Mar, and one Lewis Innes from my Lord Huntlie, by Mar's order.[24]

The fault was actually Drummond's for joining the rest of his command to the Marischal's squadron up at the Gathering Stone, rather than drawing them off to the right wing. In effect the result was that, instead of covering the right flank of the army as originally intended, Drummond's four squadrons were initially standing on the left of the army, and so Sinclair was summoned to go across to the right to replace them. Had the second line of infantry then formed directly behind the first line, the two wings of cavalry would simply have been transposed. Instead, as we have just seen, what should have been the second line of infantry extended the front line on the left of Drummond's squadrons, in hasty conformity with Argyle's men.

Any help for Hamilton should therefore have come from those squadrons standing uselessly in the centre. Unfortunately, at the critical moment, Drummond had ridden off after Mar and the right wing, which was then in the process of demolishing Argyle's left. He was thus at some distance from his command and oblivious to the crisis when he waved his sword for them to follow and join in the pursuit:

> These poor gentlemen on that signall, wheel'd the four squadrons to the right, on the ground betuixt the enemie's line and that where our's was draun up, and, in wheeling, came with their flank close to the ennemie's foot, who gave them a fire in the flank that brought doun eighteen of Huntlie's tuo squadron, or of the whole, but the loss fell most on Huntlie's, and all this doe nothing, for it had not cost them one man had they attackt those after their first fire, and not given them time to charge [load] as the Highlandmen did; but not to attack at all is still worse. This fire and the former made the tuo rear ranks of Marischall's squadron make volt face back to Pearth, and occasion'd Huntlie's tuo to make but one in the evening, a good many of them taking the same route.[25]

In all, according to Sinclair there were eighteen of Huntly's men killed and their commander, Irvine of Drum, badly wounded. Huntly himself, by popular report (and at least one scurrilous ballad) was one of the runaways – and so too was Seaforth. He had begun the battle standing well to the rear with his personal escort, and as soon as Argyle started moving forward they bolted back towards the river.

As for the unhappy infantry, without that cavalry support they were doomed, because Argyle was able to come in on their open flank. The immediate result was that the whole of Hamilton's wing crumbled and cascaded backwards. Some regiments, including the Camerons and the Stewarts of Appin, may not have stopped running until they were across Allan Water.

Yet for the most part it was still a retreat rather than a rout. It was reckoned as two miles from the scene of that first clash to the river. According to Robert Campbell's life of the duke: 'in that Space they attempted to rally again near a dozen times'. If there was exaggeration in that, it was pardonable enough in the circumstance, Sinclair reflecting:

I have often wonder'd to see so few killed on all that ground over which he [Argyle] pursued with his dragoons. The onlie reason I can conceave was, his being obliged to go about the morass, which gave our people a great advantage in the flight doun hill, and that the frost was strong enough to bear them on foot, when the dragoons horses sunk deep in the moor, our's in the meantime getting over the river of Allen.[26]

Some units certainly held together in the early stages of the retreat at least. There is a tradition recorded on the Clan Macrae memorial on the battlefield that two of Seaforth's companies were all or most of them killed. More typical perhaps was the experience of Tullibardine's Regiment. He himself was serving as a brigadier and so passed command of his regiment to the young Earl of Strathmore. When the regiment gave way, Strathmore seized its colours and rallied a small party of about seventeen or so, who promptly attracted a volley for their pains. Wounded in the belly, Strathmore was 'goeing off' when he was first captured and then murdered – 'shott thro' the heart after he askt quarters'.[27] As a whole, casualties among the Jacobite leadership were cripplingly high as they tried in vain to rally their men. Strathmore's uncle, Auchterhouse, was killed at the head of his brigade, while both Lord Strathallan and his brother, Logie Drummond, were captured, and similarly Lord Panmure was 'takne, walking at his own leasure and so very ill cut in the head that he was left for dead in a house by the ennemie'.

With some rebel units stubbornly failing to run away, Argyle responded by ordering Major-General Wightman to support him with the infantry of the right wing. His official report duly spoke of the general following him with five battalions, by which he presumably meant he expected Wightman to bring down both Forfar's Brigade and Grant's as well.

Wightman himself on the other hand, having brushed aside the Jacobite horse in the centre, stated that he 'march'd after him as fast as I could with a little above three Regiments of Foot' – not five. While he was doing so, Wightman continued, he heard a great deal of firing from the direction of the left wing and sent his aide-de-camp across to find out what was happening.

The officer was not long in returning with the worst possible news. The left wing was gone.

Chapter 13

A Battle Lost and Won
Sheriffmuir Part 2

ARGYLE'S LEFT WING HAD in fact suffered a disaster even more swift and catastrophic than that which he himself visited on the Jacobite left wing, and for pretty much the same reasons.

'The Duke of Argyle was no less embarrassed on his side', remembered James Keith. 'His army was not yet entirely formed; the rear, which was to have formed his left wing, was yet on their march, and showed us their flank, which being observed by Lieutenant-General Gordon, he order'd our troops immediately to charge . . .'[1]

However, Gordon was at first extremely reluctant to do anything of the sort, no doubt because he was waiting until his own left came up. Therefore, although the redcoats were passing just 200 yards to his front, he at first insisted on staying exactly where he was. With his usual sarcasm Sinclair suggested there was some uncertainty among the Jacobites as to who Argyle's men really were 'and some cried out it was my Lord Strathmore's colours'. To which Sinclair scathingly retorted they were union colours and sarcastically asked 'if any of ours had granadeer caps and bajonets, or red coats . . .'[2]

Instead the order to attack came directly from Mar himself, who had decided to place himself on what was now the right wing of his army. As he explained, modestly speaking in the third person for the benefit of his readers:

> The Earl of Mar placed himself at the Head of the Clans, and finding the Enemy only forming their Line, thought fit to attack them in that Posture; he sent Colonel William Clepham, Adjutant General, to the Marquis of Drummond, Lieutenant-General of the Horse on the right, and to Lieutenant-General Gordon on the Right of the Foot, and

Major-General David Erskine, one of his Aids de Camp, to the Left, with Orders to March up and attack immediately: And upon their Return, pulling off his Hat, wav'd it with a Huzza, and advanc'd to the Front of the Enemy's form'd Battalions; upon which, all the Line to the Right, being of the Clans, led on by Sir Donald Mac-Donald's Brothers, Glengarry, Captain of Clan-Ranald, Sir John Maclean, Glenco, Campbell of Glenlyon, Colonel of Broad-Albin's, Brigadier Ogilvy of Boyne, with Colonel Gordon of Glen-Back, at the head of Huntley's Battalions, made a most furious Attack.[3]

As a piece of self-congratulatory Jacobite propaganda it read splendidly, but Sinclair remembered it slightly differently, and at the point when 'General Gordon received a message from Mar, Captain Livingston of Dumbarton's regiment, bidding him with great oaths, to attack the enemie before they were formed',[4] a substantial part of the Jacobite Army was still not yet properly formed up either. As we have seen, some of them were still double-quicking towards their start line on the left in an increasingly disorderly fashion. Other men, after a brisk firefight, were already being charged and scattered by Argyle's cavalry.

In fairness to Mar, waiting patiently for his whole line to form would have accomplished little, since Argyle would still have launched his own counterattack against the Jacobite left at the moment when he did. Unfortunately, however, like the duke he too had lost sight of the bigger picture and may also have been distracted by a famous incident.

No sooner was the order to advance given than Allan MacDonald, the Captain of Clanranald, was shot from his horse, fatally wounded. He was apparently the only Highland officer to go forward on horseback. This was perhaps because he was acting as a brigadier, or simply because the order to attack caught him unawares. Either way, down he went, and in full view of his clansmen.[5] Unsurprisingly the advance momentarily faltered, but a variety of eyewitnesses then described how MacDonnell of Glengarry immediately rushed forward, shouting: 'Revenge! Revenge! Today for revenge and tomorrow for mourning!'

Discarding their plaids the clansmen set off down the hill at a furious pace and as Sinclair declared:

The order to attack being given, the tuo thousand Highlandmen, who were then drawn up in very good order run towards the enemie in a disorderly manner, always firing some dropeing shots, which drew upon them a generall salvo from the ennemie, which begun at their left, opposite to us, and run to their right. No sooner that begun, the Highlandmen threw themselves flat on their bellies, and when it slackn'd, they started to their feet. Most threw away their fuzies, and, drawing their suords, pierced them everie where with ane incredible vigour and rapidity, in four minutes time from their receaving the order to attack.[6]

Within eight or nine minutes Mar too reckoned it was all over 'and we could neither perceive the Form of a Squadron, or Battalion of the Enemy before us'.

Disaster

The distribution of the casualties among Argyle's men was very uneven, with most falling among just two regiments in Clayton's Brigade. General Wightman made a point of relating that 'Morrison's is one of the unfortunate Regiments that were not form'd, and suffer'd most'. Lieutenant-Colonel Peter Hamers, two captains, four lieutenants, three ensigns, four sergeants and ninety-seven men were killed; another captain and thirteen men were wounded, and two officers and ten men taken prisoner, out of a total of 240.[7] Nevertheless, despite being 'not formed' it evidently stood and fought for it was afterwards rewarded by being granted the title 'The King's Regiment'.

Similarly, Montagu's Regiment had its commander – Lieutenant-Colonel Herbert Laurence – and Captain John Edwards taken prisoner. Two other officers – Captain Thomas Humble and Captain Bernard – were missing, 'and a considerable number of privates killed'. This amounted in all to a total of eight officers and 108 NCOs and men killed, wounded or prisoners.[8]

In Grant's Brigade, seemingly bringing up the rear of the column, there were also considerable losses. Orrery's Scots Fusiliers suffered heavily, losing Captain Walter Cheissly, Lieutenant Richard Hayward and Lieutenant Thomas Michelson, together with three sergeants and eighty-five men killed. In addition Captain Robert Urquhart of Burdsyards was badly wounded and taken,[9] and a sergeant and twenty-four men were also returned as wounded.[10]

In marked contrast, however, Clayton's own regiment lost Captain William Barlow, Captain Michael Moret and Lieutenant Edward Gibson all taken prisoner, but otherwise had just a lieutenant and six men killed and fourteen wounded.[11] Likewise in Grant's Brigade, Egerton's Regiment escaped equally unscathed, with just a sergeant and twenty-one men killed, and only Captain John Dancer and fourteen men returned as wounded.[12] Disgustedly, Argyle afterwards complained to Townshend that 'some of our Troops behaved as ill as ever any did in this world' and then went on to grumble that if it came to another battle they would most likely just fling away their arms again, which rather suggests both regiments bolted at the first onset without troubling to put up any kind of a fight.[13]

Confirmation of this swift and total collapse also comes in the account of the fighting on this wing contained in Rae's history, seemingly obtained from General Whetham himself:

> The Left of the King's Army, commanded by General Whetham, observing a great Cloud of the Highlanders break thro' the Centre close by them, and gathering apace, could make no guess of their Number, they standing so thick and confused, and intercepting their View so as they could neither hear nor see what was acted upon the Right, which the Circular Ground on which the Army stood would have of itself impeded without any other Obstruction, and all Communication or Intelligence by Aid de Camp or otherwise being intercepted, made them firmly believe that the Duke and the Right of the Army were either entirely beat, or at least surrounded by the Rebels; nor did they find themselves in a Condition to resent it or rescue them, in case it had been so.[14]

In other words the rebel right wing overran Clayton's and Grant's brigades in short order. With the exception of Morrison's Regiment, the whole lot promptly dissolved into a great intermingled mob of clansmen and fugitives who continued rolling down the hill, under the gaze of the appalled government left wing cavalry under Whetham. Yet at the same time, thanks to the convex slope of the hill, they were invisible to Argyle and Wightman on the right.

To make matters worse, admitted Argyle, 'the Rebels pressed so hard on our Battalions on the Left, that they were disorder'd and oblig'd to fall in amongst the Horse'.[15] That no doubt accounted for the left-hand squadron of Stair's Dragoons and perhaps for Kerr's Dragoons as well. Although Colonel William Kerr was wounded and had his horse shot from under him, only one other man from his regiment was returned as wounded.[16]

Nevertheless Whetham essayed at least one counterattack, apparently at the head of Carpenter's Dragoons,[17] and not only succeeded in fetching off a remnant of Morrison's Regiment, which was still fighting, but also 'charged some of their Horse on the Right, and carried off a standard'. This was confirmed by Sinclair, who related that: 'Those of Marischall's, who followed in the pursuite, fell in among some dragoons, who did not retire so irregularlie as they folloued; their standard was taken, and nine of them killed.'[18]

That unfortunately was seemingly the limit of Whetham's ambitions. Afterwards it was put about that he retired only as far as Dunblane, a move tactfully explained by Argyle as responding to reports that the Jacobites were intending to slip around onto the Stirling road. Instead, an unknown officer of Blackadder's Glasgow Volunteers, guarding Stirling bridge, disgustedly reported that 'Colonel Keir was for staying on a Plain till they could hear what was become of the Generall. But Whitham giving all over for lost came to Stirling bridge about 3 a' clock or thereby.'

To arrive there so early, Whetham can hardly have lingered long in Dunblane. As the officer of Blackadder's Glasgow Volunteers continued:

> You may easily imagine what consternation wee were in, to see men and horses running for three hours time, three miles in length, abundance having thrown away their arms, and some their coats, especially all the three regiments that came from Ireland (so far as I remember). But at four o'clock a gentleman came riding pretty hard up to the Bridge, giving account that the duke was on the field, obliging the enemy to retire and only wanted the rest of the forces to make a compleat victory.[19]

A Battle Lost and Won

Sinclair meanwhile claimed to have received orders from Mar to bring his cavalry down off the Stony Hill of Kippendavie and move forward to seize Causewayhead, in order to cut off the fugitives' escape. But, while James Keith sourly grumbled that the ground was so bad where they stood that Sinclair's three squadrons 'cou'd never be brought to engage', Sinclair justified his inaction by pointing to a worrying development in the Jacobite rear.

Belatedly learning of the disaster on the army's left wing, General Wightman had duly 'slackened' his march and acquainted the Duke of Argyle, who was still well ahead of him at that point and urgently calling for infantry support to help him finish pushing the Jacobites across Allan Water. Some rebels had already crossed, but other units were proving stubborn and victory had yet to be sealed.

The news from Wightman undoubtedly came as a profound shock to Argyle, but he immediately disengaged and fell back on his foot, whom Wightman kept 'in perfect Order, not knowing but my Rear might soon be attack'd by the Enemy that had beat our Left, which prov'd to be the Flower of their Army'. Once reunited they resolved to put a brave face on the matter, turned to the right about and warily set off back up the hill towards the Jacobites.

Mar of course was in exactly the same situation. His left wing, under Hamilton, was broken and entirely out of the fight, while his right was everywhere victorious, but for the moment out of control. By his own account they pursued the redcoats for about half a mile 'killing and taking Prisoners all that we could overtake'. At length some of the fugitives managed to make a stand on a 'little hill' below Dunblane, which might be Drumdruills. While the deep valley of the Wharry Burn proved a deathtrap, it must also by the same token have prevented Gordon's Highlanders scattering too far and wide in pursuit of the hapless fugitives. Consequently for once it might have been possible to rally the clansmen, and perhaps push into Dunblane itself. It was not to be. Instead word came to Mar that there were still substantial bodies of redcoated troops moving about on the Sheriffmuir behind them. Thus he too ordered his horse (or at least Drummond's battered squadrons) to wheel around, and 'having put the Foot in Order as fast as could be', he marched after them and began heading back up to the battlefield.

Nearing the top of the moor the first thing the Jacobites saw were the two squadrons of Portmore's Scots Greys, busying themselves in shooting up some of the runaways from the Marischal's squadron. By Sinclair's account it was a tense moment as he:

> . . . marched on with the three squadrons softlie towards them. After being within tuo or three hundred paces of them, in a fair field, they halted first, and we halted. Where they halted, they were within fiftie paces of the prisoners of their foot, which we had taken in the beginning, and were all got about a little house, looking on. I must doe our gentlemen justice to say they called, Advance. I bid them have patience, and leave it to me, suspecting there might be some more on the slope behind them; for we had seen them appear all at once; nor did I know how near the Duke of Argyle was to them, and, for another reason, thinkeing it very possible they might pierce us, because we neither would march close, or with a straight front, and if they beat us, they'd neither allow our foot or horse, who were all strageling, to get together . . . Had they advanc'd to me, I had nothing left but to goe on at a full trot, which I took care to instruct the gentlemen to doe as soon as I gave the order; for it's a certain rule, that whoever have the quickest motion give their horse weight by that motion, and have ane advantage in the shock, provided they can keep a straight front . . .
>
> After looking at one another for some time, our foot begun to assemble and draw nere, at least some four hundred, I believe three or four; and some few of the horse, who came back, drew up in the rear of my squadron, as if they design'd making a fourth rank. On seeing the foot, I order'd to advance to the enemy, and they wheel'd and went off.[20]

So far so good, but on gaining the crest Mar then discovered to his dismay that Argyle had patched together a new battle line of his own, with his remaining foot in the centre, Portmore's Dragoons on the right and Evans's Dragoons and some of Stair's on the left. They even had two cannon, placed in front of the dragoons. It seems most unlikely that they had been manhandled all the way over the moor to Allan Water and back, and so were most likely two of the Jacobite guns, abandoned without ever reaching the battlefield. Be that as it may, the whole lot then proceeded to take up a reasonably strong position facing south, that is, back the way they had just come, among 'some Enclosures and mud Walls, which would serve for a Breast-Work in Case they were attack'd'. Exactly where this might have been is tolerably uncertain, although James Keith makes the interesting assertion 'that we discovered the enemy posted at the foot of the hill among mud walls, on the same ground where we had layen the night before.'[21] As he and the Marischal's troop had come down from Ardoch with Hamilton and spent the night on the moor, rather than in Kinbuck, the walls in questions were probably around the Whitestone steadings.

At any rate by now the light of the short November day was fading fast, and if Mar was to snatch a last-minute victory he needed to move quickly. Instead he hesitated. Afterwards it would be said that John Gordon of Glenbuchat cried out for 'ane hour of Dundee', but Keith, who was to become no mean soldier himself, had a more sanguine recollection of that evening:

> The Earl of Mar, sent immediately an officer to reconnoitre them, and at the same time assembled the General officers and heads of Clans, to consult whither he shou'd attack them again; but the officer having reported that their numbers were equall to ours, and the Highlanders, who were extreamly fatigued, and had nothing to eat in two days, being averse to it, it was resolved to keep the field of battle, and to let the enemy retire unmolested.[22]

Needless to say some bitter recriminations followed and have continued ever since. James Keith reckoned that the officer sent out reconnoitring had seriously overestimated Argyle's numbers: 'For he having taken his remarks from the number of coulours than the space of ground they occupied, made his report the enemie was betwixt two and three thousand foot strong, when in reality there was no more than three battalions, not making in all above one thousand foot.'[23] The mistake he attributed to Argyle's twin subterfuges of displaying captured colours as well as his own, and stretching his line by forming only two deep instead of three. Neither of course is admitted by Argyle or his officers, and it seems more likely that the additional colours were brought in by stragglers from his broken regiments.

Sinclair for his part claimed that the clansmen argued that since they had done all the work so far, it was now time for the horse to show their mettle. Likewise Campbell, in his biography of Argyle, had an interesting and wholly plausible story that the Highlanders 'were headed by Glengarry, and that he, upon being ordered to attack these Battalions returned for Answer that the Clans had done enough and that he would not hazard them to do other People's Work (meaning the Horse)'.

It may well have been so, and certainly Sinclair and his three squadrons had thus far been little more than spectators, but horse could not charge foot standing secure behind walls. Keith surely had the right of it in asserting that exhaustion and reaction had set in. With better leadership the Highlanders might indeed have been roused for that one last effort, for it was not courage that was lacking but the grim determination in adversity that characterises professionals.

The Hurly-Burly Done

In marked contrast, Argyle's men were vastly encouraged by the Jacobite refusal to renew the battle, and afterwards Wightman crowed: 'I am apt to conjecture their Spirits were not a little Damp'd by having been Witness some hours before of the firm Behaviour of my Foot and thought it hardly possible to break us.'

They could hardly stay there forever of course, and after a time Argyle began extending his right, in hopes as he put it of regaining contact with his missing left wing. In reality there was little or no prospect of that, and Wightman rather more candidly wrote that 'as Evening grew on, we incline'd with our Right towards the Town of Dumblain in all the Order that was possible. The Enemy behav'd like Civil gentlemen and let us do what we pleased.'

At first the Jacobites stayed on top of the moor, which afterwards gave them some scant grounds for claiming a victory, but once darkness set in reality intruded. They were faced with another night in the open, lacking food and now clothing, let alone shelter. What was more, half the army was missing. Correctly reasoning that the missing left wing might have fallen back on Ardoch, Mar resolved to do likewise. There he had hopes of joining not only with the runaways but also with Rob Roy MacGregor's men and the missing brigade of Athollmen.

As a result, next morning it was a thoroughly bemused and mightily relieved Argyle who was able to move undisturbed back onto the battlefield, to recover his surviving wounded, pick up a few prisoners and collect a substantial quantity of muskets and other weapons. In all, he claimed fourteen colours and standards taken, four pieces of cannon and some tumbrels (two-wheeled carts used for carrying ammunition), the six bread wagons, which made up Mar's entire supply train, and upwards of eighty prisoners.

In return Argyle was reckoned to have lost twenty-three officers and 366 men killed, and ten officers and 144 men wounded, exclusive of prisoners.[24] The majority, as we have seen, fell in just three regiments on the left wing. The victorious right escaped virtually unscathed, with Forfar's reporting just one officer and eleven men killed; Wightman's had seven men killed and five wounded; and Shannon's one officer and five men killed and a further five wounded.

As to the cavalry, General Evans himself received a cut in the head from someone, perhaps with a Lochaber axe. His regiment, having been badly shot up at the outset of the battle, returned one officer and nineteen men killed and four officers and twenty-nine men wounded, including Lieutenant-Colonel Hawley (variously reported as shot through the body or in the arm or the shoulder) and Captain John Farrer (with a broken thigh bone).[25] Portmore's Scots Greys reported Captain Patrick Robertson and a quartermaster wounded, and just two troopers killed and four wounded. On the left wing, Carpenter's had seven men killed and nine wounded, while Kerr's suffered just one man wounded, besides their commander. Stair's for their part reported seven men and twelve horses killed and six men and fifteen horses wounded – most of them probably falling upon the squadron on the left wing.

The proportion of senior officers lost is notable. Two brigadiers fell: Evans (at the head of his dragoons) and the Earl of Forfar (who was shot through the knee at the outset of the action). By the time the latter was found he had also been 'cut in the head with ten or twelve strokes from their broadswords, after quarter'. Having been carried to Stirling, Forfar died there on 8 December.[26] Another colonel, William Kerr, was wounded, and three lieutenant-colonels – Hawley, Hamers and Lawrence – were wounded, killed and captured respectively. One of the more unfortunate was Argyle's brother, the Earl of Islay, who joined him as a volunteer just half an hour before the battle began and was shot in the side and in the arm for his pains. Close proximity to the duke may in fact have been decidedly unhealthy, because one of his aides-de-camp, Captain George Armstrong, was also killed.

In return, the duke rather hopefully estimated Jacobite losses at 'about 800, among whom there are several Persons of Distinction'. Mar countered by admitting to have lost only sixty, but at best that might have been all he could get account of, for there is no doubt that his real losses were very much higher and were masked to a considerable extent by the virtual disintegration of his army afterwards.

The erstwhile left wing fared worst, of course, with a brigadier – Patrick Lyon of Auchterhouse – killed and at least four battalion commanders lost. The Earl of Strathmore, as we have seen, was wounded while leading Tullibardine's Regiment and then murdered while asking for quarter. His lieutenant-colonel, John Walkinshaw of Barrowfield, was luckier in being taken prisoner. Lord Panmure was badly wounded with a cut in the head, captured, paroled and then eventually rescued by his brother, Harry Maule. Seaforth's major, John Murchison, was also killed, while Mackenzie of Fraserdale was wounded. Similarly the commanders of both battalions of the Marquis of Drummond's Regiment – Lord Strathallan and his brother Logie Drummond – were prisoners, and together with more than a dozen other officers were taken to Stirling.

Many of the junior officers and 'gentlemen' who were afterwards listed as taken also appear to have belonged to Seaforth's Regiment, confirming the anecdotal evidence that it was hard hit – or at least fell apart badly. Otherwise, nearly all the prisoners belonged to Lowland regiments or to Tullibardine's Athollmen. Meanwhile the clansmen on the left, evidently not only ran away faster but rather further than anyone else, and had got the length of Auchterarder before stopping.

Eventually the other Jacobite units converged on Braco, and there Mar found himself facing another problem. Not only were his surviving men hungry and exhausted after their recent adventures, but their remaining strength was rapidly being sapped by the bitter cold. As James Keith remarked, they had lost much of their clothing during the battle. Before they went into action they naturally discarded their heavy plaids and other impedimenta. Those who had gone in on the right may have had some opportunity to recover them afterwards, but not so those on the left. Therefore when Mar eventually got them all back to Perth it was decided that they 'cou'd not resist the violent cold of the season, and were therefore sent with their officers home, not only to be new cloathed but to bring back those who had fled straight from the battle to the mountains'.[27]

Necessary though this might have been, it also served to place a gloss on a wave of desertions. Traditionally Highlanders were accustomed to returning home after a battle, even if they had been victorious, but it was not just the ordinary clansmen who left. Seaforth and Huntly, both of whom fled from the battlefield, also soon found excuse enough to go north.

These departures, together with the immediate losses in the battle itself, effectively crippled Mar's army. Although subsequently joined by a handful of regiments, which for one reason or another missed the fighting, the Jacobites were in no condition to renew the half-hearted offensive, even against an equally weakened Argyle.

The songs would famously declare:

> There's some say that we won,
>
> And some say that they won,
>
> And some say that none won at a', man,
>
> But of one thing I'm sure,
>
> That at Sheriffmuir,
>
> A battle there was, that I saw, man.
>
> And we ran and they ran,
>
> And they ran and we ran,
>
> And we ran, and they ran awa' man.

Nevertheless there was no doubting on either side that it was Argyle's victory. Learning of the Jacobite advance he had moved out of Stirling to engage them head on with an army inferior in numbers. By the end of the battle, although his left wing had certainly been swept away, the rebel army was effectively shattered. It was a costly victory, but there was no doubting the British Army had established a moral ascendancy over their opponents, which would not be challenged for thirty years.

Chapter 14
Arrivals and Departures

THE PERCEPTION THAT SHERIFFMUIR was a drawn battle rests as much on the anticlimactic aftermath as on what actually happened on the moor. After it, the Jacobites under Mar retreated to their base at Perth, while Argyle led his army back to Stirling. Athough both were back where they had started, there was a crucial difference in their situations. For the Jacobite rising to succeed, Mar needed to win the battle; for the rising to fail, Argyle merely needed to deny Mar that victory. In that respect the outcome of the battle was clear enough. Although the rebellion was still some months dying, to all intents and purposes it ended at Sheriffmuir — just as surely as it did at Preston and Inverness. Shots were still fired and men still died, but there were no more battles.

There is no doubt that Mar's army still outnumbered Argyle's, but it was effectively shattered. Many of his men had run away during the battle or afterwards, abandoning irreplaceable arms, ammunition and clothing. The Duke of Wellington famously remarked that all soldiers will run away now and again, but that the good ones will come back again. In this case, far too few came back again, and once the rot set in it proved all too infectious among those who remained. In particular, the loss of so many senior officers proved crippling. In regular units they were simply appointments, usually relatively easily filled by promotion or transfer. The rebel units, however, were very much the personal following of their officers. Consequently once those officers were slain, captured or otherwise incapacitated, their tenants, vassals and clansmen all too often considered their reluctant obligations discharged.

It was little comfort that there were a number of units still available to Mar, who had not taken part in the battle for one reason or another. There was the garrison left in Perth; and the two battalions of Athollmen who had not returned in time from Fife. There was also a battalion under Rob Roy MacGregor, and soon Keppoch would turn up with another fresh battalion. None of them, however, can have inspired any confidence. With the exception of Lord Ogilvy's Regiment the Perth garrison comprised a couple of provisional battalions cobbled together from odd remnants of those units involved in the Forth crossing. Rob Roy's people had been present at Sheriffmuir, but had studiously avoided coming anywhere near the battlefield, and neither of the other battalions had exerted themselves to arrive in time. They were a poor exchange for what had been lost.

There were other factors as well. With some few exceptions, the surviving leaders were not soldiers. They had hoped to effect a revolution in the state simply by mobilising their followers. At first they had enjoyed some success, but when forced to fight a battle, there is no doubt that the sheer violence and the loss of so many friends came as a profound and demoralising shock. It was, in short, an experience few of them were keen to repeat.

Peace Feelers

Unsurprisingly then, in the days after the battle there was a widespread desire to find a way out of the situation. Some of the more circumspect, such as Breadalbane, discreetly withdrew their men almost at once. In neighbouring Atholl, the duke was gratified to find his authority returning as his tenants and vassals looked to him once more for protection. External factors were at work also. The recapture of Inverness and the concomitant loyalist ascendancy in the north very quickly saw both Seaforth and Huntly return home, ostensibly to protect their lands. They were not the only ones.

Indeed so profound was the rebel collapse that, within days, feelers were being put out to ascertain whether Argyle was empowered to offer terms. Indeed Sinclair claimed that Huntly had even very quietly raised the prospect with him on the morning of the battle. Whether this actually happened is far from certain, for Sinclair was prone to parading his pessimism. Nevertheless, he commented: 'I knew very well that if we did not get terms with our suords in our hands, we could never expect anie'.[1] Now in the aftermath of the battle, Mar was persuaded to agree to request those terms while he still had an army at his back. Accordingly the senior government prisoner, Lieutenant-Colonel Herbert Lawrence, was sent off to Argyle, informing him that the rebels were prepared to enter into negotiations 'if he had power to treat with them'.[2]

Lawrence's news came as a profound but very welcome shock. Argyle and his officers had just rather gloomily concluded that their army was in no condition to fight. They had no confidence that, if it came to another battle, those who had run away would not run away again. If the rebels were to resume their advance, it would be necessary to evacuate Stirling and retreat southwards. Instead it suddenly appeared that a rebel surrender was a real prospect. What was more, Lawrence also brought a second, secret message from Huntly, Sinclair and some of the other more reluctant rebels, offering 'that if they might separately have his Majestie's mercy they would break off from the rest'. Either alternative meant that the rebellion could quite literally be all over by Christmas. Even if negotiations with Mar should fail, the defection of Sinclair and his colleagues would precipitate a general collapse.

Not surprising, Cockburn, the lord justice clerk, delightedly declared 'here is good news, peace', but alas he spoke too soon. To the mortification of both Argyle and the Scottish political establishment, in a letter dated 6 December 1715 Argyle was bluntly informed that the king did not consider that 'in the present situation and circumstances of affairs, it is consistent with the honour of his government, or the future peace and quiet of his good subjects that the rebels should be admitted to any terms but those of surrendering their persons and entirely submitting to his Majesty's pleasure'.[3]

The peremptory rejection of both overtures had the slightly paradoxical effect of ensuring that the rebellion would go on, while at the same time encompassing its ultimate failure. It certainly contributed to Huntly's decision to return north, where he and Sir Robert Gordon of Gordonstoun rounded up sufficient men to threaten Inverness and then astutely bargained that threat into a negotiated submission to the Earl of Sutherland. Perhaps significantly Sinclair accompanied him north and soon escaped to France by way of Orkney. Others, however, reckoned that, if no mercy was to be offered, they had nothing to lose by continuing the fight. In taking this decision rather than the opportunity to escape, many of them were influenced by a last cruel twist. James Stuart, the Chevalier de St George and would be King James VIII, arrived in Scotland at last.

The Chevalier

Like his son thirty years later, James brought nothing with him. Indeed in contrast to the famous seven men of Moidart, he landed at Peterhead on 22 December 1715 with just two!

There is no doubt that his arrival, though tardy, at first had a stiffening effect. In a short time, however, his followers would be complaining of his gloomy and depressed nature. Yet it is hard to see how it could be otherwise, because not only was the army so painstakingly created and nurtured by Mar now in a very sorry condition, but also winter had arrived and set in hard. There was no realistic prospect of James leading a renewed advance through deep snow. Instead, all that could be done was to try and make good the earlier losses with a view to renewing operations in the spring. Burgh councils and clan chiefs alike were instructed to levy out men and forward supplies, but it soon became clear there was no enthusiasm for a renewed effort.

In any case, that was precisely what the British Army hoped to frustrate. Argyle had never fully enjoyed the confidence of his government. So soon after the Union it was politically imperative that the commander-in-chief should be a Scotsman. Therefore Argyle got the job precisely for that reason rather than on the basis of his comparatively limited military experience. As it happens he did prove to be far and away the best man for the job. Unfortunately his incessant requests for men, money and supplies, justified as they were, won him no friends at court. Furthermore his readiness to accept the rebel peace overtures only confirmed an unreasonable impression that he was 'soft' on them. Now that the Scottish rebels had been defeated by a Scotsman, it was time for a new commander who could be relied upon to finish the business properly. In early December he was found in the person of Lieutenant-General William Cadogan.

Cadogan had served in Flanders under the great Duke of Marlborough as quartermaster-general. As such, while no mean soldier in his own right, his true talents lay in staff work, transportation and logistics. It was ostensibly in this capacity therefore that he was originally sent up from London. There could be no question of sacking Argyle after his victory, but he was rather pointedly advised that, with Cadogan on the spot, he was free to return to London whenever he wished. Instead, determined to see the business through, and no doubt also to inconvenience his detractors, the duke doggedly stayed on.

Political machinations aside, Argyle also had sufficient men coming in at last to be able to act as he wished. Two regiments of dragoons – Newton's and Stanhope's – were ordered north from Preston at the end of November and arrived in Glasgow at about this time. So too did the long-promised Dutch troops. The first contingent of about 3,000 men arrived in Leith on 17 December, with the rest following shortly afterwards. They soon found gainful employment. Using the threat of a naval bombardment to persuade the Jacobites to evacuate

Burntisland, Argyle thrust in a garrison of his own on 22 December, comprising levies from Edinburgh under Sir Robin Montgomerie and a detachment from a Swiss regiment in the Dutch service.[4]

This sudden switch to a more aggressive stance seems to have come as a surprise to the rebels, for a party incautiously arrived in Dysart shortly afterwards intent on seizing some horses. Instead a mixed party of Swiss and fencibles jumped them, killing two and taking seven. The following day Lieutenant-Colonel Cathcart came to Dunfermline again with his Scots Greys, but this time they occupied the place as a garrison of their own, largely to keep in check another placed by the Jacobites in nearby Falkland.

None of them sat idly, and throughout January a series of minor skirmishes rippled across Fife. Before Sheriffmuir the rebels had become accustomed to roaming as they pleased through the old kingdom. Now control slipped out of their grasp as loyalist partisans backed up by small detachments of Dutch and Swiss regulars became increasingly assertive.

Not that the loyalists had it all their own way. At one point Rob Roy carried off a neat ambush at Markinch, near Kirkcaldy. Upon 'misinformation' that a party of about twenty Highlanders were plundering the place, twelve Swiss and eighteen of the Kirkcaldy militia boldly set out from Leslie to deal with them. Directed towards an enclosure by their treacherous guide: 'Owr men came up and fyred briskly and kild two of the rebels, but when they saw themselves surrounded by 160 armed men they all asked qwarters but two of the Swise quho were at lenthe desperately wownded and taken and ane of them is since dead.'[5]

Afterwards it was insinuated that the defeat was down to the incautious behaviour of those left in charge at Leslie in the absence of their commander, Captain Innes. While it was no doubt embarrassing, however, it was still by any reckoning a pretty trivial affair and quite overshadowed in a matter of days.

On 23 January Argyle and Cadogan reconnoitred the roads north as far as Auchterarder. Although the snow reportedly came up to their horses' bellies, they agreed that an advance was practicable. Using local people to clear the roads, Argyle proposed to commence his offensive on 27 January.

Forewarned of their coming, the Jacobites began burning all the villages between Dunblane and Perth in the early hours of 25 January. Auchterarder was the first, and all the inhabitants were turned out into the falling snow as their houses burned. Then came Blackford and Crieff. Dunning and Muthil were burned by Lord George Murray on the night of 28 January and Dalreoch next day – a Sunday. Then to finish off the exercise, a second visit was made to Auchterarder in order to destroy those few houses missed the first time around.

All in all it was a sorry business – and ultimately a futile one too. The justification for the exercise was to frustrate Argyle's advance by depriving him of any shelter for his troops. Cadogan, however, had not only ensured there was sufficient tentage for the army, but he had also assembled a train of coal carts to provide them with fuel for their fires. When it was realised by the rebels against all expectation that Argyle and Cadogan were on the march a fraught series of arguments ensued. Many of the remaining Jacobites were still for fighting, but for the most part their leaders had decided to put an end to the affair.

Despite being heavily fortified, Perth had fallen to Cromwell's army in just a matter of days in 1651 and the rebels were only too well aware that their own defences were far less formidable. On 30 January James came into the city from nearby Scone, where he had been hopefully planning a coronation. The next morning at about 10 a.m. the Jacobite army began evacuating Perth, marching on the ice straight across the frozen river Tay. Once on the other side they proceeded to Dundee and then up the coast to Montrose. There the Chevalier took his leave on the night of 4 February, and returned to France. It was, in truth, the best thing he could do.

Sinclair recalled that when the news of James's arrival in France had first been confirmed, Huntly responded: 'Now there's no help for it, we must all ruine with him: would to God he had come sooner.'[6] And that was the essence of it. However ready they might be to abandon the cause and seek terms, they could not in all conscience abandon the man himself, however hopeless that struggle. His departure resolved that dilemma.

Mar and some of the other leaders went with James, and it fell to General Gordon to guide the army northwards. All the while Argyle steadily followed after, trailing just a day behind for the most part but making no real attempt to overtake them. At length, Argyle halted at Aberdeen on 8 February, while the rebels made their way unmolested to Strathbogie. Colonel Hay of Cromlix had been sent ahead to meet with Huntly in hopes that they might combine their forces. Unsurprisingly the response was a flat refusal. Huntly had already decided to seek terms for himself and for his vassals, and he certainly was not going to do anything stupid at this late point.

A few rebel leaders nevertheless still expressed optimism. Seaforth, for one, foolishly raised his followers again, but it was hard to gainsay Huntly's sensible attitude. At Ruthven in Badenoch, on 14 February, General Gordon sent a letter to Argyle hopefully asking once again for a general indemnity.[7] Afterwards they all dispersed to their homes, or fled abroad. In early January Argyle had been given permission to return to London. Now, his job done, he at last did so, turning over command to Cadogan on 27 February. He for his part ventured on what amounted to a tour into the Highlands rather than a military expedition, before heading south as well, in late April, without a shot fired.

The End of a Bad Affair

The fact that the remaining rebels were willing to submit was now regarded as enough. Sufficient prisoners had already been taken at Preston and elsewhere to serve as an example. In the end there were about thirty executions in all, largely among those taken at Preston. Kenmure and Derwentwater were both beheaded. Forster would have been hung if he had not proved to be cleverer than he is usually credited, by making his escape. Wintoun likewise managed to slip out in disguise, while Borlum and a few of his officers eschewed subtlety by fighting their way out of jail. After going abroad Borlum returned clandestinely to Scotland on a number of occasions but was finally arrested in November 1727. Confined as a state prisoner in Edinburgh Castle he remained there until his death in 1743, at the ripe old age of eighty-five.

For the most part an obscure exile awaited the escapees. Some such as Wintoun and Forster died in penniless but genteel obscurity. Others such as Mar first danced at the phantom court of King James and then turned double agent in an attempt to seek pardon. It was a vain hope, of course, and he died at Aix la Chappelle in 1732. The Keith brothers, rather more honourably, sought for their bread under other monarchs – the Marischal as a diplomat and James as a field-marshal in the Prussian service. Both made their peace with the regime, but neither ever returned home again.

A few did have a happy ending. Notwithstanding that earlier reluctance by the government to let Argyle discuss terms, the swift collapse of the rising was succeeded by a desire for an equally swift return to normality, rather than exercise retribution. On the whole, the rebels got off lightly in the circumstances. Carnwath, originally sentenced to death, was reprieved – and so too was Lord Charles Murray. Even some of the exiles, surprisingly many in fact, were eventually allowed to return. A few were unrepentant. Many of the leaders of the last rising in 1745 would be men such as Tullibardine, Lord George Murray, Lord Strathallan, Lord Pitsligo and John Gordon of Glenbuchat, who had all been pardoned after 1715. Others, including the Master of Sinclair, repaid that clemency by very pointedly avoiding any further involvement in Jacobite plotting.

There of course it should have ended, but the Stuarts still maintained their claim to the throne beyond all expectation. In 1745 the clans rose again, and this time there was to be no mercy.

Appendix 1
The Jacobite Regiments

IN MARKED CONTRAST TO the attention lavished on the Jacobite army of 1745, very little has been published on the army levied in 1715. This appendix is therefore aimed at providing an annotated listing of all known major units. It should be noted that it is deficient in respect to the accounting of officers. In many cases it is known that certain individuals served under a particular commander and may well have been accounted officers. However, unless a rank or position is specifically documented, they are not included in the listings below.

Cavalry

Angus-shire Squadron

Raised and commanded by James Carnegie, 5th Earl of Southesk (1692–1730). Sinclair claimed he turned up at Perth with just thirty mounted men, but the 13 October muster shows it to have been one of the stronger cavalry units with 100 troopers.[1]

Earl of Carnwath's Troop

Part of Kenmure's army raised in Nithsdale by Robert Dalziel, Earl of Carnwath (1687–1737). Actual command was exercised by his uncle, James Dalziel.[2]

Earl of Derwentwater's Troop

Raised by James Radcliffe, Earl of Derwentwater (1689–1716) in Northumberland. Actual command was exercised by his brother, Charles Radcliffe, and Captain James Shaftoe.[3]

Captain Robert Douglas's Troop

Raised in the Borders by Robert Douglas, and accounted part of the English Jacobite army under Forster, although substantially composed of Scots.[4]

Fifeshire Squadron

Raised and commanded by John, Master of Sinclair (1683–1750) and by his own accounting the best disciplined of the cavalry units. It was ninety strong at the 13 October muster.[5]

Captain John Hunter's Troop

Raised by John Hunter in the Tyne valley and may have been the best of a sorry bunch. According to Patten, Hunter had a commission to raise an Independent Company in Queen Anne's time, but not receiving half pay afterwards he avoided summary execution at Preston and later escaped from Chester Castle.[6]

Marquis of Huntly's Regiment

Two squadrons raised in the northeast of Scotland by Alexander Gordon, 5th Marquis of Huntly (1678–1728); 400 were mustered at Perth on 13 October 1715,[7] but one of the squadrons was very poorly mounted and sent home to patrol the Aberdeenshire and Banffshire coast. The regiment's lieutenant-colonel, Alexander Irvine, the son and heir of Irvine of Drum, was badly wounded at Sheriffmuir.[8]

Lord Kenmure's Troop

Raised in Nithsdale by William Gordon, Lord Kenmure (1672–1716) and also designated the First Troop. Surrendered at Preston.

- Known officers included:
  Captain Hon. Basil Hamilton[9]

Captain Philip Lockhart's Troop

Part of Kenmure's army, raised in Nithsdale by Lockhart, a brother of the Earl of Carnwath.[10]

Earl Marischal's Squadron

Raised in the eastern part of Aberdeenshire and the Mearns by William Keith, the hereditary Earl Marischal of Scotland.[11] Some 180 men were mustered at

Perth on 13 October 1715.[12] The squadron appears to have been badly cut up at Sheriffmuir, losing its standard. Sinclair claimed that, after Huntly returned home, the Marischal tried to persuade some of his cavalrymen to join the squadron, but got no takers. A third troop was ordered to be raised in Aberdeen in January 1716, but although officers were nominated it seems unlikely the troop was completed.

- Known officers included:

Lieutenant-Colonel James Keith[13]

Captain John Bannerman (Aberdeen troop)[14]

Lieutenant David Adie (Aberdeen troop)

Cornet Robert Burnett (Aberdeen troop)

Quartermaster Alexander Bannerman (Aberdeen troop)

Merse Troop

Part of Kenmure's army. Raised in the Merse (Berwickshire) by Hon. James Hume, brother of the Earl of Hume. Born in 1699, he was, as Patten remarked, 'not very capable of having the Command of a Troop, as well on account of his Age, as other incapacities'.[15]

Perthshire Squadron

Commanded by Robert, Lord Rollo (1679–1758) and recorded as seventy strong at Perth on 13 October. Present at Sheriffmuir but otherwise does not appear to have been much noticed in the histories of the time.

Stirlingshire Squadron

This was one of the first units to be raised, and was formed of those mounted men present at the raising of the Standard; it was commanded by James Livingston, Earl of Linlithgow (1674–1723). While officially designated the Stirlingshire Squadron it was more usually known as the Standard Squadron, since it had the duty of carrying it. For that reason it was recruited with two or three men taken from each of the other cavalry units. The squadron was seventy-seven strong at the muster on 13 October 1715.[16]

Edward Tyldesley's Troop

Raised in Lancashire by Edward Tyldesley of Myerscough. According to tradition it marched behind his grandfather's old standard, which was green with the Tyldesley crest – a pelican vulning itself, surrounded by a gold laurel wreath.[17]

Lord Widdrington's Troop

Raised in Northumberland by William, Lord Widdrington (1678–1743) but actually commanded by Thomas Errington of Beaufront.[18]

Earl of Wintoun's Troop

Commanded by George Seton, Earl of Wintoun (1678–1749), although it is unclear whether it was raised in Nithsdale or comprised Lothian and other gentlemen who followed him.

- Known officers included:
  Captain James Dalziel[19]

Captain Charles Wogan's Troop

Charles Wogan was an Irish officer, confused by Patten with his younger brother Nicholas.[20] The troop was raised in Northumberland at the outset of the English rising.

Infantry

Earl of Breadalbane's Regiment

Two battalions raised by John Campbell, 1st Earl of Breadalbane (1636–1717). Served under Gordon of Auchintoul in the west and afterwards at Sheriffmuir, where Mar reckoned them 400 strong under the command of John Campbell of Glenlyon.[21] The regiment had withdrawn from the Jacobite army by the end of November 1715.

Cameron of Locheil's Regiment

Ewan Cameron of Locheil himself was far too old for adventures by 1715 and the regiment was commanded by his sons John and Donald. The regiment was late in joining the rebel army, but was said by Mar to have been 300 strong at Sheriffmuir. There it appears to have departed the battlefield early and at some speed. Strangely enough the 22 November ration warrant credited the regiment with then being 400 strong.

- The Locheil colours were red with three gold bars. Cameron of Glendessary's 'ruddy banner' – seen at Dalcomera in 1689 and still preserved at Achnacarry – is red with a central green panel depicting the full heraldic achievement, differing from Locheil's arms only in having an arm and sword for a crest rather than a sheaf of arrows.

- Known officers included:

Lieutenant-Colonel John Cameron,   Major Donald Cameron[23]
    younger of Locheil[22]

James, Marquis of Drummond's Regiment

Chiefly raised in the Strathallan area, between Perth and Stirling, by James Drummond, Marquis of Drummond,[24] this was a large but not particularly effective regiment with a complicated history. Sinclair alleged that Drummond's vanity led him to organise it in three battalions in the French style, but it would appear that there were only two. One was commanded by Lieutenant-Colonel Thomas Drummond of Logiealmond (otherwise known as Logie Drummond) and the other by William Drummond, Lord Strathallan. Both battalions were assigned to Borlum's expedition, but few or none of Strathallan's men made it across the Forth and the greater part of Logie Drummond's men also turned back. Of those who crossed the Forth, some were taken during the crossing and, although subsequently rescued when Borlum captured Leith, they appear to have been left there when he evacuated the place, as they had lost all their arms and equipment. Both battalions fought at Sheriffmuir, where Logie Drummond and Strathallan were captured.

- As Sinclair sneered that Drummond wanted to be considered a Highland chieftain, it may be supposed that his men were clothed accordingly.

- Known officers in Logie Drummond's Battalion included:

Lieutenant-Colonel Thomas Drummond   (taken at Preston)
    of Logiealmond[25]
                                              Lieutenant Alexander Drummond
Captain David Drummond (taken at   (taken at Preston)
    Preston)[26]
                                              Lieutenant Archibald McLachlan
Captain John Carnegie (taken at Preston)
                                                  (taken at Preston)
Captain Alexander McGrowther
    (taken at Preston)   Lieutenant William McGrowther
Lieutenant James Drummond   (taken at Preston)

- Known officers in Strathallan's Battalion included:

Lieutenant-Colonel William Drummond,
    Lord Strathallan[27]   Major Thomas Arthur[28]

Gentlemen Volunteers

This was an *ad hoc* unit raised in the Edinburgh area when Borlum came over the Forth, and according to Patten probably comprised two companies.

- Known officers included:[29]

  Captain James Skene[30]

  Captain Lachlan MacLean

  Lieutenant David Stewart

  Ensign John Dunbar

Marquis of Huntly's Regiment

Two battalions raised in the northeast of Scotland by Alexander Gordon, Marquis of Huntly. One battalion, commanded by John Gordon Glenbuchat, appears to have been raised in Strathbogie and Strathavan. The other battalion, commanded by James Ogilvie of Boyne, seemingly comprised Huntly's 'Low Country people' raised in eastern Aberdeenshire. This battalion may also have included some of the men credited to the Earl Marischal. Supposedly 1,200 strong in mid-October 1715,[31] Mar's account of Sheriffmuir credits the regiment with only 400 men. This dramatic drop in numbers is explained by Sinclair's assertion that most of them had deserted two days earlier.

- An intelligence report in the summer of 1715 spoke of Huntly providing coats and tartan trews for his levies. A surviving white colours bearing the Gordon arms surmounted by a ducal coronet was carried by Glenbuchat's regiment in 1745 and almost certainly by this regiment in 1715 as well.

- Known officers included:

  Lieutenant-Colonel John Gordon of
  Glenbuchat[32]

  Lieutenant-Colonel James Ogilvy of
  Boyne[33]

Sir Donald MacDonald's Regiment

Raised by Sir Donald MacDonald of Sleat (d.1718) in the Western Isles and initially attached to Seaforth's forces before coming south to fight at Sheriffmuir. Sleat himself, pleading illness, had returned to Skye, and in consequence the regiment was commanded there by his two brothers, John and William. Mar credited the regiment with 700 men at Sheriffmuir, but the 22 November ration warrant gave a rather more realistic total of 430.[34]

MacDonald of Clanranald's Regiment

Raised by Allan MacDonald, Captain of Clanranald, serving in the west under General Gordon and then at Sheriffmuir, where Clanranald was shot dead at the very outset of the battle. Mar reckoned the regiment as 565 strong on the morning of the battle, but by 22 November it was down to 400.[35]

MacDonald of Glencoe's Regiment

Raised by John MacDonald (or MacIain) of Glencoe and serving initially with General Gordon in the west and then at Sheriffmuir, where Mar reported them 150 strong. There is no further reference to their service. Traditionally the Glencoe men marched behind a bunch of heather tied to a pole rather than a more conventional flag.

MacDonald of Keppoch's Regiment

Raised by Coll MacDonald of Keppoch in the west but avoided fighting anyone. Savagely plundered Glen Urquhart on the grounds it belonged to the Laird of Grant, but wilfully ignoring the fact many of the Glen Urquhart men were serving in Glengarry's Regiment. Briefly joined the main army after Sheriffmuir and recorded as 250 strong on 22 November.[36]

MacDonnell of Glengarry's Regiment

Raised by Alexander MacDonnell (or MacDonald) of Glengarry,[37] serving under General Gordon in the west and afterwards at Sheriffmuir. Mar said they were 460 strong there, but the 22 November warrant evidenced only 300.[38] A fairly substantial part of the regiment was actually made up of the Glenmoriston and Glen Urquhart Grants.

- Known officers included:
  Captain John Grant of Glenmoriston[39]   Lieutenant Alexander Cumming
  Captain Aeneas MacDonald of Aughtera[40]   of Dalshangie[41]
  Lieutenant William Grant of Corrimony

MacGregor Regiment

Raised in the name of Alexander MacGregor (alias Drummond) of Balhaldie,[42] by the celebrated Rob Roy MacGregor early in the rising. Initially served under General Gordon in the west. Although present with the army, the regiment contrived to take no part at all in the Battle of Sheriffmuir. A local tradition places

Rob Roy and his men at a place called Culling, near Cromlix, to the west of the battlefield and on the other side of the river Teith. From there they could join either side, by way of the ford at Kinbuck or the bridge at Dunblane, but being unable to discern the winning side they remained there throughout the day.[43]

Laird of Mackintosh's Regiment

Raised in the Inverness area by Lachlan Mackintosh of Mackintosh, but included an Aberdeenshire contingent under Farquharson of Invercauld. This regiment was a major component in Borlum's expeditionary force. According to Patten it comprised thirteen companies each of fifty men before the major desertions at Langholm.[44] Just 295 officers and men surrendered at Preston.

- Known officers, all taken at Preston, included:

Colonel Lachlan Mackintosh of Mackintosh[45]

Lieutenant-Colonel John Farquharson of Invercauld[46]

Major John Mackintosh[47]

Captain Lachlan Mackintosh (snr)

Captain Farquhar McGillivrey

Captain Angus McBean

Captain Robert Shaw

Captain Duncan Mackintosh

Captain William Mackintosh

Captain Angus Mackintosh

Captain Lachlan Mackintosh (jnr)

Captain Francis Farquharson of Whitehouse

Captain Lachlan MacLean

Lieutenant William McGillivrey

Lieutenant John Farquharson of Kirkton

Lieutenant John Mackintosh

Lieutenant Farquhar McGillivrey

Lieutenant John MacBean

Lieutenant Angus Shaw

Lieutenant Benjamin Mackintosh

Lieutenant James Mackintosh

Lieutenant William MacQueen

Lieutenant John Mackintosh

Lieutenant Duncan Mackintosh

Lieutenant John Abercromby, aide-de-camp

Lieutenant ( ) Skene, aide-de-camp

Lieutenant David Stuart

Lieutenant William Mackintosh

Lieutenant John Mackintosh, aide de camp

Daniel Grant, adjutant

David MacQueen, paymaster

William Shaw, quartermaster

Sir John Maclean's Regiment

Raised in the Western Isles by Sir John Maclean (1670–1716).[48] Served throughout the rising and said by Mar to be 350 strong at Sheriffmuir. Its casualties must have been negligible because rations were issued for the same number on 22 November.[49]

Earl of Mar's Regiment

Raised with a good deal of difficulty by John Erskine, Earl of Mar, on his Aberdeenshire estates at the very outset of the rising. His vassals were reluctant to turn out, and recruiting was badly damaged by the refusal of John Farquharson of Invercauld to serve under him. Consequently it was never a large unit, which makes it all the more surprising that it was assigned to Borlum's expedition. Even then only a detachment under Major Forbes actually made the crossing, while the rest of the regiment occupied Burntisland. Consequently just eight officers and twenty-eight men surrendered at Preston.[50]

- Known officers included:

Lieutenant-Colonel Peter Farquharson of Inverey[51]

Major Nathaniel Forbes (taken at Preston)[52]

Captain John James (taken at Preston)

Captain Donald Ferguson (Farquharson?) (taken at Preston)

Captain John Gordon (taken at Preston)

Lieutenant John Cattanach (taken at Preston)

Lieutenant Henry Lumsden (taken at Preston)

Lieutenant Robert Gordon (taken at Preston

Lord Charles Murray's Regiment

One of the battalions of Athollmen, raised and commanded by Lord Charles Murray, a son of the loyalist Duke of Athole. Assigned to Borlum's expedition, 137 officers and men surrendered at Preston.

- Known officers, all taken at Preston, included:

Colonel Lord Charles Murray[53]

Lieutenant-Colonel John Murray, Master of Nairne[54]

Major James Stuart

Captain James Menzies[55]

Captain Alexander Menzies

Captain Donald Robertson

Captain John Robertson

Captain Patrick Robertson

Lieutenant Alexander Menzies

Lieutenant Adam Reid

Lieutenant John McEwan

Lieutenant Duncan Campbell

Ensign John Stuart

Ensign John Ratson

Ensign Alexander Stuart

Ensign John Robson

Ensign James Raton

Ensign John Stuart

Lord George Murray's Regiment

One of the battalions of Athollmen, raised and commanded by Lord George Murray, a son of the loyalist Duke of Athole.[56] Just 230 strong at the Perth muster on 13 October, it was sent into Fife shortly afterwards and did not fight at Sheriffmuir.[57]

Lord Nairne's Regiment

Another of the battalions of Athollmen, this time raised and commanded by William Murray, Lord Nairne. Assigned to Borlum's expedition, not all of them made it across the Forth. Of those who did, 122 officers and men surrendered at Preston, indicating a very high level of desertion.

- Known officers, all taken at Preston,[58] included:

  Colonel William Murray, Lord Nairne[59]   Captain James Stuart

  Lieutenant-Colonel John Stuart of   Captain James Robertson
      Kynachan[60]   Captain John Stuart

  Major ( ) Blair   Captain Robert Stuart

  Captain Alexander Robertson

- Patten's list for this regiment concludes with Archibald Butler 'the Lady's Darling, tho' mangy in the Rebellion'.

Lord Ogilvy's Regiment

This regiment was formed, according to Sinclair, from Ogilvy's tenants in Kirriemuir and Glen Prosen and those of Sir James Kinloch from the Dundee area. The regiment was 351 strong at Perth on 13 October but did not fight at Sheriffmuir as it was assigned to the garrison.[61] Afterwards it appears to have been disbanded in the Dundee area rather than follow the army north.

- A blue colours with a white saltire in the centre, a thistle and the motto *Nemo me impune lacessit* was carried by a regiment raised by his nephew, David, Lord Ogilvy in 1745. It survives and may actually be a relic of the original unit. Similarly a blue colours bearing the Kinloch motto *Sursum tendo* (and probably his arms as well) was captured at Culloden and may also have been carried in 1715.

- Known officers included:

  Colonel James, Lord Ogilvy[62]   Lieutenant-Colonel Sir James Kinloch

Lord Panmure's Regiment

Initially raised in Angus or Forfarshire by James Maule, Earl of Panmure. At Perth it was combined with a contingent from Deeside brought in by Patrick

Lyon of Auchterhouse, since they were neighbours to Panmure's people in Glenesk. The 13 October muster at Perth recorded 415 men in the camp at Perth, which made it one of the larger regiments.[63] Sinclair approvingly noted: 'It must be said, nobodie engaged in that affair gave half the application to their duty, or disciplining their regiments, as my Lord Strathmore and Panmure.'[64] Unfortunately the regiment appears to have largely fallen apart as a result of Panmure's being badly wounded at Sheriffmuir.

- Known officers included:

Colonel James Maule, Earl of Panmure[65] Major ( ) Leslie[67]
Lieutenant-Colonel Patrick Lyon of Captain David Gardin[68]
 Auchterhouse[66]

Robertson of Strowan's Regiment

Raised in Atholl by Alexander Robertson of Strowan (1669–1749), and joined Mar at Kirkmichael in mid-September 1715. Some 203 men were mustered at Perth on 13 October, and the regiment subsequently fought at Sheriffmuir.[69]

Earl of Seaforth's Regiment

Raised in north of Scotland by William Mackenzie, Earl of Seaforth.[70] Engaged in rather inconsequential operations in the north before joining the main rebel army in time to fight at Sheriffmuir. Its strength and organisation are uncertain. Mar's printed account of the battle credited it with 400 men in three battalions, but this probably included a contingent of Frasers, which returned home two days earlier.

- Known officers included:

Lieutenant-Colonel Alexander Mackenzie Captain Colin Mackenzie of Kildin[73]
 of Fraserdale[71] Captain John Maclean, adjutant[74]
Major John Murchison[72]

Stewart of Appin's Regiment

A clan regiment raised and led by Robert Stewart of Appin. Took part in the blockade of Inverary and was afterwards at Sheriffmuir, though apparently 'but ill armd'. It was 260 strong there according to Mar's printed account, but a warrant for issuing rations dated 22 November credited the regiment with just 180 men.[75]

- In both 1689 and 1745 the Appin Stewarts marched behind a blue banner bearing a yellow saltire, so undoubtedly did so at Sheriffmuir as well.

Stewart of Invernytie's Regiment

Raised in and around Grantully by John Stewart of Invernytie. Was 267 strong at Perth on 13 October, but subsequently sent into Fife and did not fight at Sheriffmuir.[76]

Earl of Strathmore's Regiment

This was a Lowland regiment largely raised by John Lyon, 5th Earl of Strathmore (1696–1715), in Strathmore itself, a farming district lying between Perth and Dundee. At Perth a contingent of 150 infantry raised by James Carnegie, Earl of Southesk was added, although he himself continued in command of a cavalry squadron. Sinclair stated that, when the regiment was formed, Barrowfield was the lieutenant-colonel and 'a Captain Walkinshaw' became major. The regiment was assigned to Borlum's expedition, but none of the three field officers made the crossing, and in consequence the regiment was commanded in England by Captain William Douglas, with the acting rank of major.[77] In all 158 officers and men surrendered at Preston, but an unknown number of others had failed to cross the Forth and afterwards formed part of a provisional battalion detailed to serve as part of the Perth garrison.

When the former city was occupied at the outset of the rising, Sinclair rather scathingly dismissed them as 'tuo hundred Low Countrie men, with old rustie muskets, who had never fired one in their lives, and without pouder and flints'.[78] He does however make a point of praising the attention paid by Strathmore to training and disciplining his regiment.[79]

- Patten, in describing the units that came south with Borlum, noted: 'This Regiment was not in Highland Dress, as the others were . . .'[80]

- Known officers included:

Colonel John Lyon, Earl of Strathmore (killed at Sheriffmuir)

Lieutenant-Colonel John Walkinshaw of Barrowfield[81]

Major ( ) Walkinshaw

Major William Miller (taken at Preston)[82]

Captain William Douglas (taken at Preston)

Captain John Scrimgeour (taken at Preston)

Captain James Balfour (taken at Preston)

Lieutenant William Lyon (taken at Preston)

Lieutenant Alexander Murray (taken at Preston)

Lieutenant Alexander Orrock (taken at Preston)

Lieutenant John Burnes (taken at Preston)

Ensign Patrick Douglas (taken at Preston)

Ensign Hugh Ken (taken at Preston)

Ensign Alexander McGiven (taken at Preston)

Ensign Andrew Ramsay (taken at Preston)

Ensign Henry Ogilvy (taken at Preston)

Quartermaster William Henderson (taken at Preston)

Marquis of Tullibardine's Regiment

Raised in Atholl early in the rebellion by William Murray, Marquis of Tullibardine.[83] Not present at the Perth muster on 13 October but reckoned by Mar to be 300 strong at Sheriffmuir. Tullibardine himself acted as a brigadier in the battle, and so his regiment was actually commanded by the Earl of Strathmore.

Appendix 2

The Government Forces

THE MAJORITY OF THE British Army was deployed in the southern part of England and in Ireland throughout the rising and only those units actively engaged in Scotland or the north of England are described here.

Units are listed by the name of their 1715 commanding officer. Some regiments passed out of existence shortly after the rising. Others went onto become more famous before disbandment or amalgamation with other units – a still-ongoing process, which renders tracing their lineage superfluous. Nevertheless where relevant the numbers allocated to certain regiments in 1751 are noted for reference.

It should be noted that, although regimental colonels were more closely associated with the day-to-day affairs of their regiments than was later the case, it was relatively rare for them actually to lead their regiment in battle. At Sheriffmuir, for example, Jasper Clayton, William Evans and the Earl of Forfar were all three of them present but serving as brigade rather than regimental commanders. Unless otherwise noted, officers' names are culled from Dalton, *English Army Lists and Commission Registers*, vol. 6.

Unfortunately, although there were a substantial number of loyalist units raised in both Scotland and England – most notably the Earl of Rothes's Horse and Colonel Blackadder's Glasgow Regiment – there is as yet very little information available beyond the fact of their existence.

A brief note is given as to uniform details where known. All regiments wore red coats, distinguished by contrasting coloured facings displayed on the cuffs and linings. Grenadiers normally wore mitre-shaped cloth caps with a facing-coloured front and a red 'bag' at the rear. Apart from the obvious fact of their wearing heavy riding boots, cavalry uniforms differed in that under the coats they had facing-coloured waistcoats and breeches, while infantry wore red waistcoats and breeches. As mounted infantry some dragoon regiments also designated one of their troops as grenadiers, who availed themselves the privilege of wearing caps. How widely this was still observed by 1715 is unknown. All ranks of the Scots Greys wore grenadier caps as a battle honour. For most regiments the royal cypher was also displayed on the front of the grenadier cap, but a number of units, including the Scots Greys, were privileged to have a badge of some description.

Infantry regiments carried two flags or colours: the King's colour was a union flag, normally bearing his cypher in the centre (regiments were not numbered at this time); while the regimental colour had the union in the canton and displayed a device or emblem of some kind in the centre of an otherwise plain sheet corresponding to the regimental facings. This device was usually chosen by the colonel and often based on his own coat of arms. Sometimes the device was a 'traditional' one, as in the case of Shannon's Regiment, which may have had a representation of Edinburgh Castle. Unfortunately regimental colours or standards at this early period are very poorly recorded.

Cavalry

Thomas Pitt's Horse

Old regiment raised in 1685, latterly known as the Queen's Bays and designated the 2nd Dragoon Guards by 1751. Served in Spain during Queen Anne's War and at Preston under General Wills in 1715.

- Red coats, buff facings

- Known officers included:

Lieutenant-Colonel James Otway	Captain George Walker
Major Richard Whitworth	Captain-Lieutenant Peter Naizon
Captain William Cosby	Lieutenant William Bland
Captain James Dambon	Lieutenant Nicholas Hutchinson
Captain Thomas Ligoe	Lieutenant Andrew Rankine
Captain Francis Naizon	Cornet William Boyle

George, Lord Carpenter's Dragoons

Old regiment raised in 1685 and designated 3rd or King's Own Dragoons by 1751. Served in Spain during Queen Anne's War. Served in North East England under Carpenter and the closing stages of the Battle of Preston. Afterwards in Scotland and serving in garrison at Elgin by February 1716.

- Red coats, blue facings

- Known officers included:

Lieutenant-Colonel Joshua Guest[1]

Major Samuel Foley (brevet lieutenant-colonel)

Captain Thomas Browne

Captain Alexander Mullins

Captain Alexander Read

Lieutenant John Hoare

Lieutenant John Smelt

Lieutenant William Smelt

Cornet Thomas Haley

Cornet John Hawksworth

Cornet William Kerr

Cornet William Ogle

Cornet Erasmus Shorter

Adjutant Philip Carpenter

Charles Churchill's Dragoons

Raised in 1715 and served with General Carpenter in northeast England and disbanded in 1718.

- Red coats but otherwise no information on uniform

- Known officers included:

Captain James Ballentine

Captain Richard Roberts

Lieutenant Stephen Otway

Richard, Lord Cobham's Dragoons

Old regiment raised in 1683, and subsequently known as 1st or Royal Dragoons. Served in Spain during Queen Anne's War and with General Carpenter in North East England in 1715.

- Red coats, dark blue facings

- Known officers included:

Lieutenant-Colonel Edward Montague (brevet colonel)

Captain John Wyvell

Captain-Lieutenant Thomas Rogers

Lieutenant Ernest Shackman

Lieutenant Samuel Southouse

Cornet William Brooks

Cornet Henry Carlisle

Cornet Charles Dilks

James Dormer's Dragoons

Raised in July 1715 and designated 14th Dragoons by 1751. Served at Preston under General Wills.[2]

- Red coats, light yellow facings

- Known officers included:

Lieutenant-Colonel Henry Killigrew

Major Solomon Rapin

Captain William Boyle

Captain Beverly Newcommin

Captain Henry Pelham

Captain-Lieutenant James Stevens

Lieutenant Peter Davenport

Lieutenant James Fleming

Lieutenant Henry Lasale

Lieutenant Jonathan Perk

Lieutenant Cuthbert Smith

Cornet Thomas Dalahaye

Cornet Thomas Ellis

Cornet Andrew Forrester

Cornet William Hamilton

Cornet Rigby Molyneux

Cornet Edward Strode

William Evans's Dragoons

Old regiment raised in 1685 and designated 4th Dragoons by 1751. Served in Spain and in Flanders during Queen Anne's War. Served at Sheriffmuir, where badly shot up, and afterwards was in garrison at Montrose.

- Red coats, green facings

- Known officers included:

Lieutenant-Colonel Henry Hawley
(brevet colonel)[3]

Major Charles Lanoe

Captain John Farrer[4]

Captain Edward Hill

Captain Berkeley Knox

Captain-Lieutenant Edward Hawley

Lieutenant Thomas Bickerton

Lieutenant George Colley

Lieutenant John Olivier

Cornet John Baynton

Cornet John Cavendish

Cornet John Curfie

Philip Honeywood's Dragoons

Raised in July 1715 and designated 11th Dragoons by 1751. Served at Preston under General Wills.[5]

- Red coats, buff facings

- Known officers included:

Lieutenant-Colonel Alexander Hamilton

Major Humphrey Bland[6]

Captain Benjamin Huffam

Captain William Robinson

Captain John Suckling

Captain-Lieutenant John Maitland

Lieutenant Charles Leman

Lieutenant Malin

Lieutenant James Maule

Lieutenant John Mitchell

Lieutenant Charles Stewart

Cornet William Robert Adair

Cornet John Burroughs

Cornet John Campbell

Cornet William Gardiner

Cornet Watts

Cornet Charles Wheeler

William Kerr's Dragoons

Old regiment raised in Scotland in 1690, and served in Flanders during Queen Anne's War. Ordered to be reduced in 1714, but two troops were transferred to Royal Dragoons and three to the Scots Greys, respectively. All five were subsequently reclaimed as a nucleus to rebuild the regiment in a royal warrant dated 3 February 1715. Designated 7th Dragoons by 1751. Served at Sheriffmuir and afterwards in Fife.

- Red coats, white facings

- Known officers included:

Lieutenant-Colonel James Sandilands,
    Lord Torphichen

Major Matthew Stewart

Captain William Crawford

Captain Lewis Dollon

Captain George Dunbar

Captain James Livingston

Captain Peter Renourd

Lieutenant James Ogilvie

Cornet James Agnew

Cornet and Adjutant William Johnstone

Richard Molesworth's Dragoons

Raised in 1715. Served with General Carpenter in northeast England. Disbanded 1718.

- Red coats, but otherwise no information on uniform

- Known officers included:

Captain Lord Henry Paulet

Lieutenant Alexander Knapton

Lieutenant George Malcolm

Lieutenant John Stourbridge

Richard Munden's Dragoons

Raised in July 1715 and designated 13th Dragoons by 1751. Served at Preston under General Wills.[7]

- Red coats, deep green facings

- Known officers included:

Lieutenant-Colonel Clement Neville

Major Samuel Freeman

Captain Heblethwaite

Captain Francis Howard

Captain Lutton Lister

Captain-Lieutenant Henry de Grangues

Lieutenant Philip Bridgeman

Lieutenant Henry Dawson

Lieutenant Francis Hull

Lieutenant Thomas Mason

Lieutenant John Molyneux

Cornet Gerald Fitzgerald

Cornet William Freeman

Cornet Charles Greenwood

Cornet Martin O'Bryan

Cornet John Watson

Cornet William Williamson

William Newton's Dragoons

Raised in 1715. Served in England but assigned as a garrison for Manchester and not present at Preston. Afterwards served in Scotland and latterly in garrison at Dundee. Disbanded 1718.

- Red coats but otherwise no information on uniform

- Known officers included:

Captain Samuel Speed

Lieutenant Thomas Carfrae

Lieutenant William Higginson

David, Earl of Portmore's Dragoons

Old regiment raised in Scotland in 1681, and otherwise known as the Grey Dragoons or the Royal Scots Greys. Designated 2nd Dragoons by 1751. Served in Germany and Flanders during Queen Anne's War. Served with some distinction under Argyle in Scotland, notably at Sheriffmuir and in Fife.

- Red coats, dark blue facings. All ranks were entitled to wear grenadier caps with the star of St Andrew embroidered on the front

- Known officers included:

Lieutenant-Colonel Charles, Lord
    Cathcart

Major Sir Robert Hay

Captain Thomas Agnew

Captain George Armstrong[8]

Captain James Gardiner[9]

Captain Patrick Robertson[10]

Captain Henry Selwyn

Lieutenant Andrew King

Lieutenant James Lothian

Lieutenant Charles Skene

Cornet John Bennet[11]

Cornet Thomas Cochrane

Cornet Alexander Forbes

Cornet George Knox

Cornet William Lawrence

John, Earl of Stair's Dragoons

Old regiment raised in Ireland in 1689 and otherwise known as the Inniskillings. Designated 6th Dragoons by 1751. In Ireland during Queen Anne's War. Fought at Sheriffmuir and by February 1716 was in garrison at Aberdeen.

* Red coats, yellow facings

* Known officers included:

Lieutenant-Colonel John Upton	Lieutenant Gervase Sibthorpe
Captain Augustus Duquery	Cornet John Burrell
Captain James Dumas	Cornet Philip Gasteen
Captain Lawrence Nugent	Cornet John Hay
Captain Alway Serjeant	Cornet William Kennedy
Captain-Lieutenant Montague Farrer	Cornet William Nugent
Lieutenant Edward Loftus	Cornet Henry Strudwick
Lieutenant Francis Mears	Adjutant Robert Wigham

Philip Stanhope's Dragoons

Raised in 1715. Fought at Preston under General Wills and afterwards came north to Scotland, latterly serving as part of the Edinburgh garrison. Disbanded in 1718.

* Red coats but otherwise no information on uniforms

* Known officers included:

Major Richard Manning	Captain-Lieutenant Marcellus Laroon

Owen Wynn's Dragoons

Raised in July 1715 and designated 9th Dragoons by 1751. Served at Preston under General Wills.[12]

* Red coats, buff facings

* Known officers included:

Lieutenant-Colonel H. Pearson	Lieutenant Jacob Warnes
Major John Dunbar	Lieutenant Edward Whitney
Captain Knox	Cornet Christopher Adams
Captain Lord Leslie	Cornet William Carleton
Captain Henry Smith	Cornet Lewis Folliot
Captain-Lieutenant Crawford	Cornet James Hill
Lieutenant Gustavus Hamilton	Cornet Pemberton
Lieutenant William Humphreys	Cornet Owen Wynne

Foot

Colonel Alexander Campbell's Independent Company

One of three independent companies serving in Scotland at the commencement of the rising. Apparently had an original establishment of 123 men besides officers, sergeants and drummers, but Treasury papers revealed that this was augmented by a further eighty-seven men during the rebellion.

- Clothed in tartan but no indication as to whether wearing trews or just plaids

Jasper Clayton's Regiment

Old regiment raised in 1685 and designated 14th Foot by 1751. Saw only garrison duty in Ireland during Queen Anne's War. Fought at Sheriffmuir in Clayton's Brigade and latterly in garrison at Dunkeld.

- Red coats with buff facings

- Known officers included:

Lieutenant-Colonel John Nicholson
Captain William Barlow[13]
Captain Thomas Harrison
Captain Stanley Monck
Captain Michael Moret[14]
Lieutenant Edward Gibson[15]

Lieutenant Robert Hansard
Lieutenant George Heighington
Lieutenant Charles Standish
Ensign John Scrivenor
Ensign Richard Sinnot

William Egerton's Regiment

Old regiment raised in 1701 and designated 36th Foot by 1751. Served in Spain and later on the abortive Quebec expedition during Queen Anne's War. Fought in Grant's Brigade at Sheriffmuir and afterwards in garrison at Dumbarton.

- Red coats, green facings

- Known officers included:

Lieutenant-Colonel Robert Innes (brevet colonel)
Major William Hargrave
Captain John Dancer[16]
Captain Francis Fleming
Captain Fitzherbert Tempest
Captain Arthur Whitmore

Lieutenant James Hurst
Lieutenant Roger Irwyn
Lieutenant John Joyce
Lieutenant James Sell
Lieutenant William Tonge
Ensign Samuel Cutts
Ensign John Hargrave

Ensign John Hope

Ensign Nicholls

Ensign Hugh Murray

Ensign Edward Whitmore

Archibald, Earl of Forfar's Foot

Old regiment, originally raised in London for the Dutch service as far back as 1572 and then in the British service since 1665. Designated 3rd Foot by 1751 and well known as the Buffs. Served in Flanders during Queen Anne's War and in Forfar's Brigade at Sheriffmuir in 1715.

* Red coats with buff facings. Colours bore a green dragon in the centre

* Known officers included:

Lieutenant-Colonel John Slaughter

Lieutenant William Reed

Major Francis Williamson

Lieutenant Thomas Seaman

Captain James Bolton

Lieutenant Benjamin Smith

Captain George Grant

Lieutenant Samuel Wilson

Captain Gilbert Talbot

Ensign ( ) Branch[17]

Captain-Lieutenant Richard Lowther

Ensign John Hayward

Lieutenant Charles Barnes

Ensign William Littler

Lieutenant Abraham Lambe

Ensign Samuel Stone

Lieutenant Robert Melville

Brigadier Alexander Grant's Regiment

Raised in Scotland in 1715 perhaps around a nucleus of an earlier regiment, which had been reduced in 1714. It initially served as garrison of Edinburgh, but later took part in Argyle's advance on Perth and subsequent pursuit of the rebels. Transferred to Irish establishment and disbanded in 1718.

* Red coats, but otherwise no information on uniform. A contemporary reference to their wearing tartan actually related to the Independent Company raised by Colonel William Grant, not to the regular regiment. Later regiments raised by the Lairds of Grant had green facings, but assignment of this facing colour to the 1715 regiment is speculative

* Known officers included:

Lieutenant-Colonel William Cecil

Lieutenant Alexander Cumming

Captain Charles Elphinstone

Lieutenant George Halfhide

Captain Lewis Grant

Lieutenant John Rutherford

Captain Hugh Sempill[18]

Lieutenant John Stirling

Lieutenant George Brodie

Ensign Alexander Bruce

Lieutenant Alexander Corbet

Ensign Alexander Graham

Ensign James Grant   Ensign Anthony Robinson
Ensign Charles Jeffreys

Colonel William Grant's Independent Company

One of three independent companies serving in Scotland at the commencement of the rising. Apparently had an original establishment of 123 men besides officers, sergeants and drummers, but Treasury papers revealed this was augmented by a further eighty-seven men during the rebellion. Served in north and at the taking of Inverness.

• Clothed in tartan

Sir Charles Hotham's Regiment

Raised in 1715. Served as garrison of Newcastle upon Tyne. Disbanded in 1718.

• Red coats but otherwise no information on uniforms

• Known officers included:

Lieutenant-Colonel Fairfax Norcliffe   Lieutenant Thomas Constable
Captain James Brandon   Lieutenant Jonathan Smith
Captain James Gee   Ensign James Blair
Lieutenant James Berbet   Ensign Richard Povey

Richard, Lord Irwin's Regiment

Old regiment raised in 1688 and designated 16th Foot by 1751. Served in Flanders during Queen Anne's War. Served as garrison of Fort William throughout the rising.

• Red coats, yellow facings

• Known officers included:

Lieutenant-Colonel John Cholmley   Lieutenant George Richardson
Captain William Hook   Lieutenant Richard Worthington
Captain-Lieutenant John Whiting   Ensign Arthur Northcote
Lieutenant Robert Bradford   Quartermaster John Smith
Lieutenant George Collingwood

Colonel Robert Monroe's Independent Company

One of three independent companies serving in Scotland at the commencement of the rising. Apparently had an original establishment of 123 men besides officers, sergeants and drummers, but Treasury papers revealed this was augmented by a further eighty-seven men during the rebellion. Served in the north and at the taking of Inverness, where Monroe was established as governor.

Edward Montagu's Foot

Old regiment raised in 1685 and designated 11th Foot by 1751. Served in Spain and on Quebec expedition during Queen Anne's War and afterwards as garrison of Fort William until summer 1715. Fought at Sheriffmuir in Clayton's Brigade, then remained in garrison at Stirling.

- Red coats, green facings

- Known officers included:

  Lieutenant-Colonel Herbert Lawrence[19]   Lieutenant William Horneck[23]
  Major Charles Irvine   Lieutenant William Mortimer[24]
  Captain ( ) Bernard[20]   Lieutenant Benjamin Snow
  Captain Henry Domerque   Lieutenant Thomas Stephens
  Captain Richard Edwards[21]   Ensign Robert Brown
  Captain Thomas Humble[22]   Ensign Christopher Irvine
  Captain Richard Tracey   Ensign Lewis La Forrest
  Lieutenant Samuel Cherry   Ensign Edward Mann
  Lieutenant James Corde   Ensign Thomas Thurland
  Lieutenant James Franks   Quartermaster Lancelot Story

Henry Morrison's Regiment

Old regiment raised in 1685. Served in Flanders during Queen Anne's War. Fought at Sheriffmuir in Clayton's Brigade and afterwards in garrison at Glasgow. Subsequently granted title 'The King's Regiment' and designated as 8th Foot by 1751.

- Red coats and yellow facings at this period, but later had blue facings as King's Regiment

- Known officers included: Captain Edmund De Fisher
  Lieutenant-Colonel Peter Hamars[25]   Captain John Farcy
  Captain James Beschefer   Captain Arthur Usher
  Captain Benjamin Cuttle   Captain Borlace Webb

Lieutenant Ball
Lieutenant John Chambers[26]
Lieutenant Robert Elliot[27]
Lieutenant Theophilus Nicholls
Lieutenant Richard Kenny
Lieutenant Thomas Redwood

Lieutenant John Turner
Ensign Justin Holdman[28]
Ensign Thomas Sydenham
Ensign Charles Tilbourg[29]
Adjutant William Boyd

Earl of Orrery's Regiment

Old regiment raised by the previous Earl of Mar in Scotland in 1678. Otherwise known as the Royal Scots Fusiliers and numbered as 21st Foot by 1751. Served in Flanders during Queen Anne's War. Fought at Sheriffmuir in Grant's Brigade and eventually in garrison at Inverness.

- Red coats, dark blue facings. All ranks in fusilier caps – similar to grenadier caps, with star of St Andrew on front. Colours carried thistle badge in centre on a red roundel surrounded by a green strap bearing the motto *Nemo Me Impune Lacessit*

- Known officers included:

Lieutenant-Colonel William Murray
Major Gabriel Montresor
Captain Walter Cheissly[30]
Captain Thomas Don
Captain George Home
Captain George Jackson
Captain Anthony Lowther
Captain Robert Urquhart[31]
Lieutenant Philip Bassett
Lieutenant David Brymer
Lieutenant Charles Clarke
Lieutenant James Cumming
Lieutenant Lewis Dick

Lieutenant Laurence Drummond
Lieutenant James Graham
Lieutenant Robert Harris
Lieutenant ( ) Hay[32]
Lieutenant Richard Hayward[33]
Lieutenant Mungo Matthew
Lieutenant Robert Mitchelson[34]
Lieutenant James Murray
Lieutenant William Nodding
Lieutenant William Ross
Lieutenant Francis Skene
Lieutenant Charles Swan

George Preston's Regiment

Old regiment raised in Scotland in 1689, otherwise known as the Cameronians and designated as 26th Foot by 1751. Served in Flanders during Queen Anne's War. Fought at Preston under General Wills.

- Red coats, light yellow facings

- Known officers included:

Lieutenant-Colonel George Baillie,
   Lord Forrester[35]
Major James Lawson[36]
Captain Alexander Ogilvie[37]
Captain Robert Preston[38]
Captain Wadham Sprague
Captain William St Clair (grenadiers)
Lieutenant Robert Barclay
Lieutenant John Blair (grenadiers)
Lieutenant Alexander
Lieutenant John Colville
Lieutenant William Dunston

Lieutenant William Dyer
Lieutenant William Ferguson
Lieutenant James Gordon
Lieutenant Francis Graham
Lieutenant Robert Pringle
Ensign George Browne
Ensign Charles Colville
Ensign William Elphinstone
Ensign Richard Harris
Ensign William Russell
Ensign Francis Scott

Richard, Lord Shannon's Regiment

Old regiment raised in Scotland in 1689 and otherwise known as the Edinburgh Regiment. Designated the 25th Foot by 1751 and latterly titled the King's Own Scottish Borderers. Fought at Sheriffmuir in Forfar's Brigade, and by February 1716 was in garrison at Aberdeen.

- Red coats, yellow facings

- Known officers included:

Lieutenant-Colonel John Middleton
Major John Grace
Captain Alexander Arnott[39]
Captain James Biggar
Captain John Broughton
Captain Acclom Milbanke
Captain Patrick Ronald
Captain Robert Walkinshaw
Captain-Lieutenant Robert Scott
Lieutenant Robert Alexander
Lieutenant and Quartermaster Robert
   Douglas

Lieutenant David Lawrence
Lieutenant Charles Maitland
Lieutenant Robert Middleton
Lieutenant Alexander Moncrieff
Lieutenant Abraham Satyre
Ensign Alexander Brown
Ensign Charles Maitland (jnr)
Ensign John Maitland
Ensign William Miller
Ensign Henry Stapylton
Ensign Charles Wilkie

Thomas Stanwix's Regiment

Raised July 1715 and employed as garrison of Carlisle. Disbanded 1718.

- Known officers included:

Lieutenant-Colonel Thomas Weld
Major James Harestreet

Captain John Carney
Captain Patrick, Lord Oliphant

Lieutenant Robert Charge
Lieutenant Robert Eaglesfield

Ensign Francis Martin
Ensign Jeremiah Tully

James Wightman's Regiment

Old regiment raised in 1688 and designated the 17th Foot by 1751. Served in Flanders during Queen Anne's War. Fought at Sheriffmuir in Forfar's Brigade and latterly in garrison at Perth

* Red coats, white facings

* Known officers included:

Lieutenant-Colonel Oliver Brook
Major Christopher Russell (brevet
    lieutenant-colonel)
Captain Andrew Pope
Captain John Rivason
Captain John Smyth (grenadiers)
Captain-Lieutenant Edward Tyrell
Lieutenant John Beaumont
Lieutenant William Cobb (grenadiers)

Lieutenant Roger Pedley
Ensign Andrew Booth
Ensign Henry Brisco
Ensign Edward Crofts
Ensign ( ) Mark[40]
Ensign Gregory Milner
Ensign Thomas Morris
Ensign John Withers
Adjutant Christopher Forster

Charles Wills's Regiment

Old regiment originally raised as marines in 1702 but remustered as a regular infantry regiment in 1715 and designated the 30th Foot by 1751. Served in Spain during Queen Anne's War. Not active in early part of campaign, but in garrison at Aberdeen by February 1716.

* Red coats, light yellow facings

* Known officers included:

Lieutenant-Colonel George Burston
Major Charles Williams
Captain Michael Midford
Lieutenant Henry Aylmer
Lieutenant Patrick Aylmer
Lieutenant William Cook
Lieutenant Thomas Daws
Lieutenant John Hobart

Lieutenant Edmund Martyn
Lieutenant William Prichard
Lieutenant Edmund Quarles
Lieutenant Teddeman Roberts
Lieutenant John Roper
Lieutenant Ventris Scott
Lieutenant Benjamin Sladden

Dutch Regiments

The Dutch units listed below served in Scotland, largely on garrison duty in early 1716.[41]

- At this period most Dutch infantry wore grey coats, usually but not invariably with blue facings, waistcoats and breeches. The Swiss regiments wore dark blue coats with red facings

- The Dutch regiments were:
  Regiment Chambrier (Swiss)   Regiment Slippenbeck
  Regiment Cronstrom   Regiment Smith
  Regiment Maye (Swiss – two battalions)   Regiment Sturler (Swiss)
  Regiment Palant   Regiment Welderen
  Regiment Raytan   Regiment Zoutland

A Particular List

of the Names of the Gentlemen Prisoners, Brought to the Castle of Stirling, 14 November 1715[1]

Lord Strathallan
[Walkinshaw of] Barrowfield
Mr Murray of Auchtertyre
Mr Thomas Drummond, brother to the Viscount of Strathallan
Mr Drummond of Drumquhary
Captain William Creighton
Mr John Ross, son to the Archbishop of St Andrews
Mr Nairn of Baldwale
Mr William Hay
John Gordon, captain
William Forbes, lieutenant
Archibald Fotheringhame, lieutenant
Alexander Garrioch, ensign
Jn. Carnegie, surgeon
Nicol. Donalson, ensign
Alex. Steuart of Innerslawie, forester to the Duke of Athole
Neil McGlasson, chamberlain to the Duke of Athole
James Steuart, lieutenant
William Adamson, lieutenant
James Robertson, lieutenant
James Gordon, surgeon
David Gardin, captain of Panmure's Regiment

Kenneth Mackenzie, nephew to Sir Alexander Mackenzie of Coull
Charles Gardin of Bittistern
John McLean, adjutant to Colonel Mackenzie's Regiment
Colin Mackenzie of Kildin, captain of Fairburn's Regiment [?]

Mr John Rattray	Mr Donald McPherson
Peter Steuart	John Morgan
George Taylor	Donald Robertson
Duncan McIntosh	Robert Menzies
James Peddie	Will. Menzies
John Forbes	John Menzies
Alexander Steuart	Will. Menzies
Donald Mitchel	Will. Steuart
Francis Finlay	Alex. McLachland
James Lyon	Patrick Campbell
Auchterlony	Hugh McRaw
Lewis Crammond	Donald McRaw
William Steuart	Christopher McRae
George Mear	John Lesley
Hector McLean	James Edgar
Alexander Mill	James Mill
John McIntosh	John Gordon
Robert McIntosh	Donald McMurrie
Hugh Calder	Murdoch McPherson
James Innes	Alexander Cameron
Donald McNauchtie	Robert Miller
Ewan McLachlan	Adam Grinsell
Ewan McDonald	Angus Steuart
Donald Robertson	John Robertson
James Keoch	John Cattinach
Thomas Robertson	John Richie, merchant in Edinburgh
Alexander Morison	
Andrew Jamison	

Captain Charles Chalmers, late of the Foot Guards, one of the Earl of
    Mar's Majors

Notes

Chapter 1

1 The best (and most indispensable) modern study of the subject is Professor Daniel Szechi, *1715: The Great Jacobite Rebellion*, London & Yale, Yale University Press, 2006.

2 Acts of the Parliament of Scotland, vol. ix, p. 5. See also Paul Hopkins, *Glencoe and the End of the Highland War*, Edinburgh, John Donald, 1986, for a good modern account of the crisis and what followed.

3 Sophia was the daughter of Elizabeth Stuart, the 'Winter Queen' of Bohemia and eldest daughter of James VI. She was also, as it happens, the sister of the one-time cavalier commander Prince Rupert.

4 Szechi, pp. 40–4.

5 Szechi, pp. 86–7.

6 Just as the famous Seven Men of Moidart in 1745 were far from alone, being accompanied by their valets and other equally anonymous servants, so too were Mar and Hamilton. Exactly how many went with them is unknown, but, according to an intelligence report, as they landed 'one of his principall servants dropt over a Plank which was laid from the boat on a Rock and was drowned in the sea'.

7 In the middle of the river Quoich (a tributary of the Dee, just above Braemar) is a large stone hollowed out by erosion to form a natural cauldron, known as the Devil's Punch Bowl, and it was in this cavity that the punch to toast the rising was brewed.

Chapter 2

1 There was however a Royal Irish Artillery and minor ceremonial units such as the Battle-axe Guards of Ireland.

2 Sir John Fortescue, *History of the British Army*, London, Macmillan, 1899, vol. II, pp. 3–7 cites fifteen regiments of foot. While the officers commissions in six additional regiments were certainly renewed by George I in 1715, it is rather less certain whether they had been reduced or at least earmarked for reduction beforehand.

3   Kerr's (later the 7th Dragoons) were something of an anomaly in that, although the regiment was broken in 1714, five of the troops were not disbanded but transferred to other units, before being reunited as the cadre of a reconstituted regiment enjoying their old seniority.

4   The army belonged of course to the Crown, but the individual regiments were raised and maintained by their commanding officers, who were granted all manner of privileges, allowances and perquisites to do so.

5   Scottish Record Office, *State Papers Scotland* (photocopy vols), RH 2/4/306/92.

6   As described this represents what might be regarded as the ideal. The number of platoons could vary according the strength of the battalion. Less than twenty men was regarded as ineffectual and more than thirty uncontrollable, hence the need to number them off on the day.

7   It may be as well to mention that the distinction between carbines as carried by Horse and muskets as carried by Dragoons lay only in the fact that carbines had a smaller bore and were not capable of being fitted with a bayonet. Otherwise there was very little difference in size. Both were long-barrelled weapons.

8   A. J. Guy, *Oeconomy and Discipline; Officership and Administration in the British Army 1714–63*, Manchester, Manchester University Press, 1985, p. 125.

9   This militia was still designated by the archaic designation 'Trained Band', which reflected the fact that they met periodically for some genteel training. As such they are to be distinguished from the full-time city guard and Edinburgh Volunteers.

10   James Allardyce, *Historical Papers Relating to the Jacobite Period 1699–1750*, Aberdeen, New Spalding Club, 1895, vol. 1, p. 39.

Chapter 3

1   The letter was later widely published as anti-Jacobite propaganda in a contemporary pamphlet: Anon., *A Collection of Original Letters and Authentick Papers Relating to the Rebellion 1715*, Edinburgh, 1730, pp. 13–15.

2   Allardyce, vol. 1, pp. 55–6. Notwithstanding this testimony they were deported to Maryland in 1716. See Frances McDonnell, *Jacobites of 1715 North East Scotland*, Baltimore, Genealogical Publishing, 2000, p. 22.

3   Both were freeholders of land. A heritor was someone who owned land by inheritance, while a wadsetter was one who obtained it by means of a wadset or mortgage.

4   Allardyce, vol. 1, pp. 50–1. The council also nominated the officers of the troop, viz: Captain John Bannerman to be captain, David Adie to be lieutenant, Robert Burnett junior to be cornet and Alexander Bannerman quartermaster.

5   Patrick Lyon of Auchterhouse, who had served in the last Scots parliament 1702–7, representing the Forfarshire barons. He would be killed at Sheriffmuir.

6   John Walkinshaw of Barrowfield, near Glasgow; his youngest daughter, Clementina, would become the mistress of Bonnie Prince Charlie.

7   John Sinclair, *Memoirs of the Insurrection in Scotland in 1715*, Edinburgh, Abbotsford Club, 1858, pp. 50–1, 78.

8   Sinclair, p. 73. Presumably, if Drummond was allowing ten companies for each of his three

battalions, they would each have numbered only twenty men.

9 Sinclair, pp. 83–4.

10 Strictly speaking he was captain-lieutenant of Preston's Regiment, the Cameronians, and so a colleague of Colonel Blackadder. The curious title reflected his position as lieutenant to the company notionally commanded by the regiment's colonel. As that worthy obviously had more important things to worry about, command of his company devolved entirely upon his lieutenant, who ranked as the regiment's junior captain for his pains. Sinclair rose no higher, because he was cashiered after successively killing two brothers named Schaw in duels. Curiously the third and surviving brother succeeded him as captain-lieutenant of the regiment.

11 What was meant by 'using them to the Drum' was getting them used to the noise of drums being beaten, which might otherwise upset them, and hopefully inure them to other loud noises such as gunfire.

12 National Archives, Kew (NA), SP 54/8/3.

13 Sinclair, p. 12.

14 Sinclair, p. 191.

15 Allardyce, vol. 1, pp. 40–1. There was nothing illegal about their holding this quantity of powder in stock, and so proper compensation was paid, or at least promised, for what was taken. Most of it was promptly shipped to Edinburgh for safekeeping, but half a ton was retained for the use of the town's militia and subsequently fell into rebel hands.

16 Sinclair, p. 45.

17 Anon., *A Collection of Original Letters*, pp. 77–8; Allardyce, vol. 1, p. 43.

18 Robert Patten, *The History of the Late Rebellion: With Original Papers and Characters of the Principal Noblemen and Gentlemen Concern'd in It*, 3rd edn, London, 1745, p. 161.

19 A. Francis Steuart (ed.), *Newsletters of 1715–16*, Edinburgh, 1910, p. 70. The same account also reckoned they were fifteen deep, but that was presumably before they had deployed from column into line.

20 HMC, *3rd Report: MSS of the Duke of Montrose*, 1872, pp. 384–5.

21 A tack was a lease, and tacksmen were leaseholders, although almost invariably hereditary ones holding their land of the chieftain in return not only for an annual rental but also an obligation for military service.

22 Loch Lomond Expedition MDCCXV, quoted in John Baynes, *The Jacobite Rising of 1715*, London, Cassell, 1970, pp. 57–8.

23 Although obviously relating to an earlier period this is graphically illustrated in the surviving 1638 wapinschaw returns for five parishes in Atholl. These listed exactly what arms were carried by each landholder and his men. As might be expected, while there were some considerable variations, generally speaking only the head of household was possessed of the full panoply of musket, sword and targe. His men usually had dirks and sometimes muskets but were otherwise rarely as well equipped and all too often quite unarmed. See John, 7th Duke of Athole, *Chronicles of the Atholl & Tullibardine Families*, Edinburgh, privately published, 5 vols, 1908, appendices x–xx.

24 James Keith, *A Fragment of a Memoir of Field-Marshal James Keith, Written by Himself, 1714–1734*, Aberdeen, Spalding Club, 1853, pp. 21–2.

Chapter 4

1 This was not a territorial earldom, but the hereditary office of Earl Marischal of Scotland. Consequently Keith (and his forebears) was never familiarly referred to as Marischal, as say the Earl of Southesk would commonly be called Southesk, but always as the Marischal.

2 Anon., *A Collection of Original Letters*, p. 15.

3 The site is now occupied by the Invercauld Arms hotel.

4 Not to be confused, as he so often is, with his father, John Farquharson of Inverey, the infamous Black Colonel, who had died in 1705.

5 James Steuart of Annat, near Doune in Perthshire, began his military career in Dumbarton's Regiment (the Royal Scots) and was appointed a lieutenant in Claverhouse's Royal Regiment of Horse in 1684, but defected to Dutch William in 1689. Subsequently served in the Scots Troop of Lifeguards until resigning in 1703 to take up the post of lieutenant-governor of Edinburgh Castle. See Charles Dalton, *The Scots Army 1661–1688*, London, Eyre & Spottiswoode, 1909, p. 136. See also: K. A. Moody-Stuart, 'Lieutenant Colonel James Steuart: A Jacobite Lieutenant Governor of Edinburgh Castle', *Scottish Historical Review*, vol. XXI, no. 81 (1924).

6 Islay to Lord Townshend, quoted in Baynes, p. 47.

7 Appointed 14 April 1712, but out of the regiment by 24 March 1714. Perhaps significantly his company commander was Lieutenant Colonel John Steuart. See Dalton, *English Army Lists and Commission Registers*, vol. 6, London, Eyre & Spottiswoode, 1904, pp. 60, 62.

8 Sinclair, pp. 30–1.

9 HMC, *3rd Report: MSS of the Duke of Montrose*, p. 378.

10 A 'stand of arms' comprised a musket, bayonet, sling and tools.

11 Appointed on 20 April 1714. Technically he was only a captain, but as such his superior status as a guardsman was marked by an automatic brevet as lieutenant-colonel. See Dalton, *English Army*, p. 51.

12 Sinclair, p. 40.

13 Sinclair, p. 45. The fifty Highlanders were those of Athole's people, who elected to throw in their lot with the rebels.

14 A captain in Stanwix's Regiment, one of those broken at the peace.

15 Tullibardine's battalion fought at Sheriffmuir, Nairne's and Lord Charles Murray's at Preston, while Lord George Murray's missed both while collecting the cess in Fife.

16 The Grants of Glenmoriston, and those of Shewglie and Corrimony in Glen Urquhart were tenants and in theory vassals of Brigadier Alexander Grant of Grant, but they appear to have made a career of defying him and following Glengarry.

17 Anon., *A Collection of Original Letters*, p. 23.

18 Anon., *A Collection of Original Letters*, pp. 48–9.

19 Anon., *The Loch Lomond Expedition with Some Short Reflections on the Perth Manifesto*, Glasgow, 1715.

Chapter 5

1 Sinclair, p. 157; HMC, *Mar & Kellie MSS*, 1904, p. 51.

2   Anon., *A Collection of Original Letters*, p. 60.

3   Sinclair, p. 103.

4   James Malcolm of Grange, a prominent Fife Jacobite, who was unsurprisingly often at odds with Sinclair both before and during the rising.

5   Sinclair, pp. 95–103. A long Scots mile is 1,983 yards, while an ordinary 'English' mile is 1,760 yards. Sinclair therefore reckoned on a round trip of about forty-five miles.

6   If the higher number is correct it would indicate that a number of Invercauld's men had indeed chosen to join Mar's Regiment rather than follow him into Mackintosh's.

Chapter 6

1   Anon., *A Collection of Original Letters*, p. 60.

2   Anon., *Jurnall of the Proceedings of the Army in Rebbellion under E. of Mar*, City Archives, Edinburgh, n.d. It reads as if the author was a member of Lord Strathallan's battalion, and, if written in the third person, was most likely Major Thomas Arthur.

3   Drummond of Logiealmond.

4   Steuart, pp. 38–9. For reasons to be discussed later they almost certainly belonged to Logie Drummond's battalion.

5   Patten, p. 11.

6   Patten, pp. 120–2 for list of Scots officers who surrendered at Preston.

7   Mar to Viscount Kenmure, dated 21 October 1715 and quoted in Sinclair, p. 145 and Patten, p. 58. Both this letter and a similar one to the Northumbrian leader Thomas Forster of the same date were intercepted.

8   Steuart, p. 44.

9   Steuart, p. 42.

10 Steuart, pp. 43–4. Patten gave Argyle considerably more infantry including detachments from Shannon's Regiment and the Royal Scots Fusiliers, but this seems to reflect what the Jacobites believed they were up against and may have contributed to their hasty departure.

11 Peter Rae, *The History of the Rebellion, Rais'd Against His Majesty King George I. By the Friends of the Popish Pretender*, 2nd edn, London, 1746, pp. 262–3. It was evidently regarded as a successful speech, for Mar later alluded to it in correspondence with Lord Kenmuir and the Northumbrian leader, Thomas Forster.

12 Patten, p. 10.

13 Rae, p. 265.

14 Patten, pp. 11–12.

Chapter 7

1   Rae, pp. 246–7.

2   Rae, p. 248.

3   Patten, slightly confusingly, said that they set up the standard at Moffat before marching to Dumfries, but then just a few lines later very firmly declared that Lochmaben was the first town on that side of the Forth where the standard was raised and the Pretender proclaimed (Patten, pp. 26–7). The rising certainly 'began' at Moffat, but it rather sounds as if the

intention was to raise the standard formally for the first time in the much more prestigious surroundings of Dumfries.

4   Rae, p. 255.

5   Patten, p. 36. He himself was not present at this time, but was to traverse the route later.

6   Patten, p. 97.

7   Patten, p. 18.

8   Patten, p. 20.

9   Errington and his brother successfully escaped from jail by tunnelling under the wall and then getting out of the town in disguise.

10 Patten, p. 21.

11 Colliers were what we would now call miners, but were often at this date still working open coal pits rather than deep mines, while keelmen carried the coal downriver on barge-like vessels termed keelboats.

12 Patten, p. 30.

13 Patten is of course speaking of the total number intended to be shipped across, rather than Logie Drummond's battalion alone.

14 Patten, pp. 42–6.

15 The Merse is a low-lying area on the eastern end of the border, bounded by the river Tweed on the south and the Lammermuir Hills on the north. It has a strong local identity, and military units raised there were traditionally known by that designation rather than the name of their commander – as was common elsewhere in Scotland.

Chapter 8

1   HMC, *Mar & Kellie MSS*, pp. 512–13.

2   Jonathan Oates, 'The armies operating in northern England during the Jacobite rebellion of 1715', *Journal of the Society for Army Historical Research*, vol. 90, no. 362 (summer 2012).

3   Sinclair, p. 191.

4   Rae, p. 271.

5   Patten, pp. 53–4.

6   Patten, p. 56.

7   Cited in Szechi, p. 173.

8   Patten, pp. 56–7.

9   National Archives, Kings Bench 8/66; Oates, p. 101.

10 Helen Armet, *Extracts from the Records of the Burgh of Edinburgh*, Edinburgh, Oliver & Boyd, 1967, p. 368. Unlike those captured in England, the men appear to have been eventually released rather than transported.

11 Patten, pp. 63–5.

12 Patten, p. 70.

13 Referred to in some accounts as Colonel Chartres. Strictly speaking he was a captain in the Scots Troop of Lifeguards, with the brevet rank of lieutenant-colonel. See Dalton, *English Army Lists*, pp. 50, 205.

Chapter 9

1   Ironically Syddall was imprisoned at Lancaster, released by the rebels, taken again at Preston and thereafter hanged. His son, also named Thomas, served as adjutant to the ill-fated Manchester Regiment in 1745, and he too was hanged after being taken at Carlisle.

2   Patten, p. 80.

3   George Keith subsequently succeeded his elder brother William as Earl Marischal, and it was his grandsons, William Keith, the then Earl Marischal, and James Edward Keith who served under the Earl of Mar in 1715.

4   Oates, pp. 95–6.

5   According to Patten, the rebels acquired six ships' cannon at Lancaster and replaced their truck carriages with new ones mounted on wheels taken from Sir Henry Houghton's coaches! See Patten, p. 74.

6   Patten's history numbers Miller amongst the prisoners as a captain, so the rank of major was presumably an acting one in the absence of the regiment's other field officers.

7   Patten, p. 85.

8   Charles Sanford Terry, *The Jacobites and the Union. Being a Narrative of the Movements of 1708, 1715 and 1719 by Several Contemporary Hands*, Cambridge, Cambridge University Press, 1922, p. 212.

9   Thomas Carter, *Historical Record of the 26th or Cameronian Regiment*, London, W. O. Mitchell, 1867, pp. 90. Patten added the curious detail that Captain Preston was already dying of consumption and reckoned that his fatal wound had only shortened his life by a matter of days.

10 There does not appear to be a morning state for the Cameronians at Preston, but as the other three regiments recalled from Ireland mustered about 240 men apiece at Sheriffmuir it would be reasonable to expect the same of the Cameronians.

11 Richard Cannon, *Historical Records of the 11th or Prince Albert's Own Regiment of Hussars*, London, Parker, Furnivall & Parker, 1843 also cited five men wounded and twelve horses wounded, but this related only to the single troop of the regiment involved.

12 Patten, p. 88.

13 Richard Cannon, *Historical Records of the 14th or King's Regiment of Light Dragoons*, London, Parker, Furnivall & Parker, 1847. The caveat should be made that some of these casualties may have been suffered by the detachments assigned to Honeywood's battalion.

14 Patten, pp. 104–5.

15 Patten, p. 91.

16 Patten, p. 97.

17 It appears impossible to reconcile exactly how many prisoners were taken at Preston. By collating lists of named prisoners, Oates reckoned there could have been as many as 1,774, but it seems likely that this figure included stragglers picked up in the countryside before and after the battle.

Chapter 10

1   This was the despatch sent from Leith hours before Borlum evacuated the citadel and headed east to Seton House

2   Sinclair, p. 132.
3   Absolutely typically, witness an agreement dated 27 September by various heritors in Easter Ross, empowering Aeneas Macleod of Cadbol and others to 'treat' with Alexander McKenzie of Dachmaluack or anyone else empowered by Seaforth and assure him that they would commit no acts of hostility against the earl, his friends, tenants and followers, providing they reciprocated. See Anon., *A Collection of Original Letters*, p. 22.
4   Anon., *A Collection of Original Letters*, pp. 103–4.
5   Strictly speaking he would not be officially restored to the title of Lord Lovat until 1730, but such niceties did not trouble him then or later.
6   Anon., *A Collection of Original Letters*, pp. 23–4.
7   Scottish Record Office, GD220/5568.
8   Oddly enough, although Hamilton's remained in garrison at Fort William throughout the rising, they too got a new commanding officer in July in the shape of Richard, Viscount Irwin. None of the titular commanding officers actually served with their regiments.
9   Patten, pp. 238–9. This is actually Lovat's account of the affair, headed by Patten as 'The Lord Lovatt's Account of the taking of Inverness; with other advantages obtained over the rebels in the north of Scotland'.
10   Patten, p. 239 (Lovat again).
11   Keith, p. 15.
12   Sinclair, p. 168.

Chapter 11

1   By comparison, the weakest of the Duke of Cumberland's battalions at Culloden in 1746 was 304 strong against an average of about 400 men apiece.
2   Sleat himself remained behind in the Inverness area, sending the regiment south under his two brothers.
3   Sinclair, p. 187.
4   Lord Ogilvy's Regiment and two *ad hoc* battalions formed of the remnants of units that had failed to cross the Forth with Borlum.
5   Sinclair, p. 203; HMC, *Mar & Kellie MSS*, p. 51.
6   Sinclair, p. 203.
7   Patten, p. 164.
8   Patten, pp. 151–2.
9   Scottish Record Office, RH 2/4/307/18, 38.
10   Baynes, p. 138, suggested Argyle spent the night in the area around Dykedale farm, immediately to the east of Dunblane, but although no doubt clear of trees at the time the ground seems rather steep at this point, and Kippenross, to the southeast, offers a more attractive location which also fits better with what followed.

Chapter 12

1   Sinclair, p. 212.
2   Sinclair, p. 212. 'His Lordship to doe him justice, which I think I am obliged in conscience to

doe, it being the onlie good action of his life, made us a very fine speech . . . and concluded it was his opinion we should attack the enemie; who were so near us, and inlarged on the whole in very stronge and moving terms.'

3   Huntly was seemingly the only one who spoke in reply, apparently expressing caution and questioning whether engaging in battle before the king arrived would actually achieve anything, but if it was an objection it was ambiguously phrased and not pressed.

4   Sir Donald MacDonald of Sleat himself was not present, being in the Inverness area at the time. The regiment was actually led by his two brothers, and consequently, due to a nice sense of protocol, it was referred to as Sir Donald MacDonald's rather than as Sleat's.

5   The standing stone almost certainly predates the battle by a millennia or two, but, human nature being what it is, the tradition that the Jacobites formed there no doubt arises from the Marischal and his men being inexorably drawn to the only landmark on the moor.

6   Keith, pp. 17–18.

7   This differs from the diagrammatic representation in Rae, p. 300, which shows Argyle's army at a later point in the day.

8   Curiously, according to Richard Cannon, *Historical Records of the 8th or King's Regiment of Foot*, London, Parker, Furnivall & Parker, 1844, the left brigade was commanded by Forfar not Clayton, but this seems unlikely.

9   According to Sir William Fraser, *The Chiefs of Grant*, Edinburgh, privately published, 3 vols, 1883, he was left behind in Edinburgh. On the other hand Rae's contemporary history explicitly names him as the third of Argyle's brigadiers.

10 Some sources suggest only three squadrons were deployed in the front line, but this arrangement is as described by an unknown volunteer under Rothes. See HMC, *3rd Report: MSS of the Duke of Montrose*, pp. 384–5.

11 Rae, p. 303.

12 In the absence of any other explanation there has to be a strong suspicion that some of the officers had slipped off down the hill to obtain a hot breakfast in Dunblane.

13 This order of battle is substantially based (with reservations) on Mar's printed account of the battle and Sinclair's narrative. Its limitations will become obvious.

14 This regiment comprised two battalions. Mar's printed account credited Seaforth with three battalions, but he appears to have been including the Frasers, who deserted two days before the battle.

15 A part of Logie Drummond's Battalion had gone south with Borlum, although he himself returned to Perth with Strathallan. Presumably he had since recruited it again.

16 Probably the most reliable guide to the strength of some of the regiments of the rebel army is a muster carried out at Perth on 13 October, per HMC, *Mar & Kellie MSS*, pp. 51, which found the foot to comprise:

Marquis of Huntly	1,200
Lord George Murray	230
Earl of Panmure	415
Lord Ogilvy	351
Strowan	203
Invernytie	267

This produced a total of 2,666 foot, albeit many of Huntly's men subsequently deserted. Murray's, Ogilvy's and Invernytie's regiments were not at Sheriffmuir, while Gordon's Highland division had not then arrived from the west. A warrant for the issue of oatmeal to certain regiments dated 22 November, a little over a week after the battle (Anon., *A Collection of Original Letters*, p. 145) gave the following figures, which for the most part reflect casualties and further desertions:

Sir John Maclean	350
Locheil	400
Appin	180
Sir Donald MacDonald	430
Glengarry	300
Clanranald	400

17 Keith, p. 10.
18 Sinclair, p. 225.
19 Sinclair, p. 225.
20 Contrarily, according to Cannon, *Historical Records of the 8th or King's Regiment of Foot*, Forfar was commanding the left brigade not the right and was fatally wounded in front of the regiment.
21 HMC, *3rd Report: MSS of the Duke of Montrose*, pp. 384–5. Unfortunately the badly bruised writer of the letter is unknown. It was left unsigned no doubt because as he explained in his final sentence: 'I'm just going to let blood.'
22 Another account in the Duke of Montrose's papers, possibly obtained in part from our bruised friend related that Evans's Dragoons were soon rallied 'and took terrible vengeance, and their Col. Halley being ill wounded in the arm (of which its hoped hee'l recover) made them give little quarter'.
23 Figures are again taken from the 13 October muster at Perth. There had no doubt been some comings and goings in the intervening weeks, but nothing of consequence other than the arrival of Seaforth's contingent.
24 Sinclair, p. 215. Being at some distance, Sinclair was obviously unaware that the Marischal had been sent up onto the ridge earlier and that Drummond joined him where he was already standing.
25 Sinclair, p. 226.
26 Sinclair, p. 225.
27 HMC, *3rd Report: MSS of the Duke of Montrose*, p. 385.

Chapter 13

1 Keith, p.10.
2 Sinclair, p. 216. It may have been wilful blindness that persuaded Sinclair's cavalrymen they were looking at Strathmore's colours, but it does suggest that the form of them was not unlike those carried by the regulars. Interestingly a flag preserved in the National Museum of Scotland, bearing the date 1716, is identical in style to contemporary British regimental colours save that the canton takes the form of a cross of St Andrew rather than a union.

3   Patten, pp. 166–7.

4   Sinclair, p. 217.

5   On the other hand Sinclair alleged that Mar was at the time keeping safely below the other side of the crest and only learned of Clanranald's fall when the dying man was carried past.

6   Sinclair, p. 217. Fuzie, or fusee to use the ordinary spelling, was a corruption of the French term fusil, denoting a firelock musket (hence fusiliers), and not as one recent writer suggested a matchlock musket requiring a slow-burning fuse or match cord.

7   Cannon, *Historical Records of the 8th or King's Regiment of Foot*, p. 49.

8   Richard Cannon, *Historical Records of the 11th or North Devon Regiment of Foot*, London, Parker, Furnivall & Parker, 1845, p. 27.

9   Captain Urquhart was 'wounded in the belly', as one report ran, 'so as his puddings hang out'. As he was too badly wounded to be moved, he was paroled on the battlefield but afterwards recovered from his injuries.

10 Richard Cannon, *Historical Records of the 21st Foot or Royal Scots Fusiliers*, London, Parker, Furnivall & Parker, 1849, p. 19.

11 Richard Cannon, *Historical Records of the 14th or West Yorkshire Regiment of Foot*, London, Parker, Furnivall & Parker, 1844, p. 23. Unlike the other battalions it had seen no action during Queen Anne's War and had instead served on gendarmerie duties in Ireland, and consequently gone to the dogs.

12 Richard Cannon, *Historical Records of the 36th or Worcestershire Regiment of Foot*, London, Parker, Furnivall & Parker, 1853, p. 22,

13 Argyle to Townshend, 21 November and 6 December 1715, partly quoted in Baynes, p. 153.

14 Rae, p. 306.

15 Patten, p. 153.

16 Dalton, *English Army Lists*, p. 209.

17 Or so it may be inferred from their returning seven men killed and nine wounded.

18 Sinclair, p. 226. Keith for his part was notably reticent about what happened to the Marischal's Squadron once the battle began and said nothing of their movements or any adventures.

19 HMC, *3rd Report: MSS of the Duke of Montrose*, p. 385. Unsigned letter dated 18 November 1715 addressed to Lieutenant John Stirling of Grant's Regiment.

20 Sinclair, p. 220.

21 Keith, p. 19.

22 Keith, p. 19.

23 Keith, pp. 20–1.

24 Official return. Rae, p. 310, provided a lower set of figures, viz. 14 officers and 276 men killed; 11 officers and 176 men wounded; and 10 officers and 123 men taken prisoner.

25 There was to be a curious parallel to this at Culloden thirty years later. As we saw in the previous chapter, Evans's Dragoons, commanded by Hawley, were badly shot up by Jacobite infantry while they themselves were prevented from going forward by a ditch and marshy ground. At Culloden, Hawley would hook around into the Jacobite rear with a cavalry brigade, only to be halted by a marshy ditch and stream, and be shot up by Jacobite infantry on the other side.

26 A story preserved in Cannon, *Historical Records of the 8th or King's Regiment of Foot*, pp. 49–50, related that he was found lying wounded and that when his captors could not carry him off they hacked him seven times with their swords to finish him off. Exactly the same thing was to happen to Colonel Robert Monro of the 37th Foot at Falkirk in 1746. Wounded and left behind, he was found by a party of Highlanders who not only cold-bloodedly hacked him to death but murdered his brother as well – a surgeon who was treating his original injury.

27 Keith, p. 22.

Chapter 14

1 Sinclair, p. 210.

2 For some reason he appears in a number of secondary sources as Lieutenant-Colonel Albert Lawrence, but the various commission registers confirm his given name as Herbert.

3 A full discussion of this lost opportunity is to be found in Szechi, pp. 160–2.

4 Anon., *A Collection of Original Letters*, pp. 83–4. The Dutch Army had a number of Swiss regiments at this time, although it would appear that most of the rank and file were in fact German or other nationalities.

5 Anon., *A Collection of Original Letters*, pp. 97–8.

6 Sinclair, p. 333.

7 In another curious twist it would also be at Ruthven where the last Jacobite army disbanded itself, after the Battle of Culloden in April 1746.

Appendix 1

1 HMC, *Mar & Kellie MSS*, p. 511.

2 Patten, p. 41.

3 Patten, p. 47. Shaftoe was shot as a half-pay officer.

4 Patten, pp. 49–50. Douglas escaped from Chester Castle.

5 HMC, *Mar & Kellie MSS,* p. 511.

6 Patten, p. 49.

7 HMC, *Mar & Kellie MSS,* p. 511.

8 He was wounded in the head and never properly recovered. After escaping to the continent, he succeeded his father as the 14th Laird of Drum in 1720 but died in exile, unmarried, in 1732.

9 Patten, p. 39. Cousin of Duke of Hamilton. Sentenced to death but pardoned.

10 Patten, p. 41. Surrendered at Preston and summarily executed as a half-pay officer.

11 (1692–1778). Escaped abroad, but latterly abandoned Jacobitism and entered the Prussian service, latterly as a diplomat. Pardoned by George II in 1758, and remained in Prussia until his death.

12 HMC, *Mar & Kellie MSS,* p. 511.

13 (1696–1758). The Marischal's younger brother. Escaped abroad and left a valuable memoir, but killed at Hochkirch while serving as a field-marshal with the Prussian Army under Frederick the Great.

14 Allardyce, pp. 50–1.

15 Patten, p. 39. Found guilty he was subsequently pardoned and died in 1764.

16 HMC, *Mar & Kellie MSS,* p. 511.

17 Patten, p. 116: 'acquitted by the Jury at the Marshalsea, tho' it was proved he had a Troop, and entred Preston at the Head of it with his Sword drawn. But his Sword had a Silver Handle.'

18 Surrendered at Preston but pardoned.

19 Brother to the Earl of Carnwath and a half-pay lieutenant who served in the old Earl of Mar's Regiment before the Revolution. Resigned from the half pay before the rising and escaped summary execution accordingly (see Dalton, *Scots Army*, p. 155). Was subsequently transported but then released on arrival in America.

20 Charles Wogan (1698?–1752) was tried for high treason but escaped from Newgate and spent the rest of his life abroad in the Spanish and Jacobite service. Nicholas Wogan (1700–1770) was found guilty but pardoned and went into the French service.

21 Glenlyon was the son of Captain Robert Campbell of Glenlyon, who carried out the infamous Massacre of Glencoe in 1691.

22 Escaped abroad and died in Flanders 1748; it was his son who led the Camerons in 1745.

23 Locheil's eldest son by his second wife. Died 1717.

24 (1674–1720). Escaped abroad and succeeded his father as Duke of Perth in May 1716, although was never recognised as such outside Jacobite circles. His elder son, also named James, was one of the principal Jacobite leaders in 1745, while his younger son, Lord John Drummond, commanded a regiment in the French service.

25 (1673–1757). Captured at Sheriffmuir but pardoned. Commonly referred to as Logie Drummond.

26 Patten, p. 121.

27 (1690–1746). 4th Viscount Strathallan. Captured at Sheriffmuir but pardoned under Act of Grace 1717. Raised troop of horse in 1745 and killed in action at Culloden.

28 The same who organised that abortive attempt on Edinburgh Castle.

29 Patten, pp. 46–7.

30 William Forbes Skene, *Memorials of the Family of Skene*, Aberdeen, New Spalding Club, 1887, p. 58. Of Halyards, Fife. Sentenced to death but pardoned, dying in 1736.

31 HMC, *Mar & Kellie MSS,* p. 511.

32 (1675–1750). Appears to have gained his fearsome reputation during the rising, but afterwards included in the Act of Grace 1717. Played a prominent role in the later rising of 1745 and afterwards escaped to the Continent.

33 Had been employed as a Jacobite agent for some years before the rising. May have held a French commission and was in consequence frequently referred to as Brigadier Ogilvy. Escaped afterwards and died in France in 1728.

34 Anon., *A Collection of Original Letters*, p. 145. The regiment appears to have fought on the right wing at Sheriffmuir and cannot have suffered too heavily. It is possible that the scale of desertion afterwards was unusually high, but more likely that Mar's estimate of 700 men was a touch optimistic.

35 Anon., *A Collection of Original Letters*, p. 145.

36 Anon., *A Collection of Original Letters*, p. 145.

37 Pardoned under Act of Grace 1717 but died in 1721.

38 Anon., *A Collection of Original Letters*, p. 145.

39 William Mackay, *Urquhart and Glenmoriston; Olden Times in a Highland Parish*, Inverness, Northern Press, 1914, pp. 229–31. Pardoned under Act of Grace 1717.

40 Mackay, pp. 229–31. Glen Urquhart company.

41 Mackay, pp. 229–31. Both lieutenants were reported by Brigadier Grant (their landlord) as being out with the Glen Urquhart company.

42 (1660–1749). Elected clan chief of the MacGregors in 1714 but probably, due to his age, does not appear to have played a prominent part in the proceedings.

43 John Monteath, *Dunblane Traditions*, Stirling, Eanes Mackay, 1887, pp. 14–17. It should be emphasised that Rob Roy and his men were situated to the west of the battlefield, not to the east as inadvertently described by Baynes.

44 Patten, p. 120.

45 Pardoned and released 1717 and died in 1740.

46 Invercauld and at least two of his officers, Whitehouse and Kirkton, were pardoned or acquitted – no doubt as a reflection of his earlier dispute with Mar and consequent ability to argue that they had been forced out.

47 Escaped from Newgate with Borlum.

48 Went north with Huntly after Sheriffmuir and died there in March 1716 of natural causes.

49 Anon., *A Collection of Original Letters*, p. 145.

50 As they comprised what had been a particularly reluctant contingent from Mar's Kildrummy estate there has to be a suspicion that they were sent over precisely in order to prevent them deserting.

51 Inverey commanded the garrison at Burntisland and is frequently confused with his father, the notorious 'Black Colonel' John Farquharson of Inverey.

52 Patten, p. 122. He was one of the few who got away during a daring breakout by Borlum.

53 (1691–1720). Renegade army officer and sentenced to death accordingly, but reprieved at the intercession of his father.

54 (1691–1770). Pardoned, was unable to succeed to his father's forfeited title, but again a Jacobite in 1745 and in consequence had to flee abroad afterwards.

55 Rendered as 'Mineries' in Patten, p. 122.

56 (1694–1760). Escaped abroad but returned to Scotland 1724. At first inclined to remain loyal to King George, but in 1745 he joined the Jacobites and served as a lieutenant-general. Escaped abroad after Culloden and died in Holland.

57 HMC, *Mar & Kellie MSS*, p. 511.

58 Patten, p. 122.

59 (1664–1726). Sentenced to death, but remitted.

60 (1665–1730). Pardoned and released.

61 HMC, *Mar & Kellie MSS*, p. 511.

62 Son of the Earl of Airlie, pardoned in 1725 and died without issue 1731.

63 HMC, *Mar & Kellie MSS*, p. 511.

64 Sinclair, p. 52.

65 (1688–1723). Escaped abroad with his brother Henry Maule, and died in Paris of pleurisy.

66 Killed at Sheriffmuir while acting as a brigadier.

67 Sinclair, p. 51.

68 Prisoner at Sheriffmuir.

69 HMC, *Mar & Kellie MSS*, p. 511.

70 Escaped, but attainted and not included in Act of Grace. Pardoned in 1726 but did not regain his lands or title, and died in 1740.

71 (1683–1750). Fraserdale was a claimant to the Lovat estates through his wife, and is also known as Fraser of Fraserdale. Reports of his death at or shortly after Sheriffmuir are exaggerated, and the feud with the Beaufort Frasers continued until his death in Leith. http://www.historyofparliamentonline.org/volume/1690–1715/member/mackenzie-alexander-1683–1755.

72 Killed in action.

73 Prisoner at Sheriffmuir.

74 Prisoner at Sheriffmuir.

75 Anon., *A Collection of Original Letters*, p. 145.

76 HMC, *Mar & Kellie MSS*, p. 511.

77 Patten, p. 15.

78 Sinclair, p. 45.

79 Sinclair, p. 52.

80 Patten, p. 42.

81 (1671–1731). Escaped from Stirling Castle and fled abroad, but included in the Act of Grace 1717 and allowed to return home.

82 Patten, p. 121.

83 (1689–1746). Actually the eldest living son and heir of the Duke of Athole but forfeit as a result of his part in the rebellion. Escaped abroad, fought at Glenshiel in 1719 and returned with Charles Edward Stuart in 1745, then styling himself Duke of Athole. However was in poor health and having been arrested after the rising died of natural causes in the Tower of London.

Appendix 2

1 Governor of Edinburgh Castle in 1746.

2 List of officers per Richard Cannon, *Historical Records of the 14th or King's Regiment of Light Dragoons*, London, Parker, Furnivall & Parker, 1847.

3 Wounded at Sheriffmuir, variously described as shot in the side or the shoulder. Subsequently commander in chief Scotland in 1746.

4 Wounded at Sheriffmuir.

5 List of officers per Cannon, *Historical Records of the 11th or North Devon Regiment of Foot*.

6 Slightly wounded at Preston. Author of very influential Humphrey Bland, *Treatise of Military Discipline*, London, private, 1727 and subsequent editions). Commanded cavalry brigade at Culloden.

7 List of officers per Richard Cannon, *Historical Records of the 13th Light Dragoons*, London, Parker, Furnivall & Parker, 1842.

8   Killed at Sheriffmuir while serving as ADC to Argyle.

9   Killed at Prestonpans in 1745 as colonel of 13th Dragoons.

10   Wounded at Sheriffmuir.

11   Lieutenant in Royal Horse Guards, 24 November 1715, so may not have been present at Sheriffmuir.

12   List of officers per Richard Cannon, *Historical Records of the 9th or Queen's Royal Regiment of Light Dragoons, Lancers*, London, Parker, Furnivall & Parker, 1841.

13   Prisoner at Sheriffmuir.

14   Captured at Sheriffmuir.

15   Captured at Sheriffmuir.

16   Wounded at Sheriffmuir.

17   Killed at Sheriffmuir.

18   Later, Lord Sempill and a brigadier at Culloden in 1746.

19   Captured at Sheriffmuir.

20   Returned as missing at Sheriffmuir, no further service traced.

21   Prisoner at Sheriffmuir.

22   Killed at Sheriffmuir.

23   Still a lieutenant in the regiment in 1740!

24   Killed at Sheriffmuir.

25   Wounded at Sheriffmuir.

26   Killed at Sheriffmuir.

27   Badly wounded at Sheriffmuir: 'Resigned by reason of wounds and infirmities 1716'.

28   Fatally wounded and captured at Sheriffmuir.

29   Killed at Sheriffmuir.

30   Killed at Sheriffmuir.

31   Of Burdsyards. Badly wounded at Sheriffmuir but recovered.

32   Returned as prisoner at Sheriffmuir, probably a mistake for Hayward, who was killed.

33   Killed at Sheriffmuir.

34   Killed at Sheriffmuir.

35   Wounded while commanding regiment at Preston.

36   Wounded at Preston.

37   Wounded at Preston.

38   Fatally wounded at Preston.

39   Killed at Sheriffmuir.

40   Wounded at Sheriffmuir.

41   Anon., *The Present State of Europe, Or, The Historical and Political Mercury*, London, H. Rhodes, 1716, vol. 27, p. 98.

Appendix 3

1   Patten, pp. 156–8.

Bibliography

Manuscripts
National Archives, Kings Bench 8/66
Scottish Record Office, GD220/5568
Scottish Record Office, *State Papers Scotland* (photocopy vols), RH 2/4/306/92

Primary Sources (Printed)
Allardyce, James, *Historical Papers Relating to the Jacobite Period 1699–1750*,
    Aberdeen, New Spalding Club, 1895
Anon., *A Collection of Original Letters and Authentick Papers Relating to the Rebellion
    1715*, Edinburgh, 1730
Anon., *Jurnall of the Proceedings of the Army in Rebbellion under E. of Mar*, City
    Archives, Edinburgh, n.d.
Anon., *The Loch Lomond Expedition with Some Short Reflections on the Perth
    Manifesto*, Glasgow, 1715
Armet, Helen, *Extracts from the Records of the Burgh of Edinburgh*, Edinburgh,
    Oliver & Boyd, 1967
Athole, John 7th Duke, *Chronicles of the Atholl & Tullibardine Families*,
    Edinburgh, privately published, 5 vols, 1908, appendices x–xx
Blaikie, Walter B. (ed.), *Origins of the Forty-Five and Other Papers Relating to that
    Rising*, Edinburgh, Scottish History Society 1916 and James Thin, 1975
Campbell, Robert, *The Life of the Most Illustrious Prince John, Duke of Argyle and
    Greenwich*, London, 1745

Historical Manuscripts Commission (HMC), *Mar & Kellie MSS*, 1904

HMC, *3rd Report: MSS of the Duke of Montrose*, 1872

Keith, James, *A Fragment of a Memoir of Field-Marshal James Keith, Written by Himself, 1714–1734*, Aberdeen, Spalding Club, 1853

Patten, Robert, *The History of the Late Rebellion: With Original Papers and Characters of the Principal Noblemen and Gentlemen Concern'd in It*, 3rd edn, London, 1745

Rae, Peter, *The History of the Rebellion, Rais'd Against His Majesty King George I. By the Friends of the Popish Pretender*, 2nd edn, London, 1746

Sinclair, John, *Memoirs of the Insurrection in Scotland in 1715*, Edinburgh, Abbotsford Club, 1858

Steuart, A. Francis (ed.), *Newsletters of 1715–16*, Edinburgh, 1910

Terry, Charles Sanford, *The Jacobites and the Union. Being a Narrative of the Movements of 1708, 1715 and 1719 by Several Contemporary Hands*, Cambridge, Cambridge University Press, 1922

Secondary Sources

Anon., *The Present State of Europe, Or, The Historical and Political Mercury*, London, H. Rhodes, 1716, vol. 27

Baynes, John, *The Jacobite Rising of 1715*, London, Cassell, 1970

Bland, Humphrey, *Treatise of Military Discipline*, London, private, 1727

Cannon, Richard, *Historical Records of the 8th or King's Regiment of Foot*, London, Parker, Furnivall & Parker, 1844

Cannon, Richard, *Historical Records of the 9th or Queen's Royal Regiment of Light Dragoons, Lancers*, London, Parker, Furnivall & Parker, 1841

Cannon, Richard, *Historical Records of the 11th or North Devon Regiment of Foot*, London, Parker, Furnivall & Parker, 1845

Cannon, Richard, *Historical Records of the 11th or Prince Albert's Own Regiment of Hussars*, London, Parker, Furnivall & Parker, 1843

Cannon, Richard, *Historical Records of the 13th Light Dragoons*, London, Parker, Furnivall & Parker, 1842

Cannon, Richard, *Historical Records of the 14th or King's Regiment of Light Dragoons*, London, Parker, Furnivall & Parker, 1847

Cannon, Richard, *Historical Records of the 14th or West Yorkshire Regiment of Foot*, London, Parker, Furnivall & Parker, 1844

Cannon, Richard, *Historical Records of the 21st Foot or Royal Scots Fusiliers*, London, Parker, Furnivall & Parker, 1849

Cannon, Richard, *Historical Records of the 36th or Worcestershire Regiment of Foot*, London, Parker, Furnivall & Parker, 1853

Carter, Thomas, *Historical Record of the 26th or Cameronian Regiment*, London, W. O. Mitchell, 1867

Chandler, David, *The Art of War in the Age of Marlborough*, London, Batsford, 1976

Dalton, Charles, *English Army Lists and Commission Registers*, vol. 6, London, Eyre & Spottiswoode, 1904

Dalton, Charles, *The Scots Army 1661–1688*, London, Eyre & Spottiswoode, 1909

Fortescue, Sir John, *History of the British Army*, London, Macmillan, vol. II (1899)

Fraser, Sir William, *The Chiefs of Grant*, Edinburgh, privately published, 3 vols, 1883

Guy, A. J., *Oeconomy and Discipline; Officership and Administration in the British Army 1714–63*, Manchester, Manchester University Press, 1985

Hopkins, Paul, *Glencoe and the End of the Highland War*, Edinburgh, John Donald, 1986

Jarvis, Rupert C., *The Jacobite Risings of 1715 and 1745*, Carlisle, Cumberland County Council, 1954

Lenman, Bruce, *The Jacobite Clans of the Great Glen 1650–1784*, London, Methuen, 1984

McDonnell, Frances, *Jacobites of 1715 North East Scotland*, Baltimore, Genealogical Publishing, 2000

Mackay, William, *Urquhart and Glenmoriston; Olden Times in a Highland Parish*, Inverness, Northern Counties Press, 1914

Monteath, John, *Dunblane Traditions*, Stirling, Eanes Mackay, 1887

Moody-Stuart, K. A., 'Lieutenant Colonel James Steuart: A Jacobite Lieutenant Governor of Edinburgh Castle', *Scottish Historical Review*, vol. XXI, no. 81 (1924)

Oates, Jonathan, 'The armies operating in northern England during the Jacobite rebellion of 1715', *Journal of the Society for Army Historical Research*, vol. 90, no. 362 (summer 2012)

Sankey, Margaret D., *Jacobite Prisoners of the 1715 Rebellion; Preventing and Punishing Insurrection in Early Hanoverian Britain*, Farnham, Ashgate, 2005

Skene, William Forbes, *Memorials of the Family of Skene*, Aberdeen, New Spalding Club, 1887

Szechi, Daniel, *1715: The Great Jacobite Rebellion*, London & Yale, Yale
    University Press, 2006
Tabraham, C. and Grove, D., *Fortress Scotland and the Jacobites*, Edinburgh,
    Historic Scotland, 1995

Index